Get It Done!

Get It Done!

A BLUEPRINT FOR BUSINESS EXECUTION

RALPH WELBORN

VINCE KASTEN

WILEY

JOHN WILEY & SONS, INC.

Published by John Wiley & Sons, Inc., Hoboken, New Jersey.
Published simultaneously in Canada.

For general information on our other products and services or for technical support, please contact our Customer Care Department within the United States at (800) 762-2974, outside the United States at (317) 572-3993 or fax (317) 572-4002.

Wiley also publishes its books in a variety of electronic formats. Some content that appears in print may not be available in electronic books. For more information about Wiley products, visit our web site at www.wiley.com.

Library of Congress Cataloging-in-Publication Data:
Welborn, Ralph, 1961–
  Get it done! : a blueprint for business execution / Ralph Welborn, Vince Kasten.
    p.   cm.
  Includes bibliographical references.
  ISBN-13: 978-0-471-47931-4 (cloth)
  ISBN-10: 0-471-47931-4 (cloth)
  1. Organizational effectiveness. 2. Organizational change. 3. Industrial management. I. Kasten, Vincent A. II. Title.
  HD58.9.W456   2006
  658.4'013—dc22
                                                            2005016419

Printed in the United States of America.

10 9 8 7 6 5 4 3 2

To Meg and the kids—Nicole, Jeremy, Jacob
—R. W.

To my parents, Ken and Connie
—V. K.

Foreword

I had spent 30 years in federal law enforcement doing technology support when in November 2001, the president and Congress moved to set up the Transportation Security Administration (TSA), transferring responsibility for aviation security from the airlines to the new agency, and giving TSA just one year to get new federal security employees in place. Along with so many other people, I had felt the helplessness of watching the events of 9/11 unfold, and not being able to prevent them. So when an opportunity came up to be part of TSA and part of the solution, I jumped at the chance to volunteer as part of the original group of the first 12 or so people who started TSA. There was a lot of uncertainty in those early days of exactly how things would unfold and what the agency would look like, but the chance to be part of making a difference, resolving issues, and just being a part of something new with the critical mission of the new and largely unformed Department of Homeland Security was something I felt I had to do.

We were faced with the need to create a brand new government agency from scratch on an incredibly aggressive time line. Congress had given TSA 37 mandates that had to occur in the first 12 months. We had to rapidly provide an improved security capability at 429 airports across the nation, and at the same time position ourselves to create over time a sustainable, scalable agility to meet the agency's mission into the future. As we first looked at the amount of work we needed to get this done, we were very aware of the monumental scale and the critical importance of what we were being asked to do—we were not at all sure how that would get done, and we looked at those 37 mandates and the 12-month timeline as a real burden. At the same time, we realized that these mandates could be used to our benefit.

There was not a lot of time to debate if we should do A, B, or C. The mandates laid out pretty specifically what had to be done and in what timeframe, so they forced us to focus on action.

I knew that we would only make this sort of radical start—from 0 to 429 airports in 12 months—by creating an organization where many autonomous but interdependent initiatives could run simultaneously. I was responsible for creating and setting up the information technology organization and solutions for TSA. I started the organizational structure with a program management perspective, hiring 20 to 30 experienced program managers and giving each of them a piece of the IT program that we envisioned having to take place. Even as I went down this path, I knew that some of the consequences would be that there would be parts of our business that were "invisible" to us—we would not always know, in the language of this book—"what connects with what, where, when, how, and how much" throughout our organization. In the initial frenetic months of the startup of TSA, I used senior program managers to create a working version of what Ralph and Vince call the "visibility throughout the organization" and to invent TSA's "executional capabilities," or in their terms, our ability to "get done what has to get done."

My visibility challenges were exacerbated because I knew that I could never hire an organization with the capability to do all of what needed to be done in the timeframe it needed to be done in. It was clear to me that my organization was going to be very flat, and would highly leverage consultants and contractors to do the bulk of the work. I planned for an IT organization of only 150 people or so, to support 50,000 users in 429 airports and our headquarters facilities. That's a very small staff, so outsourcing was going to be a major part of the solution, with all of the execution challenges that that entailed. With our initial staff and a prime technology outsource partner, we launched our "red, white, and blue" technology rollout approach: the red phase involved deploying notebook PCs with dial-up access and cell phones and pagers at 429 airports; the white phase added connectivity via Local Area Networks (LANs) within airports and Wide Area Network (WAN) links from the airports to headquarters; finally the blue phase was to define the technologically enabled airport of the future.

When I accepted the Eagle Award—an award given to a person in government who makes an outstanding contribution to federal information technology—on behalf of my team at TSA, it was for the enormous amount of work we had accomplished in such an extraordinarily short time. Even then we faced implementing our white and blue packages—consolidating our infrastructure progress, putting new technologies into place, and defining/extending our threat perimeter to understand where besides airports and other transportation hubs TSA needed to spend its time. Our task was to move to the stage beyond startup, to establish, in Ralph's and Vince's words, a lasting "DNA of Execution" and create an agency with the vision, the alignment, and the cadence to improve and change with the changing threats into the future.

That's where this book comes in. General Colin Powell has said, "Leadership is the art of accomplishing more than the science of management says is possible." I believe this is true, yet, I also believe that it is every leader's job to push forward the science of managing his or her business. In this book, Ralph and Vince write a lot about what they call the DNA of Execution—the ability to mobilize resources effectively and efficiently to implement strategic initiatives and to balance the inherent tension between managing costs and creating innovation. During the startup days and months of TSA, we had a surfeit of execution capability, thanks to the many people who felt as I had watching the events of 9/11, and who wanted to contribute. Because we were born in the blood of the 9/11 incidents, I found remarkable people offering to come to TSA. Fully 50 percent of the people on my team came from the private sector, many, like me, wanting to make a difference after the events of 9/11. They came knowing there was some risk or uncertainty about exactly what they were getting into. They were, and are, extremely dedicated people, and equally importantly are attached clearly to the mission of TSA: Our job as leaders is to transmit that to our employees and make a clear connection with what they do for a living and how it benefits the mission of our organization. With that, it is also critical that we enable them with the tools, the techniques, and the information to actually achieve their mission.

A gap often exists between what executives require and the reality on the ground. Getting people from different parts of a business, or an agency, to work together effectively is often difficult to do. Operational demands, budget cycles, changing priorities, division-of-labor silos, protection of turf, crises-of-the-day, among other things, perpetuate this "execution gap" making it more and more difficult to be responsive to the changing needs of your constituents and markets. Ralph and Vince demonstrate how to bridge this gap in a surprisingly nonthreatening and effective way. While many books have talked about the need for creating a "culture" of execution, *Get It Done!* shows the pragmatics of how to make such a culture real. This is a book not to be missed and to be read each time you hear the phrases "That's not my job," "I don't see how we're going to get that done," or "I'm not clear what we're supposed to be doing . . . or how to work with those folks." In others words, whenever you need to "get things done that need to get done."

Ralph and Vince have a real winner here—they don't just tell us why execution is important, but they give us some practical reasons why it doesn't happen, frameworks to evaluate the causes of failures, and approaches to making it happen. *Get It Done!* needs to be read. I hope it sells a million copies.

PAT SCHAMBACH
Former Associate Undersecretary and CIO
Transportation Security Administration

Preface

The eighteenth-century British philosopher David Hume said (admittedly slightly paraphrased): "After considering the difficulties of [getting stuff done], I felt that the effort led into a morass from which . . . the only escape was to climb out, clean oneself off, go home, have a good dinner, and forget all about [work]." His actual quote referred to his challenges in building a pragmatic philosophy. He was attempting to counter what he considered the "disconnect" between theory and reality—between what people said "ought" to happen and what "actually" happened. What he was encountering is no different from what many of us encounter every day—namely, a significant disconnect between what is supposed to happen at work and what actually does happen. Gaps exist between what executives and managers say they want to get done and what really gets done, gaps that lead to frustration and delay, irritation and finger pointing. There are many ways to explain and close those gaps, but they all boil down to a common challenge: how to get stuff done that needs to get done. And, as many of us have experienced, that's a hard challenge to meet. But it's a challenge that needs to be and pragmatically *can be* met. This book reflects our efforts and results, our actions and impacts, our insights and lessons on meeting these challenges.

Despite all that has been written, all the money spent, all the effort expended, and all the frustration engendered, the difficulty of getting done what has to get done—of "executing" to use a hot word of the day—remains an enormous challenge. Our book takes a new tack, based on a simple insight on how to think through and consequently take action differently and in a way that helps bridge the disconnects that permeate businesses. A friend of ours once said, "If you have simple answers to complex questions, then you are left with simple answers." True enough. But if you have "simple insights" into complex problems supported by robust tools and methods, then you have a way to cut through the complexity and get to work.

Acknowledgments

It's one thing to have a different perspective; it's another to have that perspective drive different, and useful, actions with measurable results. It's the latter that we all need—and the challenge David Hume took up. Neither the perspective nor the resulting actions could have happened without lots of involvement, interaction, challenges, contributions, and results made by our clients, colleagues, and competitors over the past few years. This book is a reflection, or more aptly, a codification and contribution, of demonstrable best practices and lessons, insights and actions, of many gifted people tackling many thorny problems, from many businesses, at many times, over many years. To all of them, we say thank you for the push to get these lessons down so that others could exploit the insights, the frameworks, and the tools to get the results as well as build the capabilities to do what we all need to be able to do more effectively—namely, get done what needs to get done.

We want to thank Trevor Davis, who you will meet in this book, a rare combination of brilliant strategist and steadfast operations director at one of the world's largest business process outsourcing operations. Trevor has worked with us through the years, providing insights and lessons, as well as an operational platform to develop, test, and refine our respective ideas about what can and needs to work where, and how to make it happen.

Thank you Doug Humphreys, an entrepreneur as much of ideas as of businesses, for your collaborative insights, ongoing encouragement, keeping the torch alive of specific ideas, and picking up the pieces of things that we dropped.

Hari Chaturvedi is a great business architect, technology architect, software engineer, and voice of reason with whom we have also worked for years. His deep involvement around the world on global sourcing and strategic technology implementation initiatives and projects has provided depth of insight into a number of the models and methods (and occasionally "madness") that permeates some of the examples used throughout this book. Hari, thanks!

We thank Albert Bressand, head of scenario development for Shell International in London, as well. He and his team, including Peter Snowden, have been gracious hosts and demanding intellects from whom we have learned much and with whom we have explored provocative options for the future.

Tim Garza, chief innovation officer at California Public Employees's Retirement System whose thoughts appear throughout the book, is always an entertaining and pragmatically challenging force around how to "bridge the disconnects" faced. Thanks to Tim for his willingness to engage himself and his team.

Appreciation goes as well to Ben Steverman, a senior architect and program manager at Fidelity in Boston. His experiences, solidly grounded in the hard reality rather than the mere aspirations of what works, are always shared with wit and music.

In addition, we want to thank the extraordinarily talented members of our team, for augmenting and implementing our often vague ideas and abstract concepts, tackling each day the "execution challenges" of real clients with real business problems. We thank them for their indulgence, freely offered insights, suggestions, challenges, and refinements regarding what works, what doesn't, and what would work better—without them, none of this would have seen the light of day. For their passion, we want to thank John Boyle, Peter Bricknell, Turab Mehdi, and ToniAnn Thomas; for their critical perspectives, we add Alex O'Cinneide, Deepak Batheja, Dan Diplacido, Jeff Silver, and; for their probing insights into the concepts and the execution of these models and frameworks, thanks go to David Bridgeland, Ron Zahavi, and Jeff Pappin.

Thanks go also to some people we consider our mentors—experts in the field who are always willing to listen, discuss, debate, and share both their expertise and their insights. Working with them has only helped our understandings and methods of getting stuff done get only more effective. Dave Sanders, a long-time friend and senior executive, has always been willing to share his broad perspective on technology trends and impacts. Thanks to Debin

Schliesman, an extraordinarily gifted architect who cannot help but see patterns in everything she does and who infuses that perspective in others. Also, appreciation goes to Muffy Gaisford for keeping us focused despite many interruptions (even though she was often, admittedly, the reason for the disruption). To Ellyn Raftery, marketing and communications officer at Unisys Corporation, what can we say? Ellyn's talent is exceeded only by her capacity for work, with an unusual sensitivity to the questions of "how," "can," and "will" marketing activities really help the people who work in the field. Her help in supporting this book has been immeasurable.

To Matt Holt, our executive editor at John Wiley & Sons, thanks again—for your confidence and encouragement to get these ideas and lessons down (and ensuring that deadlines were kept and momentum maintained). And to Shannon Vargo, thank you for your (hopefully apparent) efforts to keep the "consultant-speak" to a minimum.

A special thanks, of course, goes to our families. To our wives, Meg and Darlene, who are beyond wonderful and whose encouragement, forbearance, and support exceed mere words to express our appreciation. To Alex and Nick Kasten, both in the process of fleeing the nest, but still willing to keep us entertained and honest. To Howard and Florence, thank you, as ever, for the continual reminders to get done what needs to get done. To Nicole, Jeremy, and Jacob Welborn, thank you so much for keeping us smiling in the middle of our chaotic attempts to juggle working with writing.

Thank you, one and all.

Contents

Introduction—Making Sense and Taking Action   *xxi*

Setting the Stage: What Is It about Execution That Demands So Much Attention? And Why Now?, xxi

What's in the Book?, xxv

What This Means to You, xxx

1 The DNA of Consistent Execution   1

Setting the Stage: Getting Stuff Done Quickly, Effectively, Consistently, 3

Extent of the Challenge: Why Is This So Hard?, 7

  Common Challenges to Getting Stuff Done, 8

Facing the Challenge: Bridging the Semantic Disconnect, 12

  Answering the Question of How, 18

  The Semantic Stack as Insight and Action, 20

  Detailing the Stack, 25

  Making It Real: Executing Over and Over Again, 28

What This Means to You, 29

2 Maps, Models, and Action— Blueprinting Your Business   37

Setting the Stage: Rippling Changes, Crippling Impacts, 39

Extent of the Challenge: Beware the Red Queen, 42

Facing the Challenge: Maps-as-Models, 45

Maps and Models—for Insight and Action, 47

The Business Blueprint—The "Where's Waldo" of Your Organization, 48

Business Blueprinting—The "What's Waldo Doing" in Your Organization, 51

Understanding the DNA—What Connects with What, Where, When, How, and How Much, 54

Bill and Carl's Hurting Hospital Group, 55

Strategy Model, 57

Watch Out for the Bus!—or Else the Company Stops Running, 73

What This Means to You, 73

3   Measurements, Gauges, and Graphs— Doing What's Important   77

Setting the Stage: From Gut Feel to Root Causes, 79

Extent of the Challenge: "Reducing the Number of Bad Outcomes", 80

Facing the Challenge: Defeating the "Corporate Antibodies to Change", 86

Lean Six Sigma—Methods and Madness, 91

Reginald Goes Lean, 98

What This Means to You, 99

4   The Pragmatics of Strategy . . . with Your Head in the Clouds and Your Feet on the Ground   105

Setting the Stage: How to Be "Strategic" Yet Still Get Stuff Done, 107

Extent of the Challenge: What You Don't Know Will Get You, 109

Facing the Challenges: "Go Not into Uncertainty Unaware, and Certainly Not Unarmed!", 113

Characterizing Business Uncertainty, 113

Answering the "So What" Question, 120

The "Pragmatics" of Strategy, or Pragmatic
Strategy, 120

Creating a New "Outside-In" Strategy, 120

Justifying an "Inside-Out" Operational Strategy, 123

Philippe and Marcus and Scott and Debbie, 128

What This Means to You, 129

5 Business Processes . . . Where Business
and Technology Meet   135

Setting the Stage: All Value Is Built in Processes, 137

Extent of the Challenge: "Doing More with More", 142

Facing the Challenge: Mutual Visibility/Useful Action, 146

Process Optimization Leads the Way, 148

Optimizing for What?, 151

Mutual Understanding, 152

What to Do, Where, and How Much, 153

Shared Vocabulary, Interdependent
Actions, 156

Tools to Get Stuff Done, 158

The Work of Process Optimization, 159

After Optimization, 164

Technology, 164

Organization Design, 164

Change Management, 165

Business Case Development, 165

What This Means to You, 166

6 Next Generation Business Process
Outsourcing . . . as Promise and Threat   171

*Setting the Stage: An Industry in the Crunch—
Beyond the Precipice or into the Chasm, 173*

Extent of the Challenge: At a Tipping Point or Just Plain Tipping Over, 174

Facing the Challenge: Decisions Made and Decisions to Make, 180

    The Contractual Crunch and the Unintended Consequences of Win-Lose Contracts, 181

    Nice New Promises/Same Old Methods, 184

    Explaining the Crunch, 187

        The Wedge Effect, 187

        The Bull's-Eye Effect, 190

        The Peak Effect, 193

    Returning to the Contractual Crunch, 197

    Next-Gen BPO—The Search for the Win-Win Contract, 198

    The Semantics of Value—Why We Need to Care, 199

        Mutual Visibility—Again, 202

    Making the Shift to Value, 207

What This Means to You, 209

    In Closing, 214

7 Secure Global Commerce . . . Managing the Tension between "Assured" and "Agile" Commerce   **217**

Setting the Stage: Mutual Visibility and Mutual Dependency, 219

The Extent of the Challenge: "Here, There, and Everywhere", 222

    75 Days, 25 Hands, 222

    Operation Safe Commerce: Starting Steps of a Long Journey, 227

Facing the Challenge: Turning the Tension into Harmony, 230

Visibility through Blueprinting, 230

Visible Commerce and Connectivity, 235

It *Is* a Small World after All, 245

What This Means to You, 246

8 Pragmatic Execution . . . in the Context
of Everything Else   255

*Setting the Stage: From Being Compelling to
Being Useful, 257*

*Facing the Challenge: Managing
the Impossible Decision, 258*

Making a Scramble Not a Scramble, 258

Creating Information Advantage, 259

What This Means to You, 262

Afterword   265

*The Pragmatics of Getting Work Done:
A Perspective from State Street, 265*

Notes   271

Index   285

About the Authors   299

Introduction—Making Sense and Taking Action

Setting the Stage: What Is It about Execution That Demands So Much Attention? And Why Now?

What is it about certain words, the word *execution*, for example? After a period of eclipse, execution is currently more than a hot word; it's a bona fide hot topic, a favorite of the press, the pundits, the analysts, and the vendors. A question is: Why now, or why again? The answer is as simple as its implications are profound; what's driving this hot topic is a cold reality—the marketplace uncertainty we all face.

Consider your own situation. If you do not feel at least some degree of unease, of uncertainty regarding your own personal and your company's ongoing competitive position, you are in the minority. Sure, there are those who know that they and their company will be around for years; that's not what we're talking about. We're talking about the competitive environment in which you and your company are located, and your place within that environment. Will you be in a stronger or weaker position given changes in your business environment, restructuring, reorganization, reengineering, repositioning, rebranding, or any other adjectives and actions that can and will impact your firm? How will you respond to these shifts? And do you *even know* what these shifts or pretipping point tipping points are and how to respond to if not anticipate them?

In a recent survey of CXOs (senior corporate executives that have "chief" in their title) and senior executives, 40 percent reported that in the past year their organizations had experienced "radical change." The uncertainty that drives this radical change is now the *only* certainty of their competitive lives, and yours. But just how prepared are you and your business to deal with it? It appears that the answer is: "Not very well prepared at all." In the same survey, 57 percent of the respondents rated their organizations as "ineffective in managing the varying scopes of change."

These responses help explain the critical need for effective execution. As we all know, businesses will *always* be faced with a significant amount of uncertainty. It is this uncertainty that creates fast-moving business opportunities—for those able to exploit them. To be blunt: Uncertainty, and the desire to seize the opportunities it creates, are the reason for the renewed attention and focus on execution. But you must develop specific capabilities to exploit those unpredictable business opportunities—indeed, the very opportunities that uncertainty creates.

But execution of what, for what? Companies have specific ways of doing what they do, and position themselves differently depending upon what type of "value proposition" they offer their customers; for example, a business may be known for innovation, low-cost, superior customer service, or combinations of these attributes. No matter the industry, however, and no matter the specific focus, all companies—private or public, commercial or government, market leader or market follower—need to manage their growth, their profitability, and the requirements placed on them for information and regulatory visibility. If you're a private company, you *gotta* grow, you *gotta* watch expenses, and you *gotta* know what's going on in your business because someone is *gonna* ask and you have to be able to answer. If you're a public sector enterprise, you're *gonna* grow, you're budget is *gonna* go up and down, and most likely that budget is *gonna* have regulatory strings attached.

So far, so good. And this is probably as comfortable as it is familiar to you. But now let's move onto less comfortable grounds to discuss what many of us experience everyday.

Once a strategy is formulated, its execution involves many people, many organizations, and many technologies. As with the parlor game of whispering a message around a circle of friends, there's almost no hope that a message (or an action), unaided, will make its way intact across the far-flung reaches of a business. A business that hopes to execute its strategy with the alacrity required in today's marketplace—to satisfy customers, the capital markets, the regulatory agencies—must seamlessly connect its strategy, solutions, products, business processes, and technology. To perform with the effectiveness necessary to compete and thrive, it must be able to mobilize resources inside and outside its organizational walls, protect its intellectual property, leverage what it does best—its "core competencies"—and reconfigure its assets to best face the market quickly, effectively, consistently.

Yet, multiple and specific challenges exist, everyday and in every corner of the business, to getting stuff done—to executing quickly, effectively, and consistently—from strategy through operations. Much has been written on execution. Much has been discussed on what an *executionally aware* company looks like, on the leadership needed, on aligning the metrics, changing the governance, altering the communications—on sets of *stuff* to do—to become more executionally competent. Taken as a whole, they describe a disciplined culture of execution critical for businesses to recognize the hard realities about the uncertainties they face and the choices they need to make.

No doubt, people need such a culture of execution to empower them to action. But culture does not reshape business processes, create applications, or build technology infrastructure. It creates the environment to do so. It conveys "what" has to be done rather than "how" to get it done. *"How to get it done"* requires an *execution framework* of tools, techniques, and methods to actually achieve the goals that the culture of execution encourages. An execution framework must be rich in (1) shared semantics and (2) connections. *Shared semantics* are critical to get everyone on the same page of understanding—to counter the business version of the parlor whispering game that inevitably confuses the understanding of what has to get done, and how to do so. *Connections* are critical so that people throughout the business understand "what connects with what, where, when, how, and by how much." We describe both of these in detail in this book. For now, the point is simply that both shared semantics and connections are critical so that each person involved in the enterprise is executing in a way that aligns to drive the strategy forward. If the culture of execution is the brains and personality of the enterprise, then the execution framework forms the bones and muscles needed to do the heavy lifting, and the nervous system that makes sure everything is playing its part in a coherent whole.

What needs to be in an execution framework? There are no end of recommendations "out there" on execution giving us lists of things to do, actions to take, governance to alter, and metrics to align. Again and again. But for many, following these recommendations doesn't work. So, we ask a simple question: Why not?

To the cacophony of recommendations, we say "stop," there has to be a different way. And there is. In this book, we take on the same issue but from a different perspective. The challenge remains the same: how do you get done what needs to get done—how do you execute—quickly, effectively, and consistently. But we start with a different set of questions:

- Are there common issues, constraints, and problems in creating a culture of execution?
- Is there an underlying strand of "business DNA" that determines executional consistency?
- And, if there is, what is it, and how can we manipulate it to get done what needs to get done to align the goals of an organization with its execution?

It is no surprise that the answer to the first two questions is a strong "yes." Answering the last question is the substance of the rest of this book. In short, knowing what this executional DNA is and manipulating it to your advantage, helps to achieve what we call "executional alignment and consistency." Our objective is simple: to guide executives and managers through creating such executional consistency so often lacking but so critical to getting stuff done.

Making sense without being able to *take action* may result in conceptual clarity and back-patting; *taking action* without *making sense* may result in the misplaced energy of "fire, ready, aim." Either by itself results in additional cost and delay, rework, frustration, and competitive atrophy. Together, connected through what we will describe as the DNA of executional consistency and Business Blueprinting, they result in doing what we want to get done—namely, what it is that "needs" to get done.

In far too many organizations, disconnects exist between what executives want to happen and what really does happen. Consequently, organizations face a nearly insurmountable challenge in aligning their goals with their execution. What is needed is a pragmatic means to overcome this challenge. Our goal is to provide you with means to do so, to bridge these disconnects and thereby help you get done what needs to get done. Knowing *what impacts what, where, when, how, and by how much*—getting the critical visibility into how strategic decisions impact business processes that engage supporting applications and underlying technology—is key to bridge these disconnects. And it is this key that we will use to unlock then manipulate the DNA to strengthen your executional capabilities.

What we have heard, witnessed, and experienced year after year, in organization after organization, and what underlies the "execution call to action" so prominent today is the need to align behavior and understand tangibly the implications of decisions made, investments proposed, and actions taken. We provide a highly tangible, case-study-intensive, and immediately applicable way to strengthen your execution capabilities—to help you close that gap between executive demands and field reality, of helping you get done what needs to get done.

What's in the Book?

So far, we have answered the question why is so much attention paid to execution and why now. We have also suggested that it is critical to identify and build the DNA of execution. But what *is* this executional DNA and how do we manipulate it to create executional consistency? Chapter 1 answers these questions. We describe what is common to so many of our executional challenges, offering a simple framework to understand those challenges and an equally simple insight to begin to overcome them. Chapter 1, then, starts to build our execution framework, helping us frame the "root cause" critical to get stuff done, effectively and consistently.

Chapters 2 and 3 move quickly from frameworks to action. They focus on what we call "the pragmatics of execution"—the elements that go into making it real. Knowing *what connects with what, where, when, how, and how much* is what we need to get done what needs to get done; such knowledge has very much become a business Holy Grail for many of us, for years. After all, when our actions are separated from those of others and their impacts remain unknown (or, as it sometimes seems, unknowable and invisible), it is no surprise that a business decision cannot be implemented quickly, effectively, and consistently. *Knowing what impacts what, where, when, how, and how much*—having the means to monitor, to measure and to manipulate the impacts of your activities and so understand the implications of your decisions—is at the heart of an execution framework. Chapters 1 through 3 describe our execution framework to realize the consistency so often lacking. It tackles head-on the execution hurdles faced in organizations.

We often face a double hurdle in our attempts to get stuff done: We seldom know either what impacts we create or how extensive those impacts are. These hurdles are rarely the result of malicious or intended actions. Often, they merely reflect that our organizations are made up of people with different backgrounds, focuses, and organizational priorities, each with their own understandings of what to do and how to get things done. These people probably share some common language and very possibly have the same organizational values and goals. Yet, as we have probably all experienced, shared language, values, and goals need not necessarily mean shared understandings of what any of these mean—much less how to use or be guided by them. Different groups of people in a business use different vocabularies, and their understandings of business issues are often very (and necessarily) different exactly because of their specialized focus within the business. Any attempt to create change runs directly into this organizational Babel that we call a *semantic disconnect*. This semantic disconnect is the core difficulty in getting stuff done.

Let's restate this: It is no wonder that it's so hard to get executional consistency—for a simple reason: *A semantic disconnect exists throughout our organizations.* Without shared understandings of what things mean, it is not possible to get the executional consistency needed, to figure out what connects with what, when, where, how, and how much, to get done what needs to get done. Now, if we pose the executional challenge this way, the question of *how* to overcome it becomes clear: Develop tools and methods to overcome the semantic disconnect. And that's precisely what our pragmatic framework based on Business Blueprinting, is about—providing the means to develop *shared semantics* that are as meaningful as they are actionable by the necessarily diverse people throughout your business.

Chapters 2 and 3 provide the tools to manipulate an organization's executional DNA. Chapter 2 describes *Business Blueprints* and some of its underlying tools, methods, and techniques to create the shared semantics across your business. This chapter focuses on answering the questions: What connects with what, where, and how? Chapter 3 extends this focus by answering the "how much" part of the "what connects with what" mantra. Lean Six Sigma is described as an example of how to identify, prioritize, and realize significant returns as relevant for product and service, sales and delivery businesses. Business Blueprinting and Lean Six Sigma form the two parts of our execution framework. Together, they provide a relevant, high-impact set of behaviors and methods to manipulate the DNA of getting stuff done that has to get done. We move quickly from describing the execution framework to demonstrating our execution framework in action.

Chapter 4 describes what businesses too often experience—a fine strategy not followed—and prescribes ways of making strategies *executionally aware*—a.k.a. "useful." How often have you shaken your head when you hear about a (new) strategy initiative while thinking (1) there's nothing new there, (2) it isn't a "real" strategy—it's just warmed-over operational leftovers, (3) it cannot be implemented, or (4) all of the above? Why is this so often the case? Often, as we like to say being met with wry grins, strategies are conceptually clean and analytically pure, but operationally useless. So, the question is: How can you *make* strategies more operationally useful and viable? How can you make your strategies *executionally aware,* or in even simpler language, just plain useful? The reality is, strategy—or some semblance of what organizations call strategy—isn't going away. Monies will be spent, resources will be used, and expectations will be set, so rather than chafing at the process and results, we need a way to embrace strategy to make it more relevant. Chapter 4 does this, focusing on how to pragmatically make strategies more relevant, more consistent, and, most importantly, more *useful*.

Chapter 5 turns its attention to process optimization. Business processes are the lifeblood of any business. Strategic goals of a business are implemented by its processes; an enterprise's technology exists to support those processes; business customers interact with its processes (hopefully) to create or at least support the value the customer wants. Business processes are sets of activities that "get stuff done." Getting this stuff done reflects the accumulated activities, experiences, and knowledge that power them. How to capture this far too often tacit knowledge, these mutations and workarounds, that are necessary to respond to changing market requirements and customer demands is a fundamental challenge to bridge the gap between strategic goals and actual activity. We explore how to tackle this challenge with a particular focus on the intersection between business and technology processes. We highlight the importance of *optimizing* business process solutions to balance the demands of the many stakeholders of a business process. We understand that for some, the word *optimization* might be associated with maximum efficiency. That is emphatically *not* our intent; efficiency is just one of many ways to judge a business process, and in today's business environment, efficiency is often not the most important of those dimensions. As we see in a detailed walk-through of the transformation of the Unemployment Insurance Division of New York State's Department of Labor, their focus on process optimization was critical in realigning the activities of the division with the needs of their citizens and providing the direction for modernization of their 30-year-old technology.

Chapter 6 focuses on business process outsourcing (BPO) and what is being called "next-generation BPO." The BPO industry is in transition. At its core, BPO has promised to take costs off of balance sheets, streamline business processes, and take advantage of existing assets (whether people, processes, and/or other forms of intellectual assets). These promises have been clear. But whether or not they have been kept is less clear. Certainly, many businesses using BPO have seen positive returns; value has been created, but much has been lost, too. What *is* clear, however, is that the transition includes movement away from a sole focus on reducing costs to a need to provide both cost-based *and* what is called "value-based" BPO services. But reducing costs is fundamentally different from enhancing value. Many of the fundamental tensions being faced in the BPO marketplace reflect its shifting focus—from costs *to* managing the demands of costs *and* value. Exploiting the BPO transition requires figuring out how to juggle these fundamentally different demands. Yet, neither this balance nor how to clearly measure the value to be realized has been figured out sufficiently. The BPO suppliers that figure it out will grab significant market share and add a powerful new tool to their competitive arsenal; their clients will gain a business advantage from a win-win relationship; and *their* customers will benefit from better and more effective services. Chapter 6 explores these issues, isolates its underlying dynamics, and shows how several businesses have begun to use the execution framework to juggle these different demands to sustain and newly create competitive advantage.

Chapter 7 focuses on what is increasingly known as *secure commerce*. In this chapter, we tackle one of the most important supply chain issues for businesses today: how to manage the tradeoff between low-cost, fast-moving global access and distribution of goods on the one hand, and the potential for personal and commercial disasters due to terrorism, piracy, and other forms of commercial disruption on the other. The security of the global supply chain—secure commerce—is an important focus of the Department of Homeland Security (DHS) and cooperating agencies throughout the world, and has spawned a thicket of new regulations affecting import/export activities. Businesses are well aware of the stakes: as a CEO of one of the world's largest privately held companies put it, "a terrorist activity in one of our cargo containers would be a company-ending event." Governments and businesses alike want to make visible what is far too often invisible across the handoffs and data, regulations and processes, applications and infrastructure at every step in the global circulation of goods. Figuring out how to manage the inherent tensions between being agile (moving quickly to take advantage of shifting opportunities) yet being secure (while adhering to increasing numbers of regulatory security requirements) is an increasingly important requirement for business worldwide. Tensions lie between increasing visibility into your supply chain while decreasing the costs and time of doing so. How well businesses manage this balance—what we call the tension between "agile but assured commerce"—will impact how well they perform. Chapter 7 looks at the experiences of several companies in their secure commerce initiatives and how the execution framework is helping them manage this tension effectively.

Chapter 8 concludes our book with a discussion of pragmatic execution. We step back and pull together the threads—from the case studies and anecdotes, the frameworks and methods, the tools and techniques—to weave the tapestry for executional consistency. We summarize key lessons from different perspectives; and we return to where we started—namely to reemphasize that any list of recommendations to create a culture of execution will only be as effective as it is possible to execute consistently, easily, and pragmatically. And doing so, we have found, depends on knowing how to *make sense* and *take action* to bridge what we call the semantic disconnect and getting the visibility and insight into *what connects with what, who, when, how, and how much*. Manipulating this DNA strand of executional consistency allows this to happen, again easily and pragmatically.

We acknowledge that "making sense" and "taking action" sound simple. And they are, as long as the latter builds on the former. To paraphrase a Chinese proverb, "In times of uncertainty, prepare for change; where precautions have been taken through understanding made, there is no peril." Making sense and taking action are at the foundation of the pragmatics of execution, a necessary requirement for effective organizational performance, for getting done what needs to get done—again and again.

What This Means to You

Jim Collins in his book, *Good to Great*, emphasized three key questions around which his lessons were constructed: what are you passionate about, what is your economic fly wheel—for example, how do you make your money—and what can you be best-in-the-world at?[1]

We have taken a similar approach of using three key considerations underlying *pragmatic execution*. The first, to paraphrase Jim Dillon, the CIO of New York, is *how to do more with more or even better, with less*. The second is *how to make the invisible visible*—the focus here on being clear on what connects with what, where, when, how, and how much. And the third is what we call *the pragmatics of execution . . .* in the context of everything else. One of our clients once bemoaned the fact that he faced the "impossible decision" between how to manage costs yet create innovation. Managing costs usually means "managing them down," which means minimizing risk and "taking stuff out"; yet creating innovation often requires "adding in" risk and "trying stuff out"—precisely the opposite set of activities. Reconciling these two, making decisions between them, appears impossible. Difficult, perhaps. Impossible, certainly not. But being able to *even have* the conversation about, much less make the decisions on, how to manage these inherent tensions between managing costs and creating innovation is what manipulating the DNA of execution allows you to do—and hence is the third underlying theme across all that we share here.

The Red Queen is a character in Lewis Carroll's *Alice's Adventures in Wonderland* and *Through the Looking Glass*. She is the character who runs faster and faster merely to keep up. We used her extensively as arguably "the" competitive metaphor in our first book that discussed models and methods (and some "madness") for creating collaborative-based innovation.[2] She remains as critically applicable here. A question for all of us is: Can we continue to run harder and harder, or need we run differently? Is the issue of "execution" one of working in a more disciplined manner or of working differently? We know that these questions sound like something so commonly asked that they mean nothing. But, there is, we believe, something profoundly simple and, because it is simple, profoundly useful in re-asking them. The answers to these questions are, of no surprise, "run differently" and "work differently." But, these are the answers you'd expect. So, what's different now? What's different is exploring and explaining, suggesting and offering how to manipulate the DNA of execution—of creating and manipulating the shared semantics—to create the alignment and executional consistency across the very (and necessarily) different parts of your organization so that you can do what needs to get done—again and again.

Benjamin Zander is a phenomenal orchestra conductor who is able to get sounds and emotions unheard of from orchestras and audiences around the world. He and his wife, Roz, have written a book, *The Art of Possibility*, that explores how merely thinking differently—or what they call "creating new categories"—opens up fundamentally new ways of understanding, then acting in ways that were unknown or closed to them previously.[3] There's a fabulous movie from 1980 called *The Gods Must Be Crazy* focused on a bushman in the Kalahari desert who encounters technology for the first time—in the shape of a Coke bottle. In it, there's a wonderful line: "things that yesterday were unknown have today become a necessity."[4] Both of these citations summarize our strong belief that the issue we're focused on—how to help you do what it is you need to get done, again and again—is less one of working harder than it is of working differently.

Simplicity is good. And effective. Understanding, and acting—making sense and taking action—of the DNA underlying executional consistency starts with an insight into what underlies so much of what bedevils us in getting done what we need to get done. And that insight is the critical need to bridge semantic disconnects. That insight is the critical need to create shared semantics *that are as meaningful as they are usable* to the necessarily different and diverse people in your organization. Using this insight *is* a new way of thinking; and based on what we have experienced, it is as powerful as it is provocative, as intuitive to grasp as it is easy to exploit to take the actions needed to get done what needs to get done—again and again.

The DNA of
Consistent Execution

Setting the Stage: Getting
Stuff Done Quickly, Effectively, Consistently

Mike is senior vice president of retail banking applications for one of the world's largest financial services organizations. We met with him to discuss executional consistency—consistently performing at scale across an organization and in alignment with organizational goals. Actually, the meeting didn't start out to be about executional consistency. We were there to talk about the main topic of this chapter: challenges businesses face to *do stuff*—to execute, to perform, or to do whatever achievement verb best suits your environment. Jim Dillon, CIO of the State of New York, frames this topic well: "I'm happy to do more with more, or less with less, but I am not even going to talk about doing less with more." Aside from clever wordplay, there is deep understanding and insight expressed in Jim's phrase: We need to figure out how to get our work done more effectively. That's the focus of this chapter, and that was Mike's reason for talking with us. Mike wanted some perspective on the DNA of execution and the relationship of shared vocabulary and semantics to getting stuff done effectively. He wanted ideas on how to reduce time and expense he incurred getting things done; and he wanted to know about tools, methods, and techniques that might help him get "more done." Note that the conversation didn't start well. The actual conversation went something like this:

MIKE: I don't have much time to spend with you, and if we're here to talk about methods and tools, I can tell you that everyone in my organization is trained and uses the Rational programming tools, and they use their Rational Unified Process for development. [Note: Rational and Rational Unified Process are a technical development environment and set of methods for doing technical modeling and analysis work.] In fact, I have more people using modeling tools right now than you have people in your entire company. So maybe we should have a cup of coffee, have a pleasant chat for 10 minutes, and then we can all get on with our day.

Us: We'd prefer tea if that's possible [since tea takes longer to prepare]. But while we're getting ready to go, would you please tell us what the major challenge you face is around this large project you're undertaking? [Okay, so we're not fully on top of our grammar in early morning meetings.]

MIKE: Well, okay [he said, pouring his cup of coffee and pointing to the tea bags]. We have a hard time keeping up with the changes demanded by the business. I have over 150 different retail banking products and underlying applications here that support all aspects of the retail bank, and we can't change, test, and get things into production fast enough to keep up with new products and features that have to get out to the market.

Us: [Now getting up and getting ready to go.] We see that problem over and over. Tell us, since you have a solid understanding of each of your applications and the products that you support, have you spent the time to look *across* your various applications and products to see if there are patterns where you can reuse things across applications?

MIKE: Hmm, great question . . . and please sit down. Give me an example.

Us: Well, you're a retail bank with approximately 150 different products you offer to your customers. No matter how different they are, at some point, each probably requires a customer to open an account with the bank—or something like that. Do you have any sense of how many separate "Open New Account" functions you have scattered through the applications you maintain? Or for that matter, how many different ways the people in the different parts of the bank actually process opening a new account?

MIKE: [Reflecting . . .] No. . . . I *don't* know. But talk to me, what can I do that would help me?

Us: Say that in your more than 150 applications there are 20 different places that "Open New Account" is required. We'd guess, based on what we've seen elsewhere and given that your company has acquired a number of other banks over the past few years . . .

MIKE: Yes! and I've gotten every one of their [profanity deleted] applications into my shop to support . . .

US: We'd guess that almost every one of those 20 "Open New Account" functions has been written uniquely, and probably each has buried in it business rules and business logic that you have to change each time the bank changes its rules, get new regulations that affect your products, or the bank changes or extends its product line.

MIKE: That's right.

US: Imagine the person-hours of maintenance you'd be able to use for other things if, instead of 20 "Open New Account" functions, you had a single function that all of your 150 products and underlying applications used.

MIKE: That would be a major savings . . . and there are lots of functions besides "Open New Account" that this would apply to. How would we get there?

US: Normally we'd tell you to start by modeling your business processes and applications—capturing the tacit intellectual property that's buried in the technology programs, the databases, and the heads of the experts who maintain them into higher-level abstractions of what they are and what they do—so that we could look for patterns of use and duplication. Given that you are using the Rational tools, you've already been codifying the information about your application portfolio into a form [models in Universal Modeling Language, or UML] that makes it more straightforward to find the patterns, figure out what is the same and what's different, and model a single function that could replace the 20 unique functions. We would start here, but equally if not more importantly, begin to understand what are the business processes that touch or are touched by these patterns. Knowing what touches what around these patterns will provide significant insight into what you can start to do, right away, and how to do it.

MIKE: All right, then [having asked us to stay for quite a while longer]. Let's start tomorrow on "Open New Account." By the time we've done that work, we'll have prioritized the next 10 business functions that we spend the most effort on, and we'll do the same thing for them.

Since that conversation, we found over two dozen functions—from the original "Open New Account" through "Research Account Dispute" and "Close Account." Each of these appeared in multiple business processes and the applications supporting the more than 150 and constantly increasing new products that were created or enhanced. Each of these as well were used by different groups using the applications that contained them worldwide throughout the retail bank. This one global retail bank—with a single global brand and an active campaign to ensure a great customer experience—actually looked like multiple, disconnected banks, none of which did business the same way. This lack of integration creates implications for many parts of the bank's business:

- *For the customer:* Often, when the customer wants to do more business with this bank, they are treated as though the bank knows nothing about them. This lack of a personal touch (or the illusion of a personal touch) means that the customer doesn't perceive any particular advantage in staying with this bank, and so is more likely to leave or is less likely to broaden his or her relationship with the bank.

- *For the employees who interact with the customer:* Since each part of the bank does things differently, an employee moving from one part of the bank to another—say from Mortgage Lending to Home Equity Lending—needs to learn new ways of doing things even though the businesses may be very closely related. This adds cost and effort to bank operations. Worse, it constrains an employee's mobility reducing their chances for new, challenging assignments and possibly making them more likely to look elsewhere for career opportunities.

- *For the employees who support the applications that support the employees who interact with the customer:* Many different implementations of similar but slightly different functionality create an environment that is prone to error, high pressure, and "death march" types of projects. This leads to burnout and dissatisfaction in the very analysts and programmers who may be the only ones who know the quirks of some particular program implementing familiar functionality.

- *For the senior executives and CEO:* Frustration because the vision of one global brand and one customer experience—a vision that he or she articulated to the board, the analysts, and the shareholders three years ago—is still years away from reality due to the expense and the time eaten up by the lack of executional consistency in the business processes and the applications that support them.
- *For the shareholders:* The extra cost and the lack of agility due to the lack of executional consistency negatively impact the company's earnings and stock price.

In this chapter, we define the concept of *executional consistency* and analyze the DNA of executional consistency—the underlying characteristics and behaviors that enable an organization to get done what needs to get done quickly, consistently, and effectively. Once we have identified the needed characteristics—and underlying DNA for executional consistency—we explore in Chapter 2 some methods, tools, and processes that can be used to create those characteristics, and in Chapter 3 we examine some methods and processes to actually change—permanently—the organization to create the capabilities of getting done what has to get done, over and over again.

Extent of the Challenge: Why Is This *So* Hard?

Here's a question for you: Just how important is being able to execute—to align your objectives with your activities? This seems like a silly question. Of course it's critical. But as many of us know, it's extremely difficult to do and not many businesses know how to do it. Conflicting organizational activities, silos, redundant processes, and confusing, if not complicated, governance policies block effective, consistent execution. More than 64 percent of C-level executives from 250 midsized to large companies in the United States and the European Union have said that being able to execute, to "react quickly to changing business opportunities, models, technologies, and processes is critical for their success," and yet is nearly impossible to achieve.[1] Key to being sufficiently responsive is the capability to execute and align executive statements of what's supposed to happen with "stuff" that must be addressed to go in the direction at the speed and impact desired. The difficulty, as we all know, lies in actually *being able* to do so—to "do the stuff" that has to be done. What *is* it about an organization that makes execution so difficult? And what is common to these difficulties?

Common Challenges to Getting Stuff Done

Common challenges to getting stuff done can be sorted into the following categories:

1. *Getting your stuff out the door—a.k.a., Reducing your cycle time:* Whether regulatory-driven or a result of disruptive technologies or competitor moves, this particular challenge manifests itself in problems getting new products or services out the door fast enough. In public sector organizations, the challenge is how to become more responsive to ever-changing legislative demands for new services, or convert an agency or department into a more "constituent-driven" organization.

2. *Integrating existing with emerging technologies—a.k.a., Getting "value" from your IT activities:* Up to 70 percent of IT budgets are spent on maintenance and redevelopment rather than on new application development, and 60 percent to 80 percent of application functionality is redundant leading to a significant drag on cost levels. Companies spend a great deal of time and money on maintaining heritage or legacy applications for a good reason: They work! At the same time, the never-ending introduction of new technology and business functions means that new technical skills are required to complement the ones we already have. The tension between *what we have* and *what we need*

to incorporate is even further exacerbated by things like exten-sive consolidation, acquisition of companies into other com-panies, and/or the result of initiating multiple projects to meet multiple objectives multiple times over multiple years. The re-sult: complex, different, and often redundant technical environ-ments compounding the difficulty of getting different systems to talk with each other, as well as both figuring out how to evolve the skill-sets of your people, and figuring out effectively how to integrate existing with emerging technologies. And on and on it goes.

These first two problems have been an ongoing challenge for the past 30 years and, for that reason, we won't spend much time on them. The following two are becoming increasingly critical, warranting more discussion:

1. *Disconnected or disappearing intellectual assets—a.k.a., Unlocking invisible value:* In too many organizations, the knowledge of how a particular process works, or of what an application actually does, is locked in the heads of one or a small number of individuals. In the next five years, more than 40 percent of the workforce in U.S. state and local government organizations will reach retirement age and re-tire with the knowledge that formed the "glue" that created whatever executional consistency exists in those organizations today.

The CIO of the Retail Banking Business Unit of a major global bank has identified *training* as one of his most strategic initiatives. He faces a crisis because much of what he called the "organizational wisdom"—the skills and know-how critical to keeping the business running, to develop, deploy, and maintain specific retail banking applications—was either "forced out or is walking out the door." Reasons cited for this drain of organizational wisdom included a combination of ongoing economic and competitive pressures on mar-gins as well as the fact that the momentum for outsourcing has re-sulted in significant (to use jargon of the day) *right-sizing* of the retail banking employee base. Training, for him, has thus become *the* criti-cal mechanism to capture as much of this *walk-around* or *walk-out-the-door* knowledge as possible.

Clark Kelso, CIO of the state of California, in his keynote address at the CIO Academy in California in late 2004, decried the demographic implications of 42 percent of state and local employees as well as over 70 percent of California chief information officers scheduled to retire within the next five years. "What will be the implications on systems maintained and developed," he queried. What will be the implications on the quality of constituent services that these systems enable as these people retire? As Clark pointed out, and a surprise to no one, many of these systems and applications are undocumented, held together merely by *tacit knowledge*— the knowledge in the heads of the people who built them and maintained them over the years.

At a late fall 2003 conference in Europe, the vice-chairman of one of Europe's and Latin America's premiere financial institutions articulated concerns about the "demographic transformation" of Europe and Latin America and its implications for maintaining a leadership position. As the graying (and increasingly, retiring) workforce in Europe meets the labor migration from North Africa and Eastern Europe into Western Europe—and these meet the "demographic greening" of Latin America and its explosive entrance into the workforce—what will be the effect on maintaining a competitive position and effective operations? So much of what people know will be lost as they retire; yet the demands for new products and services will explode in urgency and need. Who will be there to train the new workforce? How, he asked, will we minimize the impact of the *brain drain* as the existing workforce moves on?

There are two specific parts to this *intellectual asset* issue. The first is recognizing the role of *tacit knowledge*—ranging from hard assets (systems, applications, and documented business processes) to soft assets (norms, values, workarounds, and undocumented business processes)—as one of the key intellectual assets of your everyday activities (more on this later). This knowledge is embedded into systems, applications, business processes, and norms of behaviors that together form the organizational glue that keeps the business together on a day-to-day basis. The second part is figuring out the *competitive half-life* of these assets, how valuable they are, and for how long. Which of these assets adds competitive advantage to you and in what areas? How long will those advantages last and what do you do with assets that no longer enhance your competitive positioning?

Geoffrey Moore, author of *Crossing the Chasm* and *Living on the Fault Line*, approaches the half-life question of intellectual assets in terms of *core* and *context*. For Moore, what is *core* to your business are those activities and instantiated assets that add shareholder value and add differentiated value; *context* activities are things that have to get done but add no direct value to your competitive position.[2] The challenge, as Moore summarizes it, is to continually evaluate your core and focus on it, and figure out what to do with your context—whether to stop it, reengineer it, or outsource it. For a quick example, ING Insurance, one of the world's largest and most profitable insurance companies, has been involved recently in developing a new policy administration system. Throughout the project, they have been as aggressively focused on understanding what their intellectual assets were as the specific functionality that had to be built. For each process and application, they have asked what type of competitive value each asset provides, for how long, and what to do about it. They recognized that answers to these questions determine if and how to exploit the asset with significant implications on both their current and future competitive capabilities.

2. *Mobilizing your T-Shirts, Turtlenecks, and Suits—a.k.a., Aligning your (inherently and necessarily) diverse teams:* Most people have encountered the frustrations of conflicting organizational activities, silos, redundant processes, and confusing if not complicated governance policies. The common cry for the need to align metrics is stifled by the operational complexity of how to do so given fundamental differences of priorities and focuses. George Colony, CEO of Forrester Research, an industry research group, humorously characterizes an organization as consisting of three types of people: T-Shirts, Turtlenecks, and Suits. In the next chapter, we reinterpret this somewhat tongue-in-cheek classification into something more tangible and actionable, but for now, T-Shirts are the operations people, Turtlenecks the marketing teams, and Suits the management folks. They may all acknowledge the same set of organizational objectives

and high-level metrics that tell how well they are doing in meeting their objectives. However, each group has its own focus, language, and orientation, making their cultures vastly different, and making each group's approach to accommodating change equally different. It is, consequently, no wonder that organizations so seldom achieve the executional consistency necessary between strategy and operations. The differences in approach, understanding, orientation, and perspectives are so different that it makes any type of executional consistency a pleasant surprise rather than an operational norm.

Facing the Challenge: Bridging the Semantic Disconnect

We have all experienced one if not all of the challenges that result from a lack of executional consistency (if not, please contact us as a case study counter example!). They create tremendous amounts of frustration and costs, both personal and organizational. So, why are these challenges so hard to address? Is there anything today that is significantly different from yesterday to allow us to take on these challenges differently? Is there a common challenge or a root cause that, if redressed, can let us actually get done the stuff that needs to get done? On the surface, their different focuses seem so diffuse as to frustrate any attempts to find common ground among them. But can we not find common ground on which to make sense and take action more effectively? The answer to these questions is the same: A strong yes. There *is* a root cause to the inability to execute quickly, consistently, and effectively, and there are methods, tools, techniques, and standards to address it. And that's what we begin to explain, and explore, in the rest of this chapter and throughout the book.

Underlying the challenge of executional consistency is something we call a *semantic disconnect*. Semantics is defined as the sharing of meanings among different people. Thus, a semantic disconnect occurs when different people take away different understandings of what has to get done to reach an objective. Given such different and disconnected understandings, it is no surprise that what results is an ever-widening *execution gap* that over time merely gets perpetuated, widened, and institutionalized. Sound familiar? Ever experienced this? Each of the challenges discussed in the previous section rests on a semantic disconnect.

Let's take a simple example in the form of an abstracted, but all-too-familiar, business interaction. John, a business operations person, has been working with Mary, a technology person, for several months on an application to assess the credit worthiness of new applicants. John represents his organization, where several hundred of his colleagues hope to use this new application to reduce the time and error rate in their processing of new card applications. Mary represents the software project team creating the application. John and Mary have been working together for the past several months with biweekly updates and occasional "friendly user" demonstrations of portions of the application as it was built.

JOHN: [after signing on to the new credit card assessment application that Mary has just submitted to him to evaluate] This isn't going to work for us.

MARY: [taken aback] John, we've been working on the requirements together for months, and I've been providing you status updates and even access to test out certain features for weeks now.

JOHN: [acknowledging the comment] That's true, but this isn't what we need here. For example, look . . . it doesn't refresh the credit configuration calculator to account for changes in the interest rates.

MARY: [a bit frustrated] But John, we worked through detailed requirements for this application. You even signed off on them, again and again. See? [She points to the requirement documents with John's signature on them.] Here is your signature. This is what you said you wanted!

JOHN: [equally frustrated, voice rising] Well, I may have said that this is what I wanted, but this isn't what I meant. I thought I understood what you were planning to build, but this application isn't what we need!

Do you know anyone who has ever had one of these conversations? Have *you* ever had one of these conversations? Have you ever heard—or said—anything like: "I heard what he/she said, but I have no idea what he/she meant." Or, maybe the question should be: Has anyone *not* heard or said something like this?

John and Mary experienced a semantic disconnect, probably due to the fact that business people and technical people have different vocabularies, so communication between them is, not surprisingly, problematic. Remember the T-Shirts, Turtlenecks, and Suits? Each of them has a specific job to do, and that job has a specific language—a way of communicating, understanding, and consequently acting—associated with it. Using job functions at the far ends of the range, to emphasize the point:

- The CEO (a Suit) uses a vocabulary that includes things like top-line growth, bottom-line profitability, share price, earnings, client or customer retention and satisfaction, and so on.

- The senior vice president of a business unit (also a Suit) uses a vocabulary that includes top-line growth and bottom-line growth for the business unit, and also things like productivity, transactions-per-headcount, utilization of resources (or efficiency of resources), customer-share-of-wallet, and so on.

- The people in marketing (Turtlenecks) use a unique vocabulary, like adoption rate, elasticity, demographic, psychographic, market message, and other terms.

- The people in the trenches processing customer-related things—the (T-Shirts) people who approve insurance claims, provide help desk support, judge the credit-worthiness of a mortgage applicant—use a vocabulary completely focused on their day-to-day job, like *validate claimant eligibility*, or *credit customer's account*.

- The analysts and programmers (also T-Shirts) who create and maintain the applications that support the people in the trenches use a technical vocabulary that includes things like system use case, Enterprise Java Bean (EJB) or XML document.

- The technology operations people who install and maintain the computing infrastructure that the applications run on use a unique infrastructure vocabulary that includes things like router blade, storage area network, or SONET ring.

Yet, and more importantly, even if T-Shirts, Turtlenecks, and Suits happen to use the same language, they often mean strikingly different things by the language used. For example, think of the word "account" or "customer." These terms often mean widely different things to different parts of an organization. Ask yourself: How many hours and dollars are spent on clarifying what these terms mean, in getting the head of the business, the IT manager, and the marketing analyst to agree on something that on the surface seems so obvious? But is it? Is an "account" or "customer" someone who purchases one of your products, receives specific services, a data structure in a database, a demographic to be mailed to, a prospect to be sold to, a statistic to be measured, an asset to be exploited, a cost to be handled, an opportunity to be positioned to, a risk to be managed, or one of a dozen other descriptions?

Which characterization is "best?" Which is most appropriate? The challenge is that each of these characterizations might be appropriate for what has to get done by the person who has to get it done. Moreover, there is seldom a way to show how these different understandings connect with each other—and impact each other. It is this connectivity that is critical to resolve the semantic disconnect across these different relevant and equally important understandings of what constitutes an account, or a customer. Creating such connectivity—demonstrating how they impact each other and thereby make sense to each other—is what we need to do to get the alignment desired and the executional consistency needed.

Okay, you say, what's different now, and how do we make it happen? Let's answer those questions in two parts: first, how to think about it, and second, how to do it—how do we make it real.

In day-to-day operations, when things are working well and the company is conducting business as usual these groups don't have to interact much. Where they do interact in the course of day-to-day business, they have worked out common semantics over time and much effort.

During times of change, however, semantic differences among different groups of people become barriers to executing consistently to make the change occur. In our earlier example, the change was that John, a member of the population in the trenches with the customer, wanted a change—specifically a new computer application from Mary, a member of the analysts and programmers population. John and his team articulated their needs in terms of their group's semantics. Mary and her team translated those needs in terms of theirs and created a computer application. We saw the result: The application initially missed the mark. Over time, John and Mary will go through a few more iterations of the application and it will perform as John and his team envisioned. However, the extra iterations add time and cost to the process and, depending on how dynamic John's part of the business is and how long it takes to get the application right, the business needs for the application may have changed by the time the application is ready, setting off another round of changes. (Not that this has ever happened in your business, of course.)

Over time, John and Mary will themselves create shared semantics; as a team of "businessperson" and "tech person" they will become much better at getting specifications and the resulting applications right the first time. They will have bridged, or at least narrowed, the semantic disconnect between them. The benefits will be substantial, but will last only as long as John and Mary are the two people working together. As soon as one or both move on to new job assignments, the semantic disconnect will open wide again, and the attendant inefficiencies will reemerge.

The same disconnect issue arises, on an even more expansive and expensive scale, when the CEO decides on a change in corporate direction. In their book *Execution: The Discipline of Getting Things Done*, Larry Bossidy and Ram Charan focus on the need for the CEO to be totally immersed in the organization and to drive the linkage among strategy, people, and operations. Ram Charan has said that "if you have a five-year vision that's good and inspiring [and] you'd better convert that vision into a two-year vision. If you don't do that, you lack the skills to be able to be an effective leader."[3]

Execution focuses on the disciplines of selecting and evaluating the right people to drive the organization, on the importance of setting goals, following up to be sure those goals are understood, measuring progress toward those goals, and rewarding people accordingly. Bossidy's application of these principles at Allied Signal—leading to 31 consecutive quarters of growth in Allied's earnings per share of 13 percent or more—speaks directly to the power of consistent execution. Our approach marries some of the ideas and practices in *Execution* with the powerful concept of *closing the semantic disconnect to drive execution pervasively through every business unit, department, and ultimately every person in a company. Execution* illustrates the potential of aligning the leadership of an organization and making each layer of leadership responsible and accountable for the performance of its part of the organization. However, even at the height of its performance, interactions like those between John and Mary were happening throughout Allied Signal every day, not due to a failure of leadership, but because workers spend most of their time and energy on doing their assigned job (their "day job"), and that job has its own demands, jargon, and semantics.[4]

Good leadership includes setting goals, setting schedules, following up, measuring results, rewarding and coaching the people involved. Yet, leaders seldom know—in detail—each interaction required to complete a set goal. There could be a smooth interaction between people who know each other well and understand a shared problem. There could be an arduous, uphill "death march" with enormous struggle and waste, absorbed in heroic efforts on the part of the people involved, late nights and weekend work, with the team meeting its goal but becoming bruised, burnt out, and disillusioned along the way. As detailed in *The Jericho Principle*, one major contributor to the difference between a smooth result or a brutal death march is the presence or absence of shared semantics among the participants.

Semantic disconnects occur again and again in organizations all over the world, leading to extra work, additional costs, finger pointing, personal and personnel frustrations, budget blowouts, exacerbated organizational silos, and (need we add) project delays that sap the organization's capability to mobilize in response to a need for change.

Now, assuming the semantic disconnect *is* the root cause hindering executional consistency, the simple follow-up question becomes *how* to semantically *reconnect*. *Consequently, the critical requirement to drive executional consistency is to overcome the semantic disconnects that permeate many of your organizational activities.* This means having the tools and methods to create common expressions to drive the executional consistency needed. It is fundamentally about creating the capabilities to ensure that strategic decisions taking place at the top of an organization are consistently executed down and throughout an organization—through its business processes, applications, and infrastructure. As we said earlier, this is not about everyone knowing everything about all parts of the business; that is neither feasible nor desirable. What *is* possible, however, is to use tools and methods to let each organization use its natural vocabulary, while at the same time understand how the semantics of each part of the organization relate to every other part of the organization. With what result? Visibility and connectivity among the different parts of the organization that help establish common understanding, align metrics, rationalize governance, streamline communication, and thereby create the capabilities for consistent execution.

This is a nice vision, but one so hard to achieve that it has become in many people's minds the business equivalent of King Arthur's search for the Holy Grail. But it needn't be: There are tools, methods, technologies, and standards that exist now, some that have been around for a while, some that have begun to mature within the past year or so. We'll explore some of these later. But first we need to describe how to think about—make sense—and take action on creating the shared semantics so sorely lacking, but so critically needed.

Answering the Question of How

So far, we've described core challenges to getting stuff done consistently, described requirements to getting it done, provided some quick examples, and presented the underlying DNA *for* executional consistency. But we have yet to describe how to look for that DNA and how to manipulate it for your purposes.

Getting stuff done consistently entails two activities. First, it requires that many people rapidly *make sense of*—understand—what it is that has to get done. Second, they must effectively *take action* by mobilizing an array of people and resources *to* execute consistently. Let's take a deeper look at what it takes for this to happen.

Change in an organization happens when someone has an idea, recognizes an opportunity, or responds to a threat that others haven't identified. The insight initially resides solely in its creator's head—in other words, as *tacit* knowledge. Taking effective and scalable action depends on taking this tacit idea and mobilizing that idea so others—ideally, many others—can understand, then execute that insight on a large scale. This capability to take action on a large scale requires *codifying* the tacit idea—turning it into an explicit form that then can be communicated, understood, and used by many others.

To illustrate this codification process, think of a chef's signature dish served at a restaurant. As long as the knowledge of how to create the dish remains the tacit knowledge of the master chef, he or she can create the dish for a handful of diners. If, however, the knowledge of how to create the dish is codified into a recipe, the dish can be created in many places by many chefs, and can become a global franchise. *That's scale, and the secret sauce is codification, the recipe to everything from potato chips to microchips.*

Tacit knowledge is one of the key intellectual assets of your everyday activities (more on this later). *Executional consistency speaks to the process of codifying tacit knowledge.* As tacit knowledge is codified, it moves from being locked away—in places like the heads of critical individuals, in software logic, or in application databases. It is captured in and usable through a growing repository, using well-defined expressions of business processes, technology enablers, and other assets. Such expressions often take the forms of models, equations, simulations, scenarios, and other forms of documentation that create the shared semantics that everyone in the organization can use to execute—consistently, effectively, and cost-effectively. (We often characterize these and other types of expressions as "grammar tools"—for a simple reason. Grammar is the inherent building blocks of effective communication, in turn necessary to have a hope of shared understanding and consequently effective action. This is why when we often hear in discussions, "oh, that's just semantics," as people attempt to dismiss-away disagreements or understandings, we quickly pounce and reply "but semantics are all we have" and why means to express them, and act *from them*, are so critical.) Tacit knowledge (*all those intangibles of what we know and experience*) itself has potentially high value, but, being inaccessible, is not scalable. *We break through the scaling limits of tacit knowledge by codifying that knowledge into the processes, frameworks, and standards where the power of scale can kick in.*

How well a company does this is the true determinant of how successfully it can execute consistently and at scale. We've reduced this claim to a simple mantra: *the more codified, the more executable; the more executable, the more scalable; the more scalable, the more consistent, aligned, and able to change rapidly, effectively, and efficiently.*

The Semantic Stack as Insight and Action

What do we mean by codification and how do we know it when we see it? One conceptual tool we use is called the *semantic stack*, a simple way of thinking about the degree of codification and its impact on what you do on a daily basis. But before describing the semantic stack, let's step back and explore the question: What do we mean by codification and how do you know it when you see it?[5]

At some point in the distant past, people began expressing themselves using words, first spoken and then written. From these words emerged common ways of speaking, shared communications, common viewpoints, shared culture, and the capability to mobilize people to effective action. So, what's different now? Not a thing! Organizations consist of people with different personalities and perspectives, different departments and duties, different ways of thinking and acting. What made and makes effective actions are the *shared understanding of what is expected, of what to do, of how to do it, and of measuring and realizing the value of those actions.* Shared semantics creates this shared understanding and enables scalable action. Why is this important? Because shared knowledge and understanding becomes more scalable and cheaper when knowledge is codified. Consequently, the degree of codification in any area is a critical measure of organizational agility, and of being able to execute consistently across the T-Shirts, Turtle-necks, and Suits. Now, back to the semantic stack.

In Figure 1.1, we show the semantic stack as a simple grid. The vertical dimension of the stack refers to different types of organizational activities. Roughly speaking, as you move from the top of the stack to the bottom of the stack, you are moving from overall corporate strategic things, through business operations, and down to the technology that supports the business. Imagine a senior executive who wants to make a change in corporate direction: that change at the top of the stack can only be realized by changes through the layers lower in the stack. Similarly, imagine a fundamental change in connectivity infrastructure, such as that resulting from the Internet. Such a change can result in change rippling upward through the stack, ultimately affecting the strategic direction of the business.

Philippe is executive vice president of Global Cash & Trade—one of the world's largest banks. His decision to expand aggressively throughout Eastern Europe is a strategic decision to take advantage of ever-shifting regulatory changes allowing financial capital to flow more freely throughout the region. Making this decision is one thing; acting on it requires concentrated efforts and aligned capabilities from his strategic intent through business process coordination, through underlying application extensions, and through network and infra-structure deployments. As we have all likely experienced, getting the

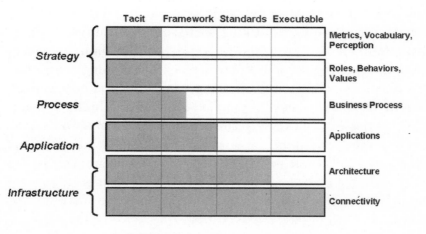

FIGURE 1.1 The Semantic Stack

alignment in terms of mobilizing activities within and across these different areas is difficult. Another difficulty lies in knowing how they connect and (will) impact each other. Philippe's decision is a "top-down" one starting from strategic intent impacting "down" into his infrastructure. But such impacts, dependencies, and constraints work the other way as well—rippling up through the stack, ultimately impacting the strategic direction of the business. Have you ever heard, or said, "we can't get that new product out the door because our network, or applications (or some other IT areas) cannot support it"? We talk much more later about this challenge and how to tackle it based on creating executional semantics.

The horizontal dimension of the stack represents the degree to which the knowledge of the layer has been codified. The further to the right, the greater the codification. The shading in Figure 1.1 gives a rough estimate of the current state of codification in each of the layers. This indicates, for example, that industry standards bodies, vendors, and the majority of global businesses have fully agreed to the standards and *shared semantics* underlying infrastructural connectivity around IP—the communications protocol that enables the Internet. Before such shared and executable semantics were created, the industry had a Babel-like environment of competing and conflicting ways of plugging into networks. Now there's a "standard" network, agreed to by most people, enabling a degree of automation and automatic execution that far exceeds any other set of organizational activity in this framework.

The upper layers of the stack remain less codified because, frankly, there is little or no agreement, within companies much less across industries, on a common way to represent activity and knowledge at those layers. Take the business process layer, as an example. We started this chapter talking about Mike's challenge of being sufficiently responsive to the market with his 150 plus retail banking products and underlying applications. The processes that Mike's technology needed to support were created over time, by different people, meeting different market needs. Mike needed a way to communicate about these processes—to express them—in a way that the business, the marketing, *and* the technical people could understand. He created business process models because without them there wasn't a consistent way the T-Shirts, the Turtlenecks, and the Suits could talk about—much less understand—what made up the business. And, without being able to do that, there was no way to be able to change the business quickly. But interestingly, while Mike recognized the importance of codifying the bank's processes, there is no industry-wide standard of doing so. Using the semantic stack model, Mike began codifying the tacit knowledge of the thousands of people at his bank and the work they did to support their customers in a way that could be meaningful and provide significant advantage to the bank. However, when Mike's bank acquires yet another bank—which it does on a frequent basis—the integration of the existing processes with the new processes will still be a challenge because there remains no cross-bank or cross-industry shared semantics of how to model processes. This is why the business process layer of Figure 1.1 is shaded.[6]

Let's compare the shading in the connectivity layer with the business process layer: while the Internet protocol specifies clearly how information flows on the network, there is no correspondingly universal way to describe business process flows, such as the process by which a credit card company takes in a customer request for a card and ends up issuing a card and opening an account or denying the card and reporting it to the credit bureaus.

The lack of codification in the upper layers of the stack means that people within those layers have higher barriers to accommodating change: When change in a layer is required, and the level of codification in that layer is low, then the people who must execute the change must first come to a semantic agreement—must close any potential semantic disconnects—about what the change is and what it means. Until that happens, many "John and Mary" interactions will *slow the process of change, and introduce ambiguity, which takes away the ability to execute consistently, effectively, and efficiently.*

Therefore, in terms of the stack, moving from *tacit* to *executable* across more and more of the layers of the stack increases the potential for executional consistency. We call this process *walking up and across the stack*.[7]

We can use the semantic stack and this process of *walking up and across the stack* to provide insight into competitive dynamics in general.

Competition results from different companies attempting to exploit a sufficiently attractive market opportunity. Initial market opportunities are usually high-margin and/or high-revenue opportunities, the results of their underlying value propositions being novel, consequently relatively unexploited or difficult to replicate, and largely embedded in the heads of relatively few people. Over time, these margins tend to get arbitraged away or shrunk as new competitors, recognizing the potential of those market opportunities, enter the competitive fray. What shrinks those margins are processes, technologies, and other activities that bring down their operational costs and allows them to become more scalable, hence executable by many. The means of driving such scalable activities is the enabling codification of those activities—of the tacit knowledge, the knowledge in the heads of few—into frameworks, into standards, into executable and repeatable activities.

So what? For now, let's highlight two things of importance. First, the stack serves as a mirror you can hold up to your business and see what is reflected back. By showing the degree of codification in a particular layer, the stack gives you a means—in an abstract but provocative way—to see how your company measures up. Again, back to Mike. Mike recognized that he had to begin to codify his processes; the bank is growing too much, is too global with too many different constituents and customers not to have widely shared agreement of what the business does, and how Mike's organization fits. "We're global . . . with the potential of fragmenting into dozens of competing companies. . . . We can't afford to do that; the risk is too great." Attempting, aggressively, to create shared semantics of what applications supported which products where, when, and how was a competitive necessity for Mike to become more effective at what the bank had to get done.

Second, the stack shows how the intellectual assets in your company are stratified, from abstract things like "business objectives" to concrete things like "connectivity" and "platforms." This is important because executional consistency comes from knowing what connects to what, when, where, how, and how much—or using the more formal language we've introduced here, from codification within a layer and codification in how adjacent layers connect with, and impact, one another. To make this point, let's focus on two of the layers of the stack—the applications layer and the business process layer—between which some of the worst semantic disconnects occur. We discuss codification within each layer, then codification between the two layers. This provides the foundation for the material in Chapter 2 where we detail Business Blueprinting—a specific set of methods, techniques, and disciplines to codify tacit or simply widely disparate knowledge both within and across the layers—across the very different organizational activities and perspectives of your T-Shirts, Turtlenecks, and Suits.

Detailing the Stack

The business process layer is where the company's production happens and where the company interfaces with the outside world, for example, its customers and its partners. A business process consists of a set of activities to get something done; processes describe the functions and interactions among people, departments, and companies defining the rules and procedures by which the company runs as well as the ownership and flow of information to get that something done. Codification in the business process layer means having clear expressions of job responsibilities, workflow, decision points, information flow, and business rules. The semantic stack indicates that the business process layer is not as codified as the application layer. One big reason for this is that there is no commonly accepted discipline for describing much less modeling, analyzing, and engineering good business process. Nor is there common agreement on even how to express "a good" business process design.

Instead, in many companies, organizational processes are documented in practices that no one actually reads. Knowledge of the way processes work is passed down as "organizational lore" over time or depends critically on the knowledge in the head of some key person(s). Executional consistency demands that business processes rapidly and precisely change as the needs of the business change, and that different parts of the organization that are doing essentially the same thing do it the same way, hopefully using common supporting technology. This requires that, like the recipe discussed earlier in this chapter, business process is recorded, understood, and accessible to everyone with a need to know. Again, such leverage was precisely Mike's motivation to do the work we have been discussing throughout this chapter.

Business process codification requires a commonly accepted way or a standard of expressing processes. Emerging languages based on eXtended Markup Language (XML), such as Business Process Execution Language (BPEL) and Business Process Modeling Language (BPML), provide a means to enable task sharing within and across organizations. Given that there is more than one way to express business processes, there remains codification to be done. Clearly though, businesses seeking agility need to begin the process of describing and defining business processes in terms that can be readily expressed, and hence understood and executed (pun intended) on to different parties in whatever standard emerges. (Skip to the next section, "Making It Real," if you want to be saved from a fairly technical discussion.)

The applications layer is where automation supports business process. Today that generally means computer applications, but can also mean physical machinery like a check sorting machine. In the applications layer, referring now to computer applications, codification translates to, among other things, clearly delineated application functionality and clearly specified interfaces between applications. Taking them one at a time:

• *Application functionality:* Applications exist to support business processes. For most of the time since people have been writing computer applications, they have focused on creating them to support one or a few linked business processes. The problem with that approach is that, in rapidly changing times, business processes need to change much faster than applications can be reengineered. For example, a new wireless telephone carrier can offer calling plans with billing in one-second increments with rollover. Legacy carriers have been challenged to respond rapidly to this competition partly because their billing applications have a legacy back to times when the telephone industry was stable (and people were billed "for the first three minutes"), and the billing applications did more than just billing for phone use—they included functionality for marketing, fraud detection, tariffs, and many things not strictly related to billing.

More recently, application development disciplines such as Object Oriented Design (OOD) have evolved that allow software engineers to understand problems in terms of clearly partitioned services. Applications created using these new engineering principles comprise discrete components, each of which implements a self-contained service that can be extended or modified with minimal impact on other components. Thus, a well-designed biller created using OOD principles can be easily modified to accommodate billing increments other than "the first three minutes." OOD and related disciplines provide codification that creates the conditions for scalable understanding and execution.

• *Interfaces:* Applications need to communicate with other applications, both within an organization and among organizations. Again using the telephone company example, opening a new customer account requires that the biller communicate with the customer care applications, with the provisioning applications that turn on new service, and with the billers of other telephone carriers. For applications to interface, there needs to be an open channel and a clear language. Codification in interfaces means widespread agreement on the communications channel and on the language "spoken" across that channel. At one time, interfaces were created one application at a time with slight regard for other application interfaces and thus, little standardization.

Over the past few years, however, the Internet and its related technologies have emerged as the clear channel for communications between applications and organizations. Along with this, languages like HyperText Markup Language (HTML) and eXtensible Markup Language (XML) have emerged as standard languages for application-to-application communications. Specific vocabularies of XML such as e-business XML (EBXML) and security assertion markup language (SAML) provide widely understood and accepted means for communicating among applications. Finally, Web Services, an emerging standard for application-to-application interaction across the Internet, provides a standard way for applications to advertise and fund functionality, connect, and communicate via XML.

Interface codification creates the conditions for agility since applications (supporting business function) can more easily and robustly communicate with other applications, meaning that as business functions change, applications can be rapidly deployed to support the change. Codification within the application layer and the business process layer allows each layer to be engineered and managed more efficiently. We stated earlier that executional consistency depends also on codification between the layers. Most business processes are supported in some way by application functionality, and conversely, most application functionality exists in support of some business processes. Thus codification between the business process and application layers means that there exists clear *traceability* between a business process and its supporting application functionality. Traceability means that the impact of a change to a business process—to support a new business opportunity for example—can quickly be translated into necessary changes to underlying applications, speeding implementations and increasing agility. Similarly, traceability means that changes in the application layer—to accommodate a new release of vendor software for example—can be evaluated quickly and accurately for possible impact to business process, eliminating nasty surprises.[8]

Making It Real: Executing Over and Over Again

Our composite made-up examples of John and Mary, the real-life ones of Mike and Clark, and possibly many of yours reflect what many of us know too well: Doing the stuff that aligns your firm's objectives with everyday activities is hard; execution is hard work, and consistent execution even harder. And, of course, there are many examples and excuses, situations and rationales for why disconnects exist both within and among the T-Shirts, the Turtlenecks, and the Suits. Yet, underlying them all, underlying the challenges to getting stuff done consistently, lies a simple but insidious disconnect: the semantic disconnect.

Here's where it gets interesting and useful. If we understand that the semantic disconnect is the root cause impeding executional consistency, then a new way of thinking, of pragmatically acting, becomes clear: *Develop the tools and methods to bridge the disconnect, creating execu-*

tional semantics that are as meaningful as they are actionable by everyone. This is not a group-think thing. Rather, it is exposing the proverbial "elephant on the table." Group-think cannot connect the semantic disconnect. Diversity of perspectives, personalities, and actions is far too critical to keep insight and innovation, excitement, and opportunities for those organizations who nurture them thriving and highly competitive. Besides, the different audiences—executives, business process owners, application writers, and so on—really do need to have their own distinct vocabularies, and understandings, for an obviously simple reason: Their jobs *are* different. Yet, respecting differences is one thing; respecting them and knowing how to marshal them in a consistent, effective, and pragmatic way another. And it is the latter we're focused on.

In the last scenes of the movie *Amadeus*, Salieri is shown scribing the music of an ill Mozart, performing the role of an amanuensis—a person who is translating the brilliant insights of Mozart into a form that can be read, interpreted, and performed by thousands if not millions of people. He is *codifying* Mozart's *tacit knowledge*—creating the platform to scale, to execute, over and over again. And that is the simple but powerful key to the semantic stack, which we will bring operationally alive with Business Blueprinting in the next chapter. Bridging the semantic disconnect entails creating tools and methods that allow the T-Shirts, the Turtlenecks, and the Suits *with their own perspectives and behaviors* to work together—based on creating a shared environment that is as meaningful to each of them as it is actionable by them all. And codifying the tacit knowledge that *is* the expression of all of these differences *is* the DNA for executional consistency and the strands to manipulate to get done what needs to get done—quickly, consistently, effectively.

What This Means to You

1. *The semantic stack is pretty abstract; what use is it to me?* We've spent this time explaining the semantic stack and the underlying concepts of codification and the semantic disconnect for two reasons: First, to provide the framework underpinning the rest of this book—the

semantic stack is the conceptual cousin of the very concrete Business Blueprint we introduce in the next chapter.

Second, to act as a "mirror" with which you can view your own organization. The semantic stack is a qualitative way for you to look at the activities in your organization and ask yourself key questions, such as:

- What are the key reasons I'm challenged to get stuff done?
- Is there something, some set of reasons, underlying or common to these challenges?
- How well documented and understood are my business processes?
- How dependent am I on a few key individuals, applications, and/or systems who hold the knowledge on how things work?
- In meetings among departments in different layers of the stack, how much time is spent wrangling over the meanings of terms and objectives? How often do people use the same term (e.g., "customer" and "account") to mean different things? How often do people use different terms when referring to the same thing?

Based on asking these sorts of questions, you can judge where you are and how far you need to go in applying the methods, tools, and techniques that we detail in the next chapters.

2. *Are you saying that everyone across the organization needs to be connected to everyone else?* No. There is a common misconception that there's no such thing as too much communication. We disagree completely. Over-communication wastes time and resources and is a poor substitute for the *right* communication. Executional consistency depends on creating the shared vocabulary and the shared semantics so that you know what communication is necessary where, when and how, and so that the necessary communication can take place with minimal effort and loss of understanding. Again, one of the challenges we see over and over again is that within "communication," there is lots said, but not much heard.

To be effective, communication needs to be understood, and actionable. But to be understood and actionable requires "talking in the language"—or delivering the content—in a way *that is as meaningful as it is actionable to whomever needs it, and critically, how they can use it.* Because the T-Shirts, Turtlenecks, and Suits all have different needs, means of understanding, communicating, and acting, creating "shared semantics" is not an issue merely of "communicating" or "communicating more;" it is one of creating a shared semantics so understanding, and pragmatic, execution can occur. This is why we focus so much on the models, the messages, the software, the business rules, the (un)documented business processes—and all the other means of "expressing" what is done within an organization—codifying what is in someone's heads so others can use it.

3. *So, "codification" is pretty key?* Absolutely. Codifying the intellectual assets in your organization to bridge the semantic gaps that naturally exist in any organization *is crucial.* How well a company does this determines how successfully it can execute consistently and at scale. We've reduced this observation to a simple mantra: *The more codified, the more executable; the more executable, the more scalable; the more scalable, the more consistent, aligned, and able to change quickly, consistently, and effectively.*

Let's expand a bit on this answer. A business's intellectual assets include knowledge in people's heads, logic buried in computer programs and databases, information in a knowledge management or business intelligence portal, and/or the processes—documented and undocumented—that you use to run your business. Codifying those assets means expressing them in a way that is (1) understandable and accessible to everyone that needs to use them directly; and (2) connected in a visible, traceable way to the knowledge and assets used by other people in the organization. The semantic stack provides a way to discuss codification, with each layer of the stack representing a distinct function of an organization that can benefit from codification (the "everyone that needs to use it" mentioned earlier); the stack in total characterizes organizations as a bunch of smaller organizations that have to work together (the reason there needs to be "a visible, traceable way" that the knowledge of one organization relates to another).

We refer to codification as the "DNA for executional consistency." The semantic stack is to executional consistency what the double-helix model is to biological DNA. Both give us a mental picture with which to begin to understand a complex and important system, and expose some of its underlying constituent elements. Neither gives a prescription for how to manipulate those constituent elements effectively to create a desired response. Much of the remainder of this book is devoted to "unpacking" the semantic stack into a set of very tangible things you can do to increase codification and thus vastly improve how to get done what you need to do to enhance the performance of your organization. Specifically, in Chapter 2, we examine in detail methods, tools, and processes that can be used to create those characteristics, and in Chapter 3 we explore some methods and processes to actually change—permanently—the organization to realize that *executional consistency thing.*

4. *This seems huge. Is there a way to get started, and do it piecemeal?* Yes. It has to be done piecemeal because it's impossible to do it any other way, and we will show how in the next few chapters. Once a part of the organization has internalized the discipline to make codification a priority outcome of any project, then every project completed increases your capability to be more executionally consistent. This means that you can start pretty much anywhere. A good way to start is to examine your top 10 strategic initiatives, "grade and shade them" against the semantic stack in terms of the degree to which the project activities are codified, and then programmatically begin with codifying the patterns you see across these top 10 projects.

5. *My organization changes constantly because of competitive pressures, changes in regulations, and changes in customer demands . . . when can I find time to "codify" things?* We would ask in response, "How can you afford *not* to find the time to codify things?" As codification increases, executional consistency increases and you can respond more rapidly, effectively, and efficiently to change. And, as hinted at in the answer to the previous question, the discipline of codifying a project at a time makes for better projects, and actually adds little or no cost. The disciplines you put in place will reduce the execution risk of each project on its own, helping you to change with predictable success. We'll see multiple examples of this throughout the rest of the book.

6. *Are there technologies and standards that can help me?* Yes, to varying degrees in different parts of the stack. We will examine this in more detail in the next chapter.

7. *If I start doing things in "standard" ways, how do I keep my differentiation from my competitors?* When we preach codification and standardization, we are talking about codifying the way *you create* your differentiation, and exploiting standards so that you can more rapidly, effectively, and efficiently create and deliver the products and services that differentiate you in the market.

8. 4. *How should leadership interact with the different layers of an organization?* Let's quote Ram Charan again regarding the plight of technology organizations as an example of one layer in the semantic stack: "IT people are forced to set their own priorities. They love to have the involvement of senior leadership. Those who have it, they are succeeding; those who do not have it, have been left behind."[9] Executional consistency means creating the capability to mobilize leadership thinking into the decision-making process of every part of the organization. Business Blueprinting lets everyone in an organization approach the solution to a business problem in a coordinated, coherent way; each sees and contributes to the parts of the problem that they can best help with, and the Blueprint connects them to the contribution of everyone else involved in solving the problem. We'll see this in detail in the next chapter.

Chapter Cheat Sheet

The Issue

Many businesses face a nearly insurmountable challenge in getting done what needs to get done, in aligning their goals with their execution. No doubt, such alignment is hard to get, and the resulting challenges to do so are significant. But why? What is it about this "executional issue" that makes it so difficult? Lots of answers are offered and recommendations made to these questions. Still, challenges continue to occur in getting the executional consistency so sorely needed but so woefully lacking. But they need not. Rather than getting bogged down in the myriad of possible explanations of why such alignment doesn't occur, let's start with a simple, but provocative question: Is there a common challenge or root cause underlying these challenges that, if understood, could serve as the starting point to overcome them and thereby build our capabilities to get the stuff done that needs to get done? The answer is yes. There *is* a root cause to the inability to execute quickly, consistently, and effectively. Understanding this underlying root cause, *what we call the DNA of executional consistency*, is critical to being able to manipulate it.

The Insight

Underlying the challenge of executional consistency is something we call a *semantic disconnect*. Semantics is defined as the sharing of meanings among different people. A semantic disconnect occurs when different people take away different understandings of what has to get done to reach an objective. In day-to-day operations, when things are working well and the company is conducting business as usual, groups don't have to interact much, and where they do interact in the course of day-to-day business, they have worked out common semantics over time and much effort. During times of change, however, semantic differences among different groups of people become barriers to executing consistently to make the change occur. Given such different and disconnected understandings, it is no surprise that what results is an ever-widening *execution gap* that over time merely gets perpetuated, widened and institutionalized.

The Phrases

Semantic Disconnect; Semantic Stack; Tacit Knowledge; Codification; T-Shirts, Turtlenecks, and Suits; What Connects with What, When, Where, How, and How Much

The Implications

If we understand that the *semantic disconnect* is the root cause impeding executional consistency, then the next step becomes clear: *develop tools and methods to bridge the disconnect, creating "shared semantics" that are as meaningful as they are actionable by everyone.* Because the T-Shirts, Turtlenecks, and Suits all have different needs, means of understanding, communicating, and acting, creating shared semantics is not an issue merely of communicating or communicating more, it is one of creating a shared semantics so understanding, and pragmatic, execution can occur. This is why we focus so much on the models, the messages, the software, the business rules, the (un)documented business processes—and all the other means of expressing what is done within an organization—codifying what is in someone's heads so others can use it. This is not an issue of changing your languages, of aligning your metrics, of changing your governance processes, of communicating more, and more. It is fundamentally about creating shared and shareable capabilities to drive consistent execution. It is fundamentally about creating capabilities to ensure that decisions taking place at the top of an organization can be and are consistently executed throughout the organization—through its business processes, applications, and infrastructure.

Maps, Models, and Action—
Blueprinting Your Business

Setting the Stage: Rippling Changes, Crippling Impacts

Mark, the COO of a large retail bank based in the Midwest, was doing his strategic planning for 2004/2005. He was working with his staff to prioritize their key business and technology initiatives. As with any bank, the potential impact of new banking regulations on their business loomed large. "Check 21," which would go into effect in late 2004, was one the larger "loomers."

Check 21 is a congressional mandate basically allowing electronic images to serve as fiduciary commitments much as paper checks do. In other words, banks are allowed to treat electronic images of checks the same, for settlement purposes, as paper checks. Check 21 is a classic case of a strategic change—from a legislative mandate—impacting the entire U.S. banking industry.

According to Mark and his team's initial assessment, Check 21's impacts would be minimal—perhaps affecting 15 business processes, with little or no impact on how the bank interacts with its customers, and some slight impact on 20 or so of the software applications that support the bank's check processing.

Check 21 is a textbook case of why businesses need to be continuously responsive to change. In this case, a government regulation is strategically impacting the U.S. banking industry generally, and Mark's business in particular. Check 21 does not mandate that any bank change its current check collection practices. However, a study by the Federal Reserve estimated that during the first 6 to 12 months of its implementation, the percentage of bounced checks would rise fivefold from 4 percent of total check numbers to over 20 percent as banks grapple with new operations. Check 21 was an excellent test of whether Mark's banking operations could *make sense of* the new regulation and then quickly, consistently, and effectively *take action on* it. Mark's challenge was straightforward: to assess how the new Check 21 rules would impact the bank's operations—its rules, policies, business processes, and underlying software applications and technology infrastructure.

Mark's team's initial assessment was way off base. When persuaded to look at Check 21 in more detail, using the approach presented in this chapter, Mark was stunned at the results: The legislative change would impact 24 business processes—several of them important client-facing processes—and was going to require modification of 71 software applications. Check 21 moved to the top of the bank's 2004 priority list! The potential cost impact of the sudden jump in exception-processing costs from the increased number of bounced checks was a clear call to immediate action. Maybe more importantly, the Check 21 experience revealed that Mark's tacit knowledge of how the business runs and how things are connected was far from sufficient to accurately and consistently make sense and take action in the face of change. Codifying the knowledge of the bank's operations and technology has now become one of Mark's highest priorities—recognizing that the Check 21 project of 2004 and 2005 will be one of many, as new regulations, market demands, pressures, and opportunities continuously appear.

The COO began to take the company on its walk across and up the semantic stack. His goal of enhancing executional consistency means that the next time a regulatory change—or any other market pressure or opportunities—comes along, he can move more effectively and with more assurance; his estimates and actions will be based on codified fact, not on distributed tacit knowledge.

In terms of the semantic stack, the Check 21 regulation forced a change in the top layer that affected the bank's strategic posture (and new opportunities) with respect to other banks: It might create a competitive advantage to provide clients with enhanced services based on electronic check processing; it could uncover an important way to take out costs and provide cheaper service; it could become a practical necessity to continue to do business with existing correspondent banks, and other benefits. However, the very *consideration* of these types of opportunities was previously impossible since so much of what was actually done was unknown. Without such visibility, there was no way of knowing what the ripple effects were, and could be, throughout the organization— precisely what was needed to be able to respond effectively.

This change in the upper layers of the stack predictably forced changes lower in the stack, specifically in the 24 business processes that underlie check processing, the people that execute those processes, and in 71 of the applications that support those processes and people.

Changes will always ripple up and down the stack. What is less obvious is what types of ripples they will be, where and when they will occur, how significant their impacts will be, and who will be impacted by them. Putting it differently, what is less well known is *what connects with what, when, where, how, and how much*. Why is this? Because the organizational silos, the governance models, the undocumented processes, the different perspectives, the misaligned metrics, the fundamental differences among the T-Shirts, the Turtlenecks, and the Suits—in short, these and any of a number of other characteristics that reflect semantic disconnects—give rise to the lack of visibility and awareness of "what gets done *over there*" as opposed to merely knowing our own stuff of "what gets done *over here*." How many of us really know what happens "over there"—in another department in any level of detail? How many hand-offs or "over-the-wall" comments do we make? How many times do we assign blame for problems "in *their* department" or merely shake our heads at the "black box" of activity that occurs "elsewhere." Or to make it even closer to home, how many times do we make these types of comments regarding our own department? How many times have we been surprised to find out things that we did or how we did them within our own area of responsibility that were previously unknown?

Let's return to our example. Mark's misunderstanding is not a surprise; it's pervasive. "I didn't even know we did some of these processes," Mark exclaimed. "I had no idea that 17 percent of our exception processing costs were associated with these types of payments." Visibility—what connects with what, when, where, how, and how much—is *the* challenge underlying the semantic disconnect. This chapter describes some of the methods, tools, and examples of Business Blueprinting, our execution framework used to bridge the semantic disconnect and to create the visibility that is critical to making both decisions and actions more effective.

Extent of the Challenge: Beware the Red Queen

We talked a lot about the "Red Queen" effect in our book, *The Jericho Principle*, at client sites, at workshops, and at speaking opportunities. We met the Red Queen, whose personal mantra is, "You have to run as fast as you can just to stay in one place, and even faster if you want to go anywhere," in the Introduction to this book. She is a fabulous symbol for the fast pace of change faced by organizations in all industries. She is also, unfortunately, emblematic of too many organizational efforts in how they respond to that change.

Relentless change is an operational reality for all organizations today and into the foreseeable future. Uncertainty from competition, from changing regulatory requirements, the impact of world events, and especially from ever-changing market demands means that organizations—both commercial and public sector—must always be ready to respond to change. We call this *the Red Queen challenge:* the Red Queen runs with organizations through the marketplace. She can be seen in the grinding commoditization process driving down margins as global competition floods into existing markets, and as consumers (or citizens) demand that organizations provide highly individuated or personalized products and services to respond to their unique needs.

As the Red Queen runs, she forces organizations to do new things that are possibly very far away from what they do best—from their existing "core competencies"—to meet new and possibly short-lived markets. Those individuals, groups, organizations, companies, and industries that will survive and thrive are the ones that can effectively shift their core competencies and market focus, that can continually recreate themselves embracing the uncertainty and turning it to competitive advantage. *The Jericho Principle* focuses on what we call the *collaborative imperative:* the further and faster companies have to change, the less likely it is that they will find the needed capabilities internally; they must look beyond their own organizational walls to mobilize resources needed to respond to specific and fast-moving opportunities.

Two benefits result from this: (1) Such collaboration becomes a means of responding more effectively, and (2) Such collaboration becomes a way to start creating new capabilities—new core competencies—faster. We also discuss the need to be able to move from a position of strength and to minimize the expenditure of resources needed to change. In *Jericho*, we argue that companies that can make sense and take action effectively, efficiently, and at scale—in other words, companies that display executional consistency—will be able to keep up, if not change the race, with the Red Queen over the long haul.

Outracing the Red Queen means using brain power much more than leg power. Using the former more effectively is why, as we explained in Chapter 1, it is an organizational priority to drive toward codifying your knowledge into standards, alignment, and common business process—to "walk up and across the semantic stack." Why? Because turning that tacit knowledge into codified knowledge means that everyone in the organization can help run with the Red Queen. That's the power of scale, created through codification.

Here's a flash of obvious insight: Businesses are complex and interconnected. Figure 2.1 shows something called a Business Interaction Model (BIM). It depicts, at a very high level, the interactions between a business (represented in the center of the diagram), its suppliers (on the left), its customers (on the right), and its competitors (on the bottom). Each of the boxes in the BIM represents an organization—either within the company or external to it. A single arrow in the diagram represents some business activity—say "Confirm Delivery"—where one organization requires action by another organization. That single arrow can represent a phone call, a dozen meetings, or a computer application talking to another application— or more typically, all of these together.

BIMs show the highest, most abstract view of the interactions among the organizations that make up the business. The BIM hides (business modelers use the phrase "abstracts away") almost all of the underlying connections and complexity that really make the business run. When something changes, the changes ripple across those connections. Not understanding these connections in detail means not

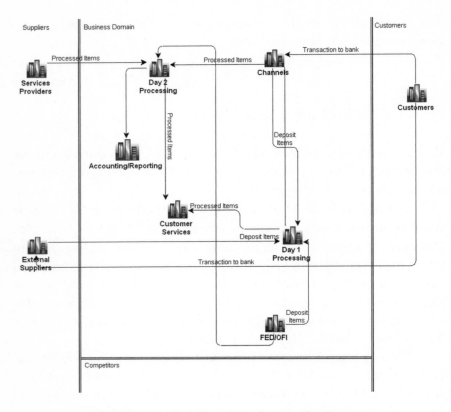

FIGURE 2.1   High-Level Depiction of a Business

knowing where the ripples will stop, or the extent of their impact. This was the problem with the initial analysis Mark's team undertook on the Check 21 implications. They did not have the visibility needed to see the full extent of change propagating throughout their business. They did not know what impacted *what, when, where, how, and how much.*

Here's another flash of obvious insight. Business problems require business solutions. Problems and solutions are tangled throughout your business, creating many, often unanticipated, interactions and impacts. The more you know about those interactions and impacts, the more quickly and effectively you will be able to make sense of a business problem and take action. We all know this.

The challenge lies in the "how" to make it happen, pragmatically. Let's start tackling this challenge.

Facing the Challenge: Maps as Models

Back to Mark and the implementation of Check 21: Mark has made codification of the knowledge of the bank's operations and technology a high priority, starting the company on its walk across and up the semantic stack. What does that mean, really? And what does it mean to create shared semantics across the T-Shirts, Turtlenecks, and Suits in a way that is as meaningful as it is actionable by them all? It means creating models of various aspects of the business, representing essential information about what the business is and how it works, while managing the level of detail so that the models are useful as tools not merely to understand and navigate, but also to manage and drive the business.

Think of how maps, blueprints, and government documents relate to a city. Travelers to an unfamiliar city use maps to help find their way around. Why? Because maps codify knowledge that resides in the heads of people familiar with wherever it is the traveler is going. They provide a scalable way to use that knowledge: Travelers can figure out how to find their way around by using the available maps. Even casual travelers use different types of maps. They may use a road atlas to find their way to the city. On the road atlas, the city is shown as a dot on some line that represents a highway. Once in the city, the traveler uses different maps to navigate different aspects of the city: a street map that gives information on the surface features the traveler is likely to care about—street names and which streets cross which other streets, major landmarks, the names of lakes and rivers, and other landmarks; a transit map showing the routes of subways, trams, buses, and other transportation; a travel guide describing restaurants, museums, and attractions. These three types of maps—street, transit, and restaurant guide—are all connected to one another through street names, addresses, and sometimes telephone numbers. Remember the notion of *what connects with what, where, when, how, and how much*—the traceability discussed in Chapter 1? Street addresses provide a mechanism for traceability among these three maps.

Of course, there is more to getting around a city than just the "where." There is also the "what" and the "when." Another type of map used by many travelers is the "What's Happening in [City]" found in their hotel room. This map tells when interesting events are happening—the Santa Lucia celebration in Malmö, Sweden, at sundown on December 13, for example. It is still traceable to the other maps by providing addresses where things will occur, but adds the critical dimensions of events of interest and the time they will occur.

Zooming in, the people responsible for making the city run use maps and drawings that show underground pipes, wires, cables, support structures, and tunnels that provide water, heat, communication connectivity, electricity, and gas. The fire department has a map of each fire hydrant in the city; it has detailed models of the fire systems in the major buildings. The city planning office has maps of the city showing the bridges and tunnels; it has planning models showing the capability of the city's infrastructure to support new development. The architects and engineers who put up the buildings have blueprints that serve as maps for everything from how the building looks from various angles through to how the plumbing, electricity, and finished woodwork are installed.

None of these maps provides a complete picture of the city; not even all of them together do so. Additional materials—documents, diagrams, subway maps, and so on—help make sense and communicate about different parts and aspects of the city. There are documents that detail the governance in the city—its constitution, laws and regulations. For each of the mechanical and electrical devices that the city depends on such as the generating plants, computers, telephone exchanges, there are drawings and specifications used by whoever's job it is to keep the lights on. Taken together, this pile of different maps and materials constitutes a set of *models* that give a view of a city. Each has its own focus and its own audience, yet all necessarily work together and are *linked* to provide an effective understanding of what has to get done and how to do so.

Maps and Models—for Insight and Action

The same holds for a business: the more information that a business knows about itself, the better the people who run that business can navigate it to make sense of changes that are coming, to understand its impact to the business, and to take effective action. What *maps* are to the group of people interested in the city, *models* are to the people who wish to understand their business.

We use the term model as an explicit, important concept with a simple working definition: *A model is a description of some thing or concept that captures the important properties of that thing or concept.* A statement attributed to W. Edwards Deming, father of the modern quality movement, is, "All models are wrong. Some models are useful." The street map is a model. It will never be mistaken for the street itself; it abstracts away certain properties of the street, for instance whether the street runs uphill or downhill. In that sense, it is "wrong." However, the street map is "useful" to a traveler to the extent that it helps the traveler navigate the city. The street map is not particularly "useful" (in the sense intended by Deming) to an architect designing a building on the street and who needs to know if the street actually runs uphill or downhill.

Because a model is not reality but a representation of reality, it is necessarily flawed and of use to a restricted set of people. The key to making a good and useful model is to capture the important properties of what you're trying to describe and hiding, or deferring, the details that are not important to what you are trying to describe. The amount and type of detail is dependent on who will use the map and what it will be used for. But generally, modelers try to avoid the sorts of problem described by comedian Steven Wright. Paraphrasing: "I bought a map of the United States the other day. The scale is one foot equals one foot. It's a b*tch to fold."

What does this have to do with your business? Think of the immense complexity of your business in operation—the thousands of interconnected parts, all of the communications among people, the tangle of technology, the relationships with each of your alliances, the obligations to each of your customers, the web of vendors and partners, the different types of employees scattered throughout—the T-Shirts, the Turtlenecks, and the Suits. There is more to your business than any one person can keep in their head. Yet, when asked, you can describe your business in a two-sentence "elevator pitch." The elevator pitch is a very high-level model of your business. When a change comes along—like a new regulation for Check 21—the two-sentence description of your business may stay the same, but somewhere in the business, things are going to change. Understanding the relationship between the impending change and its impacts—between some cause and lots of effects—means you can execute effectively. Lacking such understanding makes change increasingly risky and resource consuming. It all comes back to *what connects with what, when, where, how and how much*—those visibility and traceability "things."

The Business Blueprint—The "Where's Waldo" of Your Organization

Suppose you could have a model of your business that captures the important properties of the whole thing, from the elevator pitch view through to the actual, nasty complexity of day-to-day operations of your business processes, applications, networks, and hardware. Such a model would, like the pile of maps of the city mentioned earlier, actually consist of multiple and different types of models. Each individual model would show important properties *of a piece* of the business in terms that the person responsible *for that piece* of the business would find useful. The models would be connected—like the street map and transit maps are connected through street addresses—by *traceability* that shows, for example, how a computer application is used by a call center staff member. The challenge is to define the set of models and the level of detail that captures the information you need—the useful properties—while at the same time hiding the details so that it is easy to place those properties in the proper context. That is what a Business Blueprint *does*.

Figure 2.2 shows our icon for a Business Blueprint. It should be clear that this is related to the semantic stack, with some of the layers combined. It's a simple and logical way to distinguish the different types of things and activities that occur in a business. There are

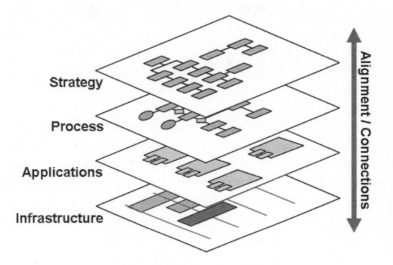

FIGURE 2.2 A Business Blueprint

"strategy" things, "business process" things, "application" things, and "infrastructure" things—all working together and held together somehow. And each of these things has its own set of people who work on them with their own priorities, perspectives, metrics, and language. In any going business, they work together, somehow. The challenge is in digging into that stack and understanding that "somehow," in other words, understanding what impacts what, when, where, how, and how much.

A Business Blueprint consists of a set of connected models that captures the useful properties needed to understand the business and predict the impact of change while avoiding the "one foot equals one foot" problem. *Business Blueprinting* specifies a set of models and methods that together can be used to represent the important aspects of any business problem, from strategy right through to infrastructure. As we said earlier, it is not reasonable—or even desirable—to expect that every person in a business will know everyone else's jargon and share their semantics. But it is as reasonable and desirable, as it is important and critical, that there be a way to create shared semantics across, with, and through these people.

Each layer of Figure 2.2 has its own ways of doing what it does and isolating what is important for it to do. Each layer has its own set of models to isolate specific activities, each aimed at a specific audience with a view of the overall business problem using a vocabulary—and ways of doing things—suited to the audience. Business Blueprinting specifies how the parts of the different models relate to one another. This relationship—or connectivity—among the different models enables a Business Blueprint to communicate the impact of a change in one model to all of the other models in the Blueprint, answering the *what impacts what, when, where, how, and how much* questions. Thus, the language of the Business Blueprint creates the shared semantics needed to create executional consistency—not by requiring everyone in the organization to understand everyone else's job but by employing specific tools, methods, and techniques for letting the groups understand that "when I say this or do that, it maps to *your* world and affects your *this* and your *that*." In this way, Mark achieves an understanding of the rippling effect of Check 21 throughout the different layers of his organization.

There's one other thing to keep in mind about models, one that we will come back to in a few pages when we talk about specific models that make up a Business Blueprint. You don't need to know how to create a model to be able to use it. It takes a cartographer to create an accurate map of the United States; but just about any third grader can use that map to find their home state. Creating models may take special skills; but once created, the models are designed to be highly understandable, usable, and—within limits—changeable by their intended audience.

So, let's step back and connect this discussion with the previous chapter. When we talk about codification, what do we really mean? We mean creating models that represent the useful properties about the business; we mean making sure that each person in the organization understands how to use the models that are important *to them*; and we mean that the models themselves contain information on how one group's models relate to all of the other groups' models so that the impact of changes in one group can be recognized and understood by other groups. By providing these shared semantics in a single set of interconnected models, Business Blueprinting tangibly helps you get done what you need to do: It enables executional consistency by:

- Getting heads mobilized around the business problem
- Meeting each group at its own level and in its own language
- Codifying each group's knowledge through modeling
- Connecting the groups together through traceability—by making explicit what impacts what, when, where, how, and how much.

Business Blueprinting—The "What's Waldo Doing" in Your Organization

A Business Blueprint can be thought of as providing four different flavors of information, each of which corresponds roughly to the needs of a particular business audience, as represented by the four layers shown in Figure 2.2. There is nothing magical about these four layers; they are logical sets of "stuff" that an organization does. What is helpful about these layers is that (1) they are intuitive, logical, and simple; (2) each has its own set of people who work in them with their own vocabulary, metrics, and behaviors, perspectives, and processes; and (3) they cleanly reflect a simple "bucketing" of stuff that has to get done. Such simplicity masks tremendous complexity but models, as we've discussed earlier, need to start somewhere to build up the "grammar" for effective execution.

The top layer of the Business Blueprint, layer 1, is the *Strategy Layer*. Models in the Strategy Layer represent things that are interesting to executive management such as the CEO or head of an organization large enough to create and execute a strategy. What does this person care about? Generally three things, as told to us by a gracious, intelligent, now-retired CEO of two large Fortune 500 companies: growth, profitability, and keeping their job (and not necessarily in that order). Models in layer 1 need to engage executives, showing the things that they care about, and providing an anchor so that each of the detailed business process and technology activities can clearly be related to goals that executives care about. This helps make sure that executives understand the context and impact of process and technology initiatives. At the same time, it helps ensure that the initiatives are indeed aligned with their objectives for the firm.

Executives, supposedly, set the vision and direction for an organization. However, the people who do the work do so by executing business processes that result in the value—the products and services—delivered by the company. Layer 2 in the Business Blueprint is the *Process Layer*, and has models of interest to these people, typically a Business Line Executive—a more operational audience than layer 1. These models express the sets of activities—the stuff that has to get done—that determine how the organization creates value (its products or services), how it services its customers, alliances, partners, vendors, and itself.

Business processes, and the people who execute them, are supported by automation for example, computer applications. Thus layer 3 of the Business Blueprint is the *Applications Layer*. The models in the Application Layer have two audiences: One of these is the people who perform the business processes, since they want to know that the applications that are created really meet their needs. The other audience is the people who have to create the applications to support those needs. Thus this layer has models with a real business flavor as well as those that are intensely technical.

Layers 2 and 3 are closely related. They are separated in a Blueprint for two reasons. First the two audiences have different vocabularies so the models in each layer are targeted to the layer's specific audience. But there's another, more pragmatic reason: For flexibility and executional consistency, it is important that the business process not be tightly tied to the underlying application. Business folks have to be able to change their processes as the needs of the business change. Technology folks have to support these changes; but they are also responsible for accommodating technology changes—for example, a vendor-required software patch that may or may not be tied directly to a business change. Each group, while dependent on each other, has its own set of concerns and issues, shared semantics, and executional consistency that they need to address. Yet, equally, and arguably more importantly, they need to be able to understand and act on what is important *to each other*. In other words, both need to be able to understand what is important, why, and how—from either direction.

Finally, the people, the applications, and the information in the company need a place to live. The models of layer 4, the *Infrastructure*, represent the physical things that the company uses to do what it needs to do as well as the services that the people and applications depend on to do their work. The physical things in the infrastructure layer include computers, databases, networks, telephone connections, and the physical machines that sit on people's desks. The services include things like e-mail, and security. As change ripples from the strategy layer through the subsequent business process and applications layer, models in the infrastructure layer need to reflect the resulting impacts on the stones and boulders of these ripples. Mark found that that Check 21 had unforeseen but significant, impacts on his server clusters (sets of computers) responsible for security monitoring and reporting. Keep in mind, also, that ripples don't start from layer 1 and move down. No matter where the changes start, at any level, there are likely to be implications (too often invisible ones) in the other layers. Just think of what happens if your mainframe or e-mail system goes down—the hue and cry by you, your customers, suppliers, and if out for long enough, Wall Street analysts.

Layer 4 models are used by the CIO, CTO, IT managers, and hardware and network engineers. IT investment is largely tied to the infrastructure modeled in layer 4; the fact that the Business Blueprint connects the models means that infrastructure investments can be tied all the way back to the strategic goals they support.

Each layer of a Business Blueprint has its own set of activities, metrics, owners, and behaviors. The challenge, as we've said several times (and will say over and over in this book), is to understand what connects with what, when, where, how, and how much. It is getting the visibility and traceability into these connections that is so critical to mobilizing very different and diverse resources quickly, consistently, and effectively. In the formal language of the models presented so far, the challenge is to mobilize the intellectual assets of all of the owners into a common expression of a problem to be solved, and to create common expressions across the layers so that the requirements and expectations at, for example, the Process layer, are equally understandable and usable to those at the Applications layer, and so on. *This creation of shared expressions of differences is the crux of creating executional consistency so critical to get done what needs to get done.*

Understanding the DNA—What Connects with What, Where, When, How, and How Much

The semantic disconnect is the fundamental challenge to getting stuff done well and consistently. Business Blueprinting is about meeting that challenge. It is fully focused on bridging the semantic disconnect by creating common expressions to drive the executional consistency as sorely needed as it is woefully lacking.

Who cares? Well, Mark does, as do many, many others. Let's think back to Mark and his Check 21 experience. In their initial analysis, Mark's team thought that the impact was relatively simple and contained. They were off by a lot. Not from lack of effort, nor of insight, nor of intelligence, nor of their knowledge of their business. Rather, they missed the real impact of regulatory change—that would have had a huge financial impact on them—because of the inherent, pervasive, and ultimately pernicious existence of semantic disconnects. Making visible what is so often invisible in organizations is a fine marketing slogan. What it means in practice is making explicit what is too often implicit in the workarounds, the exceptions, and the stuff that is in too few heads or embedded deeply in too many applications. Getting this stuff "out" in a form that can be used by everyone in the business is the core challenge of doing stuff consistently, the result of overcoming the semantic disconnects, and the opportunity to do what you need to get done, again and again.

Think of tracing implementation of Check 21 through a Business Blueprint. The connected models give immediate visibility to the extent of the change. Understanding quickly and accurately the extent of a change means that you can anticipate and *make sense* of potential consequences. With what implication? Better likelihood of taking action with less risk and more alignment among your very different teams. How so? Because you know *what connects with what, where, when, how, and how much* so that there are few surprises.

We examine the Business Blueprint in more detail in the next section looking at how some of the key models in the layers fit together and relate to the Blueprint Stack. We'll look at examples of traceability—the *what connects with what* mantra—to show that the impact of changes made in one layer of the model by one constituency are properly reflected in the other layers so that no one is surprised and the entire set of people interested in the business problem can execute quickly, effectively, and consistently.

Bill and Carl's Hurting Hospital Group

Bill is CEO of a national hospital group that provides primary care, specialized care, and related medical and social support services. Bill's board of directors is demanding rapid changes in how business is being conducted; the group has been experiencing less-than-satisfactory performance in their collection of reimbursements for certain categories of patients and health coverage plans. Carl, the director of hospital operations, is feeling the pressure even more since he is responsible for billing and collections, the group's major pain area. The board has been very clear with both Bill and Carl: Make the hospitals in the group more efficient, with an aggressive focus on making billing and collections systems consistent across all of the entities in the group—hospitals, hospices, and outpatient centers—or else.

Figure 2.3 shows the key models in Bill's and Carl's Business Blueprint and relates them to the Business Blueprint icon. We'll walk through some of what Bill and Carl have done given their strategic challenges and changes using the models and we'll show how they have helped meet the board's demands, and Bill's and Carl's personal objectives, quickly and effectively.

Carl and his team established some key business objectives for a dramatic improvement—a "transformation" in their parlance—in billing and collections performance. This included standardizing

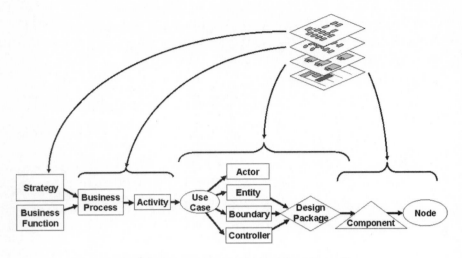

FIGURE 2.3   Bill's and Carl's Hospital

on a single, nationwide, commercial software application. Their success measures included reducing the "time to bill" by over 50 percent, increasing collections by 30 percent, reducing the number of bills requiring human intervention by 50 percent, and enabling continuous innovation and process improvement. These are aggressive goals. The group was able to quickly start their initiative; that was the good news. But they quickly had bad news; they ran into some thorny problems leading to unpleasant surprises and unacceptable service disruptions. They realized that they did not sufficiently understand the dependencies between some of their business processes and their supporting applications, and consequently were unable either to anticipate or respond quickly to the impacts of changes. These problems were exacerbated by a not-surprising reluctance to change key legacy systems for fear of setting off a disastrous chain reaction and exacerbating an already spiraling-out-of-control situation.

In terms of Business Blueprinting, a solution to the hospital group's business problem potentially affects all four layers—of which we'll highlight certain parts:

1. *Changes to strategic goals:* One strategic goal of this initiative is to increase the group's performance in collecting reimbursements.
2. *Changes to business processes:* The processes related to billing and collecting needs to change to become more automated, responsive, and accountable.
3. *Changes to applications:* There is a stated goal to settle on a single, nationwide, vendor-provided application platform.
4. *Changes to infrastructure:* Though not called out explicitly, changing the processes and applications will likely result in changed requirements for infrastructure services.

Remember the enablers of executional consistency, and how these models help achieve it, as we prepare to walk through the changes that will result from the hospital's goal to improve collections.

Visibility, the capability to see the impact of change across the business, is crucial to achieving executional consistency. The models in a Business Blueprint create visibility by connecting models that represent what the business does to the various audiences that need to know it. Knowing *what impacts what, where, when, how, and how much* is critical in any effort that by its nature requires the attention and cumulative brainpower of people who do not naturally speak the same organizational language. Having such knowledge is further complicated by any change or transformation that will take multiple iterations to get it right. Changes in one part of the business are represented by changes to one or more models with rippling changes to other models. Blueprinting helps ensure that all models stay in sync and that changing the models is not unacceptably labor intensive.

Too often strategy is thought of as a soft and squishy topic. While the road to creating strategy may indeed be soft, messy, and full of ambiguity, the strategy, once arrived at, can be articulated crisply as a set of related business goals, objectives, initiatives, and success measures.

Strategy Model

We start with one of the hospital's stated business drivers: to improve its performance in capturing revenue. One of the strategies for

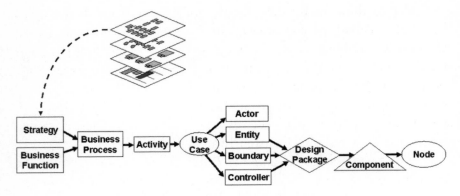

FIGURE 2.4   The Intended Change

capturing revenue is to improve the group hospitals' performance in collecting insurance reimbursements from third-party insurance providers. The strategy box in Figure 2.4 details the Business Goals model, shown in Figure 2.5. The Business Goals model ties strategic business goals to more tactical goals—not in a soft "strategic" sort of way, but in a clear hierarchical relationship.

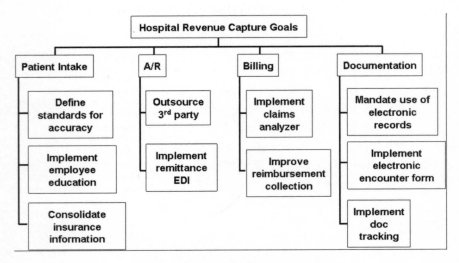

FIGURE 2.5   Business Goals

Where does the Business Goals model come from? It is created by what is called a Business Architect—someone who understands the business and has the ability to depict or "architect" how the business interacts with its environment and underlying processes. This business architect works with executives to express their goals and strategic initiatives in a tight manner that can be understandable to people with different perspectives and, equally if not more importantly, can be acted on, consistently and quickly.[1]

The business goal to *Improve Reimbursement Collection* must be implemented by people and/or systems executing one or more business processes. It is the role of the business architect, working with subject matter experts from the business, to determine which business processes will be involved in the implementation of this goal. In the scope of the business initiatives that the hospital is undertaking, many business processes are involved and need to be modeled—over 30 processes in all.

Traceability connects a business goal with the business processes that implement that goal. Figure 2.6 shows the resulting connection between the business goal *Improve Reimbursement Collection* and the business processes that implement it. Thinking of this in *making sense* terms, rather than having to search through 30 processes that might be related to the strategy, Blueprinting focuses attention specifically on the few business processes that are directly affected.

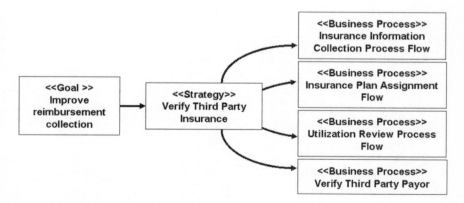

FIGURE 2.6 Business Process Impact of Intended Change

In this particular case, performance in collecting third-party payments can be improved by improving the *Verify Third-Party Payor* business process; analysis showed that the third-party insurance verification service being used by the hospital was missing a significant percentage of patients covered by a third-party insurer. The hospitals decided to modify the *Verify Third-Party Payor* business process to add a second, independent, verification service.

What is the impact of adding another verification service? The *Verify Third-Party Payor* business process will change, and with it there will likely be changes in the underlying automation that supports the process. To keep things in perspective, Figure 2.7 shows where we are in the overall Business Blueprint. To see the impact of the proposed change, we need to look at the details of the *Verify Third-Party Payor* business process as it exists now. This process is shown in Figure 2.8.

The business process model in Figure 2.8 depicts the activities needed to perform the business function *Verify Third-Party Payor*. This type of model is also known as a "Swimlane" model because it shows, in lanes separated by the horizontal lines, who or what business function is responsible for performing the activities in the process, where the activities are depicted by the boxes, each activity described by an action verb and a noun. Again, our intention here is not to describe, in any detail, the "content" of the hospital group

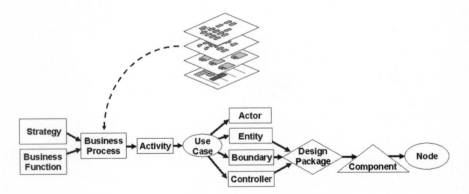

FIGURE 2.7 Walking the Blueprint

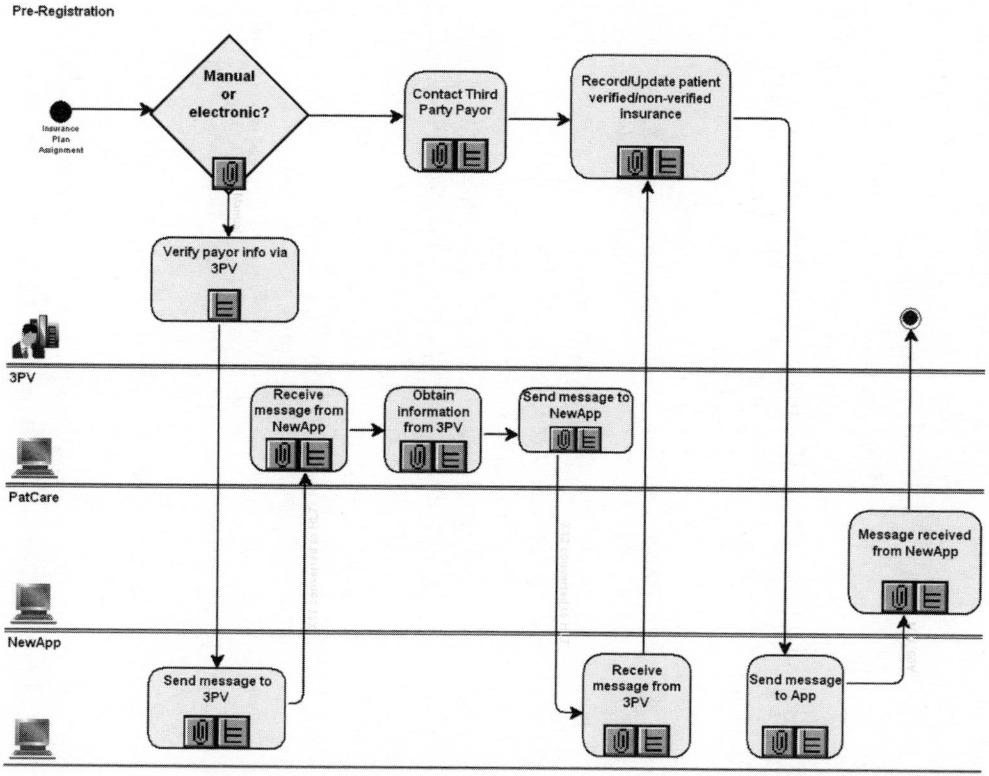

FIGURE 2.8 Business Process Swimlane

process but rather illustrate a "method" of how these models—that express specific business activities—can be used to make visible what connects with what, where, when, how, and how much. Two observations arise at this point that illustrate the need to start creating the shared semantics across the T-Shirts, Turtlenecks, and Suits:

1. What goes into this, or any, particular Swimlane model is often a debate among different people involved. This challenge of designing a Swimlane model includes determining how much detail should go into the model, what to hide, and how to capture what is "left out." The goal is to make sure that the model is, as Einstein once said about any way of thinking about the world, "only as complicated as it needs to be—and no more."

2. Having agreed on "what's in/what's out," the next debate is over labeling each activity and entity (thing) with a verb and noun—to indicate "what" is impacting "what" (the nouns) and "how" they are doing that (the verbs). Just imagine the debates *this* engenders. We've described before how hard it can be to define even supposedly clear things like "customer" and "account." Multiply this complexity by adding other "things" and "actions"—all of which have to be indicated and labeled in a way that's meaningful to everyone in the room—and you quickly appreciate the complexity of this process. And yet, so too can you (hopefully) appreciate the power and potential of creating such shared understandings of what others and eventually everyone agrees that these models, and consequently, actions mean (and not incidentally, should be). This process is painful. Yet, it's critical. Pulling out the (usually widely varying and deeply held) assumptions and beliefs—the tacit knowledge that we *all* bring into such discussions, and that *always* frames our actions—is a challenge. Yet, the explicit and tangible, shared and (most importantly) shareable, understandings that result from this process far, far, far outweighs the difficulties of creating them.

Mark Monmonier recently wrote a book on how the Mercator map was developed. From the time the world was discovered to be spherical in shape and not flat, cartographers have struggled with the problem of how to depict its three-dimensional curved surface on a two-dimensional piece of paper. Monmonier's book describes the dilemmas and processes of creating "shared semantics" of how to depict our spherical, three-dimensional world in a manner that anyone who looks at a Mercator map can say, "I get it, I understand what the world looks like and where I am, and how I can get to where I need to go."[2]

Creating a Swimlane, or any model, forces an excavation of often deeply held and rarely communicated understanding of what the business does, and what is important from people with very different perspectives on the business. Whether this is "putting the moose on the table"—as a client of ours likes to put it—or making visible what is invisible, the intent is the same: Codifying the tacit knowledge into a form that is understandable to all. Sure, this takes discourse and debate. But the process of making it tangible—of putting it down in a form that can be touched, scratched, printed, simulated, refined, and ultimately agreed on—is the purpose and the power behind creating shared, and executable, semantics. But enough of the theory, back to the models.

Business Process models can be created in more than a single level of detail. For example, Figure 2.9 shows nested models where a single activity such as *Schedule Surgery* is drilled down to more detail; the *Schedule Surgery* activity is itself composed of multiple activities and decision points (represented by diamonds with a question in them). By starting at a very high-level business process description and providing more and more detail in "drill-down" models, a set of Business Process models allows an interested person to take in a high-level view to set perspective, yet still provide the detail to satisfy more specific needs.

Carl's initiatives required the involvement not only of his direct reports and others throughout the hospital group but also of insurance vendors who are the source of the third-party payments so important to Carl. Insurance companies have their own processes; they think about the business in their own terms. Getting agreement on how to depict the high-level model—of what was important—was a challenge. But, said Carl, it was "significantly worth the effort since it was clear that many of us had our own assumptions about what we were doing that was inconsistent and ultimately contributing to the

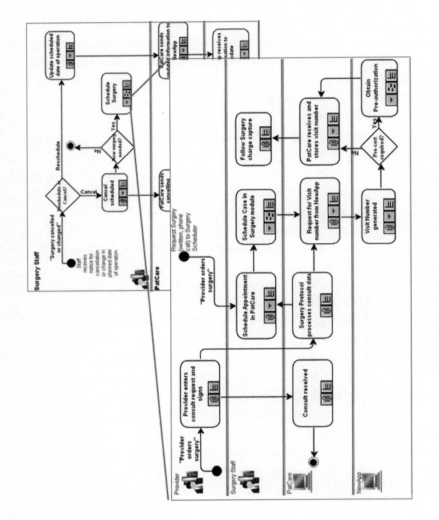

FIGURE 2.9 Diving into the Swimlane

problems we were all having." Drill-downs, having more detail along each of the flows within the Swimlane, strengthened the confidence and commitment both to the process and, interestingly, to the models created because as one person put it: "The topic sentence [the high level model] was clear and the additional details simply augmented what we had agreed made sense."

Swimlane models are packed full of information showing business activities, the major things that affect process flows, and the people—known as "actors"—that perform the activities in the business processes. Back to Figure 2.8, adding another independent third-party verification service would be represented by adding another Swimlane to the diagram. In the existing process, the current verification service is represented by the Swimlane labeled *3PV*. In the "to be," or future state, process, there will be one additional Swimlane for the new provider, and that Swimlane will have pretty much the same activities as the 3PV Swimlane. Critically for assessing the impact of the change, the process model shows clearly that the 3PV activities interact with the activities in the Swimlane labeled *NewApp*. With what implication? Simply that activities in the *NewApp* (which happens to be the commercial computer application the hospital settled on) Swimlane will have to change to send messages to a second verification service, and receive messages back from that service. Also, the activity *Record/Update Patient Verified/Non-Verified* will need to be modified to accommodate new conditions that arise from having another verification service, such as what to do if the two services do not agree.

What does Carl have so far? Three things: He has visible, clear, and tangible expressions of (1) the business goals of the transformation, (2) the cause and effect relationship among the business goals and business processes, especially *Verify Third-Party Payor*, and (3) the multiple activities contained in it needed to perform the business function *Verify Third-Party Payor* in the context of the business process they support. Figures 2.6 and 2.10 together illustrate the full relationship. When looking at Figure 2.10, keep in mind that there are well over a hundred activities that have been modeled as part of the hospital's overall improvement efforts. Figure 2.10 lets the person analyzing the impact of adding another

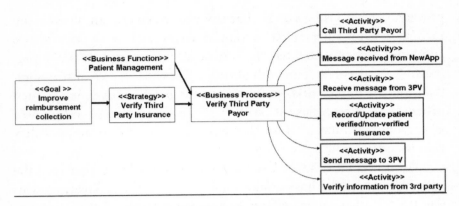

FIGURE 2.10   Process Impact on Activities

third-party verification service to focus *only* on the few activities that might be affected. Think about this in terms of your projects and only focusing on what is important. How many times have you said, like Mark, the executive assessing the impact of Check 21, "I think X number of activities might be impacted but I'm not sure." One huge benefit of explicitly *knowing* what connects with what, when, where, how, and how much lies in being able to use your scarce resources, and time, much more effectively.

Back to the models.

As Carl's team discovered, the activity *Record/Update Patient Verified/Nonverified* needed to be modified to accommodate two possibly conflicting sources of information. The people performing that activity use a computer application to assist them. Figure 2.11 shows this: the *Use Case* "Assign Insurance Plan" represents the place where some computer application supports some business activity. *Use Case* is a technical term for the simple concept of expressing the interactions between people and applications in terms of how they are "used," hence the name. What is particularly

FIGURE 2.11   Process Impact on Technology

powerful about Use Cases is that they, themselves, can be used (no pun intended) to bridge the semantic disconnect between T-Shirts and Suits each of which has their own, often respectively incomprehensible, languages. The reality is that these two sides of the organization are more alike than not and highly dependent on each other. Both sides focus on "stuff that has to get done" and on how that stuff "gets used." The Use Case gives them a way to codify that focus.

In Blueprint terms, a Use Case serves as the bridge between the process (usually the businessperson's) layer and the application (usually the technology person's) layer. The notion is that business activities, which may be carried out by people (e.g., a call center representative) or a computer (e.g., an interactive voice response system) are supported by automation. As shown in Figure 2.12, a Use Case describes the interaction between an actor—the person or system performing some business function—and the automation—typically a

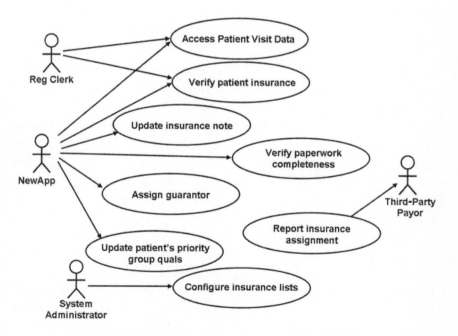

FIGURE 2.12 Technology Supporting the Process

computer application—that supports the actor in carrying out the business function. The Use Case shows actors as stick figures; usually an actor is a human performing some business activity though other computer applications can also be actors. The actions of the automation—typically a computer application that supports or (in the case of developing a new system) will support the actor in carrying out the business function—are depicted in the ovals by a simple verb-noun statement. The same process of building shared semantics is as necessary for Use Cases as it is for the Swimlanes described earlier. Namely, while Use Cases require simple verb-noun statements, the debates and discussions over what different people think these verbs and nouns should be are often far than simple. These debates, however, are necessary, again, to codify what is tacit, to create the shared understandings so critical for consistent execution.[3]

In addition to what he already accomplished, Carl's team now has (1) designed a Use Case model that details the interactions of people with the applications that support them, and (2) isolated, explicitly, the important connections to focus on. The hospital models have over 20 Use Case models for various applications that are used by the hospital's employees. But Figure 2.11 shows clearly that there is only one Use Case that might be affected by the proposed change to this activity. Once again, the traceability in this Blueprint creates a shared understanding of what's involved when it's time to get stuff done saving time and money, and reducing the time required for analysis and delivery.

Use Cases are the gateway to software implementation, raising yet another critical consideration about the information in a Business Blueprint. Figure 2.11 shows clearly that the *Record/Update Patient Verified/Non-Verified* activity is supported by one Use Case. Looking ahead a bit: Changes to the activity will change how people interact with underlying applications, and it's likely that the application functionality itself will change. In short, at that point, a software developer can set about writing code. But there's a huge catch to the preceding description, and Figure 2.13 shows what it is.

While the *Record/Update Patient Verified/Non-Verified* activity is supported by exactly one Use Case, "Assign Insurance Plan," that same Use Case supports, directly or indirectly, numerous other business activities. So what? Think of the software developer modifying

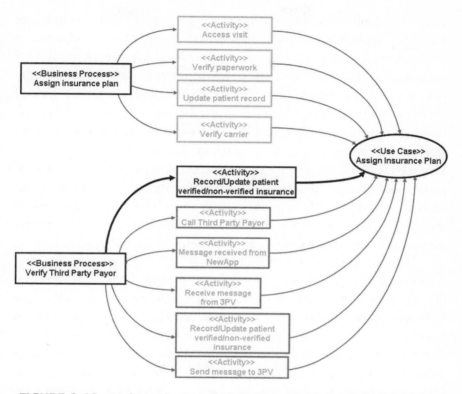

FIGURE 2.13 Making the Invisible Visible—Unintended Consequences

the application software that supports *Record/Update Patient Verified/Non-Verified.* Any change that programmer makes may have an affect on any of the other activities supported by the Use Case. If programmers do not know specifically the activities supported by the software they are creating or changing, they cannot be sure whether a change to support one activity causes an unintended impact to another, probably unrelated activity. It is just such unintended consequences that make software development and integration costly, time consuming, and error-prone. By exposing the connections in its models, the Business Blueprint helps ensure that consequences are more intended than not. Emphasizing this point, making visible what is way too often invisible—namely, getting clarity of what impacts what, when, where, how, and how much—we minimize the risk and decrease the likelihood of unintended consequences.

Moving past the Use Cases, we get to the technical parts of the Business Blueprint. As mentioned earlier, the benefits of modeling in the technical implementation arena are well established and well documented, so there's no need to go into detail here. That said, it is instructive to follow the model trail to the end to illustrate the full range of Business Blueprinting benefits.

In Figure 2.14, the Use Case (the bridge between the business view and the technical view) connects to a set of models known collectively as *Analysis Classes*. (We are truly in geek-land at this point, so feel free to jump to the end of this section; that said, we're going to skim through this at a level that it might be useful for you to know.) With apologies to people who create object-oriented models and systems for a living, we'll give a brief description.

The easiest way to think about *Entity-Boundary-Controller* is in terms of the "guts" of the application being created, the user interface that the actor—typically a human—interacts with, and software that mediates between the two. The *Entity* models the "guts" part of the application that has the application logic—the "stuff" in the application that understands how to actually solve the problem at hand in the business domain. The *Boundary* models the part of the application that provides the user's view—the user interface—into the functionality modeled by the *Entity*. The *Controller* determines, based on rules and context, how the user will actually see the user interface. The reason for the three pieces is to make it easier and more flexible to reuse parts of the system design and the application once it is written.

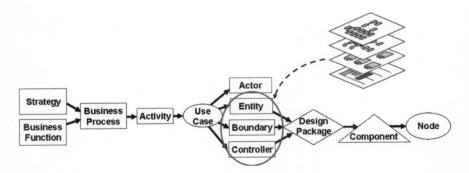

FIGURE 2.14 Designing the Technology

Why should anyone other than a programmer care? Because proper use of the information in these models can be the difference between reusing common software functionality and re-creating duplicative functionality which is wasteful. To illustrate, say the *Entity* is a model for a problem domain like *Maintain Patient Medical Data*. There may be multiple actors who need to *Maintain Patient Medical Data*—physicians affiliated with the hospital, unaffiliated physicians, nurses, technicians, health insurance representatives, and others. Each of these actors probably has different levels of things they can see and change. For ease of use, the system will want to present a unique interface to each. But there's only one underlying set of logic to maintaining patient data. So using the *Entity-Boundary-Controller* Analysis Classes lets one piece of application functionality serve multiple views, with the *Controller* holding the knowledge of which view to use in which circumstance. This way, different people get to see what is useful for them, and arguably only them.

Figure 2.15 shows how Analysis Classes lead directly to software running on a server. The *Design Package* model exists to let technology folks group software, possibly many pieces of software, into logically related packages. Figure 2.15 shows how a single design package

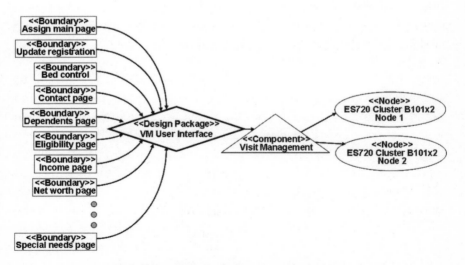

FIGURE 2.15 Packaging the Technology

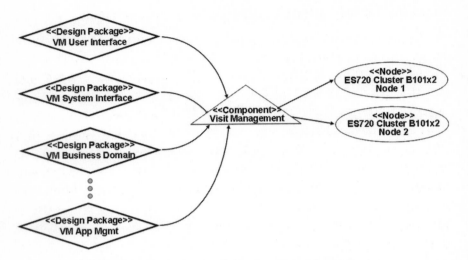

FIGURE 2.16   Technology Impact on Infrastructure

can contain the software from a number of analysis classes, and as Figure 2.16 shows, a software component, created from several design packages, ends up running on a computer—two different nodes in this case, for reliability purposes.

Again, who cares? Carl does. Look at it from the perspective of the data center manager and the person who needs to actually perform the *Record/Update Patient Verified/Non-Verified* activity. If a computer node goes down, how does the data center know who to call? Does your business know what business processes are affected by activities on which computer server? Part of the problem Carl and his team discovered was that data center operations occasionally *did* go down. This was easy to verify; the computer screen would freeze, an application would lock up, or data could not be pulled up. A challenge arose each time in terms of not knowing quickly where to look to diagnose, then fix, the problem. Which computer node went down, impacting which applications, stopping what customer processes? Who knows this type of linkage—quickly, easily, visibly?

This hospital now knows. In fact, if you think back through the connections of the models, Carl and his team actually understand how the processing power of one of the data center servers—say *ES720 Cluster B101x2 Node 1*—relates to their business goal of improving the collection of third-party reimbursements.

Watch Out for the Bus!—or Else the Company Stops Running

"If Sue gets hit by a bus, we're out of business." Who is your Sue? Do you want to be so critically dependent on a single person? Are you? Here's another of our mantras: Getting stuff out of the heads of the few provides the power to do much by the many. Or, using the language of our framework, so far, building shared semantics is critical to drive consistent execution. And this latter thing—this consistent execution thing—needs no longer be a fruitless quest. Re-defining the fundamental challenge of executional consistency as that of semantic disconnect creates a new way of thinking, and subsequently, acting on how to create it. How? By creating methods and using tools to create shared semantics that are as meaningful as they are actionable by your necessarily diverse teams.

As we've described in this chapter, Business Blueprinting is a pragmatic way to create such shared, and actionable, semantics. Each layer in a Business Blueprint has models relevant and appropriate to a specific audience with their own set of activities and responsibilities. These models provide different perspectives or views, sets of which provide a complete understanding of the solution to a business problem much as different types of maps highlight different things about a city. A key challenge is to (1) connect these different types of maps *within* a layer (as we all know, there are often significant differences, semantic disconnects within any particular layer—within the technical community, for example) as well as (2) connect *between* the layers (bridging the semantic disconnect between business-folks and technology-folks). This chapter worked through some of models necessary for Carl and Bill to execute their respective tasks from layer 1 through 4. It's hard work to be sure. But what is interesting is that it is: (1) doable, (2) actionable, (3) explicit, (4) tangible, (5) scalable, and (6) useful—as Carl and Bill will attest.

What This Means to You

1. *This seems like a lot of work.* That's not a question. Still, it is a fair observation. Creating and maintaining detailed, accurate models

of the business and its supporting technology requires real effort and expense. Our goal in this chapter has been to show that a relatively few models can represent a lot of invaluable information about your business to help you make sense and take action. Our experience is that, aside from a one-time cost in training and tooling, this doesn't add cost or time. Rather, it rather introduces good engineering hygiene into transformation initiatives, reducing risk and creating better results. Over time, the accumulated intellectual property directly saves time, effort, and heartache.

2. *How important are modeling tools?* It is not practical to model without the proper tools, in this case, modeling software for the business models as well as the technology models. Increasingly, the models created by tools from different vendors can interoperate thanks to an aggressive standardization program on how to represent modeling data in a tool-independent way.

3. *How do I start?* Pick a project at the top of your priority list, pick out the two or three critical business processes involved in that project, and get to it. See the Experiential Workshop discussion in Chapter 5 on how to start quickly as well as to create a working team around the process change that accompanies almost every project. Engage an experienced facilitator and a business modeler with knowledge of your business to guide you through the first few projects and use those projects to build the expertise in your own staff. And recognize that there is a different way to "think about" and consequently "take action" regarding how to get done what needs to get done.

4. *Do I need to Blueprint everything?* Absolutely not. Our motto is "as much as necessary, and no more." Don't even think about Blueprinting "the whole business." It's a waste of time, and not possible to boot. Instead, use Blueprinting to clarify the parts of the business that are changing, while the projects are going on. We've found that the models we've described in this chapter capture most of the value of codification for most projects with a reasonable amount of effort. There are lots of different types of models that you *can* create; the trick is to know which ones are valuable to you. This book, and an experienced modeler, can help you figure out which types are relevant and useful.

Chapter Cheat Sheet

The Issue

The fundamental challenge to getting stuff done well and consistently is that of the semantic disconnect. If we define this challenge—and the DNA for such executional consistency—this way, then the way to meet this challenge becomes clear: create tools and methods to create shared expressions that are as meaningful as they are actionable by everyone—the T-Shirts, Turtlenecks, and Suits. And this is what Business Blueprinting is all about: bridging the semantic disconnect by creating common expressions to drive executional consistency.

The Insight

A *Business Blueprint* consists of a set of connected models that captures the useful properties needed to understand the business and predict the impact of change made in one part of the business on another, from strategy through infrastructure.

The impacts of change—from shifting market demands to increased customer requirements—will always ripple throughout an organization. This is well known. What is often less well known is what types of ripples they will be, where and when they will occur, how significant their impacts will be and who will be impacted by them. Why is this? Because the organizational silos, the governance models, the undocumented processes, the different perspectives, the misaligned metrics, the fundamental differences among the T-Shirts, the Turtlenecks, the Suits—in short, these and any of a number of other characteristics that reflect semantic disconnects—give rise to the lack of visibility and awareness of what actually occurs throughout an organization. Consequently, it is no surprise that it is extremely difficult if not impossible to understand, much less anticipate, how changes in one part of an organization will impact other parts. Blueprinting tackles this issue. It makes

(Continued)

visible what is far too often invisible. And it does so by creating the "shared semantics" that are as meaningful as they are actionable by your teams with their (necessarily) different focuses, priorities, and processes.

The Phrases

Business Blueprint; Blueprinting; Models; Traceability

The Implications

Making visible what is so often invisible in organizations is a fine marketing slogan. What it means in practice is making explicit what is too often implicit in the workarounds, the exceptions, and the stuff that is in too few heads or deeply embedded in too many applications. Getting this stuff "out" in a form that can be used by everyone in the business is the core challenge of doing stuff consistently, the result of overcoming the semantic disconnects, and the opportunity to do what you need to get done, again and again.

Blueprinting is a way of explicitly codifying the knowledge of the solution to a business problem. Applied diligently each time a business problem is solved, Blueprinting creates a cumulative, connected set of knowledge—intellectual property in the form of models—that, one business challenge at a time, can grow to describe your entire organization. This visibility and understanding of how your organization operates constitutes a permanent competitive advantage in your capability to understand the impact of decisions before you make them. It further enhances your capability to react rapidly, effectively, efficiently and consistently to the demands of change—in other words, to achieve executional consistency.

Measurements, Gauges, and Graphs—
Doing What's Important

Setting the Stage: From Gut Feel to Root Causes

Reginald inherited a business in trouble. The business, IPSL, is an outsourcing utility that processes bank payments—primarily checks—from the point where the check leaves the teller window through the point where the exchange of funds occurs. The business was something of an enigma.

In some respects, it was very successful. The result of a successful and productive industry partnership, IPSL was created in the late 1990s and by 2002 boasted many of the largest banks in Europe as its customers. By 2003, the business was processing over three-quarters of a million items each day for banks across Western Europe.

But fundamental problems loomed despite this success. As a business process outsourcer, IPSL had grown over a period of time by adding customers—banks—and their check-processing employees that those banks were outsourcing. As we'll show in detail in Chapter 6, for a business process outsourcing deal to be successful—for it to be a win-win proposition between, in this case, IPSL and the banks—two critical elements are required. First, the outsourcing company must be able to create efficiencies of scale to drive costs down below the costs that its customers incurred to do the same work. Second, the outsourcing company must be able to provide a level of service that meets the expectations of those customers. IPSL was losing on both counts. Its productivity, as measured by the number of items processed per employee was very low—less than half of the target productivity of 7,000 items per employee. At the same time, IPSL was not creating happy customers, repeatedly failing to meet the requirements of its service level agreements and incurring substantial financial penalties as a result. Further compounding these easily quantifiable measures, intangible problems were brewing. IPSL was struggling with the problems of not having integrated the workforces from its four major bank clients resulting in four sharply distinct cultures across their more than 500 employees with resulting low morale and growing high absenteeism.

Reginald took charge in 2002 with IPSL at a crossroads. He and his team recognized that IPSL needed to increase its productivity to meet its cost and profitability targets. They also recognized that the IPSL business processes too often failed to meet the needs of IPSL's customers; there were aspects to the processes themselves that needed examining and fixing to make certain that every business process was focused on a specific customer outcome and to "reduce the number of bad outcomes" (using one of Reginald's favorite expressions). Finally, they came to arguably the most important realization of all: Over the years since its creation, the employees, management, and executives of IPSL had made decisions based on "gut feel" rather than "root causes." Decisions were based more on hope than on fact.

Extent of the Challenge: "Reducing the Number of Bad Outcomes"

In confronting these sorts of problems, IPSL was, and is, not alone. Approximately 80 percent of the gross domestic product (GDP) in the United States—and a growing proportion throughout the world—comes from delivery of business services. Case studies show that when companies deliver services, fully 50 percent of the total services costs come from work that adds no value to the end customer.[1] "Services" in this context includes parts of companies that we might otherwise consider to be manufacturing. For example, Lockheed Martin is an aerospace manufacturing company, but they have found enough service processes in their company—customer requirements, maintenance, support, sales, concept development, and so on—that they have completed more than 1,000 initiatives to speed and streamline service processes.

Companies spend vast amounts of money executing the processes by which they service their customers and keep the lights on. Take spending on logistics alone—on shipping, freight forwarders, third-party logistics companies such as UPS, airlines, and shipping lines. Annually, businesses spend approximately $2 trillion on logistics. Wherever there is $2 trillion of commerce, there are vast amounts of money to be saved. There is no business that is not affected by logistics spending. For companies that are involved in importing or exporting goods, the processes surrounding logistics can be Byzantine—as we will see in Chapter 7, the regulatory environment is changing rapidly and processes across many different enterprises are increasingly linked. Clearly, improving logistics processes, and the ways that businesses procure logistics services presents enormous opportunities to save money.

Saving money is only part of the opportunity for improving a business. The notion of what it means to "improve" includes things like reducing costs and increasing productivity, but also includes improvements to offer better service to customers, and grow the revenue of the business. The "vocabulary of value" as it pertains to business process outsourcing (BPO) relationships, and the importance of creating partnerships with vendors that focus on both cost reduction *and* value creation will be covered in more detail in Chapter 6. For now, we just note that "reengineering," or "improvement" has picked up an excessive connotation of cost-cutting and efficiency improvement. Indeed, this is where process improvement began: In the immediate postwar years as the economy of Japan was getting back on its feet, Japanese manufacturers needed to be able to do more with less—they had few human resources and scarce financial resources. Toyota, especially, focused on disciplined, process-focused approaches to production, and minimizing the resources—people, processes, technology, and money—that added no end value for the customer. They created shared semantics, tools, and techniques for streamlining processes, and focused on adding value to the customer, resulting in what became known as the "Toyota Production System."

The Toyota Production System, which has since been generalized into something called *Lean Manufacturing*, began in response to scarce resources. But it was developed fully mindful of things that add value to the customer. Its impact on the automotive industry is well known. Western auto manufacturers began to play catch-up around Lean and quality activities in the 1980s, but the advantages from Japan's head start have proven difficult to surmount. In 2002, Toyota became the first non-U.S. manufacturer to sell more than two million cars in the United States, and, in 2003, Toyota passed Ford Motor to become the world's second largest carmaker. In 2004, Japanese auto manufacturers reached a major milestone—30 percent of the cars sold in the United States were from Japanese manufacturers. Why? According to Tatsuo Yoshida, analyst at Deutsche Securities in Tokyo, "Japanese carmakers are offering highly competitive products at reasonable prices." Simple enough—over the second half of the past century, by systematically focusing on value and quality in their production processes, Japanese car makers have overcome enormous economic and cultural obstacles to dominate the car industry. All this is well-known and well-trodden ground. But this is an important starting point from another perspective into how to create and drive (pun intended this time) executional consistency.

Opportunities for better execution will only increase, and with them, so too will the challenges of executional consistency. As we discussed in the first two chapters, competitive pressures and market uncertainties drive companies to innovate faster and farther from their core competencies. Never-ending pressures from competition means that each time a company creates an important innovation, competitors rapidly, and inevitably, rush to benefit from it. For the innovative companies, executional consistency allows them to conserve their organizational resources. Ongoing innovation can be nurtured by making sure that resources are put on those things and activities that add value to their customers; this customer-led determination of where to use resources ensures that they are used both effectively and efficiently.

And executional consistency in the innovation process itself means that innovative companies can more consistently bring innovation to market allowing the innovative company to take advantage of the larger margins that innovation allows.[2]

For the competitors of innovative companies, a daunting challenge lies in rapidly responding to the competitive moves of the innovative companies. Getting the resources you need to respond quickly requires shared semantics and a shared framework for execution. Because "follower" companies do not enjoy the same margin advantages that innovative companies do, they are further challenged to focus on profitability and productivity through cost takeout. Thus, we see that the very nature of competitive dynamics drives companies toward the need to execute consistently, effectively, and efficiently.

Along with this, companies' business processes are becoming inexorably interconnected. In *The Jericho Principle*, we introduced what we called the Collaborative Imperative. Simply put, the Collaborative Imperative says that you gotta collaborate—that no one can any longer do it all alone. Different types of collaborative relationships exist; each is designed to take advantage of a specific business opportunity and each involves different ways of sharing risks and rewards of doing so. Knowing what type of collaboration is relevant when and for how long is key to continually take advantage of specific innovation opportunities.

Arriving at the same result along a somewhat different path, Shoshanna Zuboff and James Maxmin envision an emerging economic system where nearly every product and service is created to satisfy the custom—"individuated"—needs of a particular person.[3] In their model, production starts with the specific need of a specific individual. Given the highly personal nature of such needs, and thus the dynamic nature of products and services in such a system, vertically integrated companies—geared toward efficiently making many copies of the same thing—will give way to multiple collaborating, or what they call federated, organizations. Federations will come together quickly and seamlessly to produce the exact thing needed to satisfy an individual. The collaborating organizations will assume all responsibility and accountability for satisfaction. This "support network" will be paid only when the individual releases his or her cash into the system, signaling satisfaction.

The Collaborative Imperative puts a heavy burden on organizations to codify the salient characteristics of their business so that they can easily move in and out of potentially close relationships with a number of collaborative partners. More specifically, collaborating companies must have shared semantics for describing all aspects of their interaction. In the support network case, these interactions are intimate indeed, because no one in the network gets paid until all have fulfilled their part in creating the product or service for the individual. Executional consistency in the face of the Collaborative Imperative means that process improvements will not be exercises for a single company. Rather, they will involve engineering processes that stretch across organizational boundaries. James Champy calls this sort of process engineering *X-Engineering*. To make X-Engineering work, companies must have a great deal of shared semantics, tools, techniques, and methods to be able to execute, and more importantly, to continually improve, in this highly interconnected environment.[4] Imagine, for example, how a new regulation like Sarbanes Oxley would ripple through such a support network.

We don't have to imagine it. There is a real-life example in the *Secure Supply Chain* initiatives that have been undertaken by the U.S. government and some commercial organizations—product companies, port operators, logistics suppliers, and so on—in the face of the threat of terrorist events in the supply chain. We examine Secure Supply Chain in detail in Chapter 7. For now, we'll make only a few observations on this topic.

First, supply chains in general entail multiple interlocking processes among members of the supply chain: the most straightforward import/export transaction for goods crossing the Atlantic to the United States requires that over 25 documents change hands between government agencies and members of the supply chain directly involved with the import/export. Second, new regulatory requirements are creating specific demands for notification, provenance, and security of both the goods in the supply chain and the information about those goods that travels through the business processes of the supply chain's members. A continual, coordinated upgrade of *all* of these business processes will be needed as these regulations become pervasive. Estimates range widely regarding the cost and effort of such sweeping changes. But there is an intriguing data point with regard to an early example of such costs and efforts. Wal-Mart's requirement that its top 100 suppliers deliver pallets of goods identified with radio frequency identifiers (RFID) will cost those suppliers, according to AMR research, $2 billion to implement.[5] Of that $2 billion, approximately $1.2 billion will be spent not on RFID tags and readers, but on technology to support the business process changes that the Wal-Mart edict will trigger—such as upgrades and integration for supply chain applications, data storage, and analytics tools. And this is only one drop in the bucket.

As we saw in Chapters 1 and 2, significant "good stuff" can happen by creating common semantics and executable descriptions of your business processes. What we add in this chapter is the need for common semantics and executable methods and techniques to *improve* business processes—improve in the broad sense that we are using in this section, including cost takeout, improved cycle time, better value to customers, and better customer experience, and better able to absorb the next regulatory volley. Business Blueprinting describes your business in detail and tells you *what connects with what*. To improve your business, you further need to *make sense* of how your business creates value for customers, to *focus all of your processes on creating value*, and to *continuously improve your business processes*. In this chapter, we show how the vocabulary, methods, and techniques of Lean Six Sigma give you the tools you need for this. Lean Six Sigma helps you improve your likelihood of successfully getting change to happen—no mean feat because, as James Champy has noted, "every large organization has the corporate antibodies to kill any incremental change program."[6]

Note to the reader: Your organization may already embrace Lean or Six Sigma, or both. If so, this chapter will show the crucial role of codification in the form of a Business Blueprint. Your organization may not use Lean or Six Sigma, nor have any intention of doing so. If so, this chapter will show how codification in the form of a Business Blueprint provides the objective data so critical for Lean Six Sigma. We use the language of Lean Six Sigma because it exists, it's well documented, it has been famously successful, and it applies to all businesses in all sectors.

In the previous chapters, we described the DNA for executional consistency—the creation of shared semantics critical to get stuff done over and over again consistently. We explained that codifying in a Blueprint *what connects with what, when, where, how, and how much* is needed to get that consistency. Lean Six Sigma is a complementary method that focuses on the "how much" part of the previous sentence. It provides additional methods and tools to maintain and extend the shared semantics as they continuously, and necessarily, evolve; it provides the "pragmatism" wrapper to our pragmatic execution framework.

Facing the Challenge: Defeating the "Corporate Antibodies to Change"

How do you go about speeding up and cutting down processes for products and services? Increasingly the answer to that question involves the methods and concepts of Lean, a concept that has its roots in manufacturing, but applies to all businesses. Lean Manufacturing came from a study by the Massachusetts Institute of Technology's (MIT) International Motor Vehicle Program that examined the significant performance gap between Western and Japanese automotive industries.[7] Superior Japanese production techniques were described as *Lean production*. The adjective "lean" referred to the way in which specific Japanese companies expended less human effort, capital investment, floor space, materials, and time in their manufacturing operations. Five core principles provide the focus for Lean:

1. *Customer value:* Define customer value from the outside-in, that is, from the perspective of the customer.
2. *Value stream:* Identify all activities used to make a product or provide a service.
3. *Flow:* Create a system where value is continuously added. Clear away obstacles that don't add value or clog the value stream.
4. *Pull:* Initiate work only at the demand and to the specific specifications of the customer.
5. *Perfection:* Continuously refine the process to improve efficiency, cycle time, costs, and quality.

Note that the words "reduce cost" do not appear. We will come back to this point later. After the study, MIT, working with leaders in U.S. defense aerospace and the U.S. Air Force, started the Lean Aerospace Initiative (LAI) in 1993. Its mission: "to accelerate the lean enterprise transformation of the entire U.S. aerospace sector." LAI aims to promulgate Lean methods and techniques throughout the industry and "encourage positive interaction among consortium members to leverage shared knowledge and create a virtuous circle between customer and supplier, with all parties reaping the benefits."[8]

But the potential benefits of Lean are not confined to the manufacturing shop. Let's go back to Lockheed Martin. A founding member of LAI, it might be tempting to think of Lockheed Martin solely as an aerospace manufacturing company. However, through application of Lean techniques to their *services* processes, Lockheed Martin has completed more than 1000 projects to improve its services. This has led to many improvements, one of which is to reduce the cycle time for its Atlas missile program from 48 months to 18 months, simultaneously driving substantial costs out of the program.[9]

Of course, Lean does not get all the credit for Lockheed Martin's improvements. In 1999, Lockheed Martin undertook an approach called LM21 (for Lockheed Martin in the twenty-first century).[10] Briefly, LM21 combines the speed and streamlining philosophy of Lean with a continuous quality improvement approach called Six Sigma. Taken together, these two form a powerful approach for improving the performance of a company. The approach is called *Lean Six Sigma* (or sometimes, Six Sigma Lean).

Lean and Six Sigma bridge powerfully together the fifth of the five principles of Lean, which you'll recall is "perfection—continuously refine the process to improve efficiency, cycle time, costs, and quality." Six Sigma is a data-driven approach that focuses on driving variability out of the processes that run a business. In other words, it's a way of doing business that uses quantitative methods—measurements, analysis, experimentation, and results tracking—to improve the performance of processes. We'll discuss Six Sigma in a few paragraphs. But first, we'll look at an example of applying Lean and Six Sigma to a business process, in this case the "deliver-to-cash" business process that collects money after the delivery of a product or service. Applying the principles of Lean naturally leads to a customer focused, streamlined process that reduces the average time for generating an invoice, tracking accounts receivable, and collecting payments.

In a specific instance, Rick, a certified project management professional and Lean practitioner, worked on the deliver-to-cash process in his company, a medium-sized manufacturer of electronic subassemblies. By applying Lean principles and tools to streamline the deliver-to-cash process, Rick reduced the average time required to post payment after the order of a product from 55 days to 37 days, and in so doing reduced the cost of processing an order from $173 to under $100. This increased the amount of cash available to the company and reduced the receivables backlog by over 50 percent. Success! However, Rick is also a Six Sigma practitioner—in Six Sigma parlance he is a "black belt"—and so he recognized that averages can mask deeper information about how a process is operating. In this case, Rick was compelled to look more deeply at the "average 37 days" measurement of performance following the Six Sigma philosophy of "torturing data until it gives up useful information."

In the case of Rick's deliver-to-cash process, a deeper examination of the average time of 37 days showed that for 70 percent of orders, payments posted in 25 days or less, but for 20 percent of the orders the time was 45 days or longer, and for 10 percent the time was 60 days or longer. On average, the company was doing better converting deliveries into cash, but there was a huge variance in the amount of time, with the 45-day and 60-day receivables dragging down overall financial performance. If Rick could find the source of the variance, he could eliminate, or at least reduce, the very long times experienced by 30 percent of the orders, improving performance still further.

Through deeper analysis of where time was spent in the deliver-to-cash process, Rick uncovered the source of the variation: a single order from someone outside the United States might include numerous products, which, depending on the size of the order, could be packed and shipped in multiple shipments. However, certain technologies, when sent to certain countries, required additional approvals and documentation—things such as an export license, consular invoice, or a certificate of origin. Whenever an order included even a single one of these technologies, the bill processing for the entire order was held up until the approval was processed. The approval process, Rick found, was itself highly variable, taking anywhere from one to three weeks. By focusing on the sources of variance in this business process, Rick was able to further reduce the average order-to-cash time from 37 days to 31 days. Equally importantly, the maximum amount of time went from over 60 days to 42 days, reducing the receivables backlog by another 35 percent, and the cost of processing an order by an additional $11. The bottom line? The combination of Lean and Six Sigma enhanced both speed and predictability.

Six Sigma was created by Motorola in the 1980s as a way of measuring, controlling, and improving the variability of a process. The actual term *Six Sigma* comes from the concepts of probability and the "normal distribution." In a normal distribution, represented in the familiar *bell curve*, the term sigma refers to the "standard deviation"—a measure of how far some data point is from the average of all the data points in a set of data. In the 1980s, Bob Galvin, chairman of Motorola at the time, developed a new standard for measuring the effectiveness of a process, based on the notion of "Defects per Million Opportunities." If an "Opportunity" is the output of some business or manufacturing process, then, per the Motorola formulation, the sigma number is an indication of how many times the output is defective. Higher sigma numbers indicate lower numbers of defects, or, equivalently, a better yielding business process. This is shown in Table 3.1.

In Rick's case, the data set was the deliver-to-cash times for all the orders placed in the year. Rick's initial work reduced the mean of this data set to 37 days. However, since 30 percent of the orders took from 45 to 60 days or more to process, in Six Sigma terms the

TABLE 3.1 Six Sigma Performance Levels

Sigma Level	Defects per Million Opportunity (DPMO)	Business Performance Percent (Yield)
1	691,500	30.85
2	308,500	69.15
3	66,800	93.32
4	6,200	99.38
5	230	99.977
6	3.4	99.99966

deliver-to-cash process was a "Two Sigma" process—in a million orders, 300,000 of them would take longer to process than is desirable (note the second line of Table 3.1). If Rick improves that to a "Three Sigma" process, "only" 67,000 orders would take so long. If Rick improves that process to a "Six Sigma" process, only 3 orders out of every million would take so long to process.

Motorola's engineers recognized the usefulness of thinking of process in Sigma terms and created a methodology and a toolset to support it. Methodology and experience are important for Six Sigma for a pragmatic reason: its usefulness depends on identifying and measuring the truly critical dimensions of the business. In more visceral terms, possibly, than Rick's technology export or Motorola's product quality, think of some processes that are closer to everyday experience. By common agreement, competitive, quality businesses in the United States run at approximately Four Sigma, or at approximately 6,200 defects per million opportunities. At Four Sigma, a payroll company would make an error in 6 of every 1,000 checks processed—probably unacceptable if the errors result in someone not getting paid or getting paid the wrong amount, possibly acceptable if the error is in a "comment" field. Even at Six Sigma performance levels, an airline will have 3.4 defects in every million passenger miles flown. Those 3.4 defects are annoying if they mean a missed connection, and unacceptable if they mean 3.4 fatalities for every million passenger miles flown.[11]

Using Six Sigma methods, Motorola has documented more than $16 billion in savings directly attributable to Six Sigma. Interestingly, at the time it was invented, Motorola thought of Six Sigma as a manufacturing-only methodology. It took them several years to realize that it could apply to their other processes as well. Over those years, Bob Galvin estimates Motorola could have saved an additional $5 billion.[12]

Hundreds of companies, including giants like Allied Signal and General Electric, have adopted Six Sigma as their way of doing business. And as we have seen, other giants like Lockheed Martin have adapted both Lean and Six Sigma into a hybrid business approach that compels both a relentless customer focus and a continual culture of improvement. As Andrew N. Parris, an Atlas Program Improvement executive with Lockheed has said, Lockheed Martin applies both methodologies in their LM21 program, "We want Lean processes operating at Six Sigma capability. That's what we're looking for in a process."

Lean Six Sigma—Methods and Madness

As we saw in Chapter 2, Blueprinting is a way of explicitly codifying the knowledge of a solution to a business problem. Applied diligently each time a business problem is solved, Blueprinting creates a cumulative, connected set of knowledge—intellectual property in the form of models—that, one business challenge at a time, can grow to describe your entire organization. The resulting visibility and understanding of how your organization operates constitutes a permanent competitive advantage in your capability to understand the impact of decisions before you make them. It further enhances your capability to react rapidly, effectively, and consistently to the demands of change—in other words, to help you get done what needs to get done.

Blueprinting provides ever-growing knowledge of *what* your business does, and *how it does it*. Lean Six Sigma shows *how to use that knowledge quantitatively to prioritize and execute projects*, and *to link metrics from project results to business results*. Applying the principles of Lean drives a business toward customer-driven processes with low (ideally zero) waiting times, and low (ideally zero) inventory. Applying the principles of Six Sigma drives those processes to consistency of execution, time after time. Six Sigma considers every business outcome to be the result of a process. It understands that all processes, inherently, have variability and uses data and statistics to understand the variability and drive process improvement decisions.

Where Blueprinting is the bone and muscle of the organization, Lean Six Sigma is the nervous system. It plays the role of the involuntary nervous system in the sense that it becomes instinctively part of everything you do, like breathing in and breathing out. It plays the role of the voluntary nervous system in that it creates the framework for thinking about which things to do, making sense of them, and then taking action. But there is a key phrase in the above two paragraphs—"applied diligently"—and Jim Champy's observation that "every large organization has the corporate antibodies to kill any incremental change program" certainly seems universally applicable. Cutting through all of these words: *What needs to happen to actually get this stuff working?*

Two things: The first is having the understanding of how the processes in a business create the value of the business. As Wipro's corporate vice president of Mission Quality, C. R. Nagaraj, said in a 2002 interview, "Six Sigma converts a business problem into a statistical problem and finds a statistical solution. It then converts the statistical solution into a business solution." Having objective, detailed information on business processes—both the "as is" process that you want to improve, and any prospective "to be" improved process, is key to achieving the kind of clarity envisioned by Nagaraj. Blueprinting, as we will see shortly, can provide such information.

The second part is what Bossidy and Charan call the *organizational will* to apply the methods of Lean Six Sigma to really make a change. Six Sigma and Lean books[13] are chock-full of recommendations on how to get organizations to actually move. There is no doubt that chief among them is the commitment from the top to invest the necessary money, create the needed behaviors, and the incentives to reinforce them. Famously, at General Electric, Six Sigma Black Belts need to prove that the problems are fixed permanently before they can claim achievement of the goals of a particular project, and up to 40 percent of the bonuses of top management are tied to Six Sigma performance goals.

Investment in the organizational commitment takes a special form in Six Sigma. Everyone in the organization requires some degree of training. But specialists are particularly needed in the organization for Six Sigma (and therefore in Lean Six Sigma):

- *Green Belts:* A team member of a Six Sigma process improvement project who has been trained in the Six Sigma methodology.
- *Black Belts:* A Six Sigma specialist, and the backbone of the leadership for process improvement teams. Black Belts are senior,

highly regarded, line personnel, who have been deeply trained in Six Sigma methods, and can serve as both team leaders and management advisors.

- *Master Black Belts:* A very senior Six Sigma practitioner, qualified to set up and run an overall corporate Six Sigma program, oversee the population of Black Belts and their process improvement projects, and to train Green Belts and Black Belts.

We mentioned earlier Lockheed Martin's LM21 initiative and that it had completed more than 1,000 improvement projects. In Lean Six Sigma terms, improvement happens in a series of discrete projects with well-defined objectives and business benefits. Each project is overseen by a Black Belt. Most, if not all, of the team members on the project are either Green Belts or receive Green Belt training during the course of the project. In organizations initially undertaking Lean Six Sigma, the Black Belts assigned to improvement projects may be Black Belts in training, with part of their training occurring before the start of a project and the remainder of the training happening at different stages in the project.

What does a Lean Six Sigma project do? It aims to improve some specific business metric by focusing on a process or set of processes, with a specific business goal as the objective. The key steps in a Lean Six Sigma project are known by their initials DMAIC, which stands for Define, Measure, Analyze, Improve, and Control. The Define step is key to a Lean Six Sigma project: a project charter is explicitly created that defines customer-oriented business problems to be solved and specific business metrics to be approved. A typical project charter will address:

- *The project name:* People need something to identify with, and at some point the project will be successful in creating tremendous business benefit and will be a poster child for best practices. The name should be short and evocative, like "Improve Accounts Receivable Performance."
- *The Black Belt* (and Green Belts) who will participate in the project.
- *The start date* and *anticipated end date.*

- *The cost of poor quality:* This is the cost associated with Defects that get produced by process variability. It may be a real cost—products that need to be scrapped, extra service hours that need to be worked to satisfy client needs in a professional services engagement, penalties that need to be paid because of a contract breach—or a more abstract cost like damage to the brand or to a customer relationship. The most telling thing in Lean Six Sigma is that, before any substantial resources are expended on a project, that project must clearly quantify the costs that will be reduced by successful completion of the project. So, for example, for the Accounts Receivable project mentioned earlier, the Cost of Poor Quality might include its quantitative impact on free cash flow or the interest expense incurred when receivables are not collected in a timely fashion.

- *Importance to the business:* Why is this project important enough that you should expend company resources in it (as opposed to the countless other projects that you could spend company resources on)? Is it a competitive differentiator? One where you critically have to be at least as good as your competitors? Central enough that getting it wrong impacts many other things?

- *The problem:* How is the process "broken?" This includes the current baseline performance, which presumably is unacceptable, and an initial cut at why this is considered unacceptable, possibly by reference to industry best practices, or by stating how this process performance is a necessary part of larger corporate performance goals.

- *Scope:* In a business, the Six Degrees of Separation principle applies aggressively. Almost every process is connected indirectly with almost every other process. Lean Six Sigma project teams always struggle with where to cut off the scope of what they will look at and try to improve, and what is beyond their ability to change in a time-boxed project. The Six Sigma Black Belt is important here, as an experienced practitioner who can help a team—who may get carried away in their zeal to fix everything—to focus on the essential improvements for *this* project.

- *Anticipated benefits:* A challenging, but realistic, quantitative statement of the business benefits from this project. Will the maximum time to collect an accounts receivable to be reduced to 15 days?

- *Measurements of effectiveness:* What are the business metrics that will be measured before and after to determine the success or the project
- *Business case:* Why is this project important, what are the consequences for not doing this project
- *Team members:* Including the project sponsor, project leader, subject matter experts
- *Stakeholders:* People not on the team, but interested in its progress and results
- *Major milestones and dependencies:* When will the DMAIC phases of an improvement project be completed, and are there any known obstacles.

There are always projects that *can* be undertaken. A key challenge for Lean Six Sigma-oriented companies, especially in the early stages of implementation, is deciding *which* projects to do when in terms of impact, which happens in the *Define* stage. An example of one company's experience will help to illustrate how important the Define step is.

When Unisys—a 100+ year old company with a complex mix of professional services, technology services, and technology products—undertook Lean Six Sigma, CEO, Joseph McGrath set out two broad areas of initial focus: Sales and Delivery. He established two senior task forces, led by members of the Unisys Executive Committee. One of the task forces focused on Sales Excellence, the other on Delivery Excellence. Each included leadership from a broad set of stakeholders from across the company: field, headquarters, sales, delivery, marketing, HR, finance, and administration, and so on. Each of the task forces was assisted by a Master Black Belt.

For one week, this senior group worked in intensive, parallel sessions—largely separate, with occasional coordination, to identify a focused list of potential initiatives for an initial set of Lean Six Sigma projects. At the end of the week, each task force had identified their top 10 initiatives and the dependencies between the initiatives of the two task forces.

The 20 or so projects identified by the two task forces were still too many initial projects for meaningful action. Joe, working with his leadership, determined that Unisys would use the most critical three or four projects from each of the two task forces as pilot projects to have immediate impact, to serve as the proving ground for Lean Six Sigma in the company, and to serve as the projects for training Unisys "home-grown" Black Belts for further Lean Six Sigma projects. To select the top projects, each task force used a prioritization/voting mechanism, where members of both task forces, the Unisys Executive Committee, and business heads each rated the relative importance of each initiative based on the following characteristics:

- Business impact—size
- Business impact—speed
- Client impact
- Incremental investment
- Complexity/interdependencies

The ratings provided a consensus opinion on the relative relationship of each initiative to the above categories, with a 9 indicating a High/Strong impact, a 3 indicating a Medium/Mild impact, and a 1 indicating a Low/Weak impact. The voting mechanism included a weighting mechanism that gives the relative importance—in the eyes of Unisys leadership—of the categories, with 5 being the most important, and 1 being the lowest importance. The relative importance of these categories—and indeed the categories themselves—can change over time as company imperatives change; for Unisys, the projects with the most Business Impact and Client Impact were favored for this first round of projects.

With the *Define* step completed, and the projects initially defined, each project team methodically proceeds through the MAIC steps of Measurement, Analysis, Improvement, and Control. The Lean Six Sigma project team is responsible for identifying the appropriate metrics based on their understanding of the business, and of Six Sigma's need for data, data, and more data. The project sponsor, a senior executive with particular passion for the area that the project is involved with, provides air cover, sponsorship, and removes obstacles. Each project has one or more full-time Black Belts who may be Black-Belts-in-training, who take the lead in applying statistical methods and tools to the data collected by the team. The team examines the data, aided by the detailed analysis of the Black Belt, for patterns, causal relationships, trends, and "root causes" for the business problem that the project was created to improve. Teams might conceive and perform experiments to confirm suspected root causes and relationships between different business factors.

Simulation of business processes is another particularly powerful technique, enabled by Business Blueprinting. Simulation gives the ability to "experiment" with business process changes without disturbing the actual business. To use simulation in business process improvement projects, the team first creates the appropriate business process models, and uses the data collected from the Measure step as performance data for the activities in these models. Typically, a robust business process modeling tool has the ability, with the necessary underlying information on activity performance, to simulate the performance of the business process, showing things like total person-time to process something, the total elapsed time something will spend in the process, and whether and where things will be delayed. Most importantly, as the Lean Six Sigma project team analyzes data (in the Analyze step of DMAIC), and posits potential Improvements, these proposed improvements can be modeled by modifying the "as is" model into a "to be" model. Simulations run on the "to be" model give an early indication of whether the proposed "Improvements" really improve things, make them worse, or—as is often the case early in a project—don't have much of an impact at all.

Lean Six Sigma project teams will often iterate through the Measure-Analyze-Improve steps incrementally making changes to business processes until the target level of performance is achieved. At that point, the team's role changes to determining and establishing the sorts of control measures needed to sustain the desired level of performance.

Reginald Goes Lean

Recall IPSL, the business example that began this chapter. Reginald and his team aggressively used the quantitative analysis and improvement methods of Lean Six Sigma to conceive, prioritize, create, and execute a set of improvement projects. They were equally committed to ensuring that the improvements really became cultural changes. IPSL did this using the connected, business-oriented models of Business Blueprinting to define the challenges, make sure that the execution aligned with its strategic goals, and capture the intellectual property created along the way to leverage it across IPSL. IPSL focused on specific operational goals for Year 1, including:

- $1 million in cost takeout—generically, "Cost Out"
- $200,000 in new revenue—generically, "Revenue In"
- Zero Service Level Agreement breaches—generically, "Customer Improvement"

Recalling the four layers of a Business Blueprint, IPSL captured these goals in a layer 1 model called a *Business Goals Hierarchy*, which served as the anchor for each of the projects undertaken, and for all of the models created, from that point forward. Reginald and team then established DMAIC projects—six in all—in the areas of *Cost Out*, *Revenue In*, and *Customer Improvement*. As part of these projects, IPSL created and leveraged business process layer and application layer models. IPSL was able to identify business patterns and reuse, eliminating process redundancies and streamlining the supporting technology by codifying its business processes and the applications that support those processes. Equally importantly, Reginald now has a baseline corporate resource of how the business runs. Such a baseline has become crucial for further automation, improvement, and for maintaining, as Reginald puts it, "organizational wisdom during personnel turnover."

These projects, some of which are still ongoing at the time of writing, have achieved substantial success. IPSL has exceeded its *Cost Out* goal of $1 million, identifying improvements that will save in excess of $1.3 million annually. Through improvements in service and cost performance, IPSL has had no SLA breaches in two years, further improving financial performance and, maybe more importantly, leading to renewed contracts with two of its major clients, thus exceeding its *Revenue In* targets.

Over the past two years, Lean Six Sigma has helped IPSL improve its performance in the eyes of its customers and its employees, with respect to industry standards for efficiency—where it has doubled its productivity—and, last but certainly not least, financially. As the improvement projects continue to move forward, IPSL's focus has broadened to include organizational changes to consolidate and maintain its achievements. It has ongoing initiatives in several areas including training, rewards and recognition, leadership and executive behavior, measurement, coaching and facilitation, and communication.

With the commitment and vision of top executives, driven by leadership and troops who are committed to making a change, Lean Six Sigma has recreated companies across all sectors, business models, and sizes. The process streamlining philosophy of Lean works tightly with the process and technology codification of Business Blueprinting. The Blueprint also provides an objective, quantified, measurable expression of what the business does and how the business operates, providing powerful support for the statistical techniques and the *Measure-Analyze-Improve* iterations of Six Sigma. As Business Blueprinting represents the state of the business, Lean Six Sigma gives the impetus and the means to improve that business. Taken together, these two approaches form the backbone of what we call pragmatic execution—of going beyond organizational desire to the pragmatics of getting stuff done—again and again.

What This Means to You

1. *Does Lean Six Sigma only apply to the largest companies?* There is no question that both Lean and Six Sigma have their roots in large companies—and large manufacturing companies at that. We've

tried to show examples in this chapter of smaller companies—IPSL is a relatively small business compared to a Lockheed Martin, and Rick's electronics company is a medium-sized supplier. The Lean Six Sigma literature draws heavily on large companies, but that's to be expected for a few reasons: first, large companies can afford to hire expensive consultants who are the people who write a lot of the literature; second, large companies have sufficient resources to dedicate large teams of senior people to projects and senior people from big companies are the people who get invited to speak about their results at the sorts of events written about by the people writing the literature; third, large companies are the only companies capable of generating the sort of "the-Golden-Gate-Bridge-contains-enough-wire-to-stretch-around-the-world-three-times" type of statistics that interest people and motivate them to undertake large change.[14] But big does not necessarily mean better nor necessarily the most relevant. Few companies of any size have the type of executional consistency they would like to have. Few companies have closed the semantic disconnect gaps. Yet, any and all of them could. The examples we're drawing from, the lessons we're highlighting, and the opportunities we're opening up are as relevant, as helpful, and as doable by any firm, of any size and in any sector.

   2. Does this only apply to big manufacturing companies? No. There is literature for improving quality across essentially all types of businesses in all sectors. Our favorite example of Six Sigma quality at the opposite end of the spectrum from large corporate high technology is the story of the tiffinwallahs of Mumbai, India.[15] As reported by Subrata N. Chakravarty and Naazneen Karmali for *Forbes:*

> *In Mumbai, India, 175,000 of the people who commute to work daily prepare their lunch ("tiffin") at home, and leave it at home in a tin container which contains a number of bowls held together in a frame. Tiffinwallahs are men who deliver these lunches each day to offices and schools throughout Mumbai, and, after lunch, return the carriers to the people's homes to repeat the process the next day. There are roughly 5,000 tiffinwallahs, and, according to Ragunath Medge, the president of the Mumbai Tiffinmen's Association, they make a mis-*

take only about once every two months. In Six Sigma terms, that's a DPMO (remember, Defects per Million Opportunities?) of 0.125, or approximately 6.7 Sigma. Per Mr. Medge, no one would pay for their service—which is very affordable and earns the tiffinwallah a good living—if they made 10 mistakes a month, which, to keep things in perspective, would be a DPMO of slightly over 1, or approximately 6.3 Sigma performance.

Now that's leverage!

Chapter Cheat Sheet

The Issue

In the previous chapters, we described the DNA for executional consistency as the creation of shared semantics critical to get stuff done over and over again consistently. We suggested that the process of codifying tacit knowledge is the DNA to manipulate and that understanding *what connects with what, when, where, how, and how much* results of that manipulation. We're left with a question, though: where do you start and how do you continuously maintain, and use the Blueprints created?

The Insight

Blueprinting provides ever-growing knowledge of *what* your business does, and *how it does it.* Lean Six Sigma shows *how to use that knowledge quantitatively to prioritize and execute projects,* and *to link metrics from project results to business results.* From this perspective, Lean Six Sigma is a set of methods and tools that focus on the "how much" of the "what connects with what . . ." mantra. It helps prioritize where to start and the process to continuously extend, refine, and use the Blueprints.

The Phrases

Process Variability; Lean; Six Sigma

The Implications

As we saw in earlier chapters, significant "good stuff" can happen by creating common semantics and "executable descriptions" of your business processes. What we add in this chapter are examples of tools and methods to improve business processes. The vocabulary, methods and techniques of Lean Six Sigma provide (1) rigorous methods to clearly understand *where* and *how* your business creates value for customers, (2) means to prioritize your resources on those processes that create such value, and (3) a process to build a "culture of execution," one based on "fact" more than "intuition." Lean Six Sigma, or other similar types of disciplines, improves your likelihood of successfully getting change to happen—no mean feat because, as James Champy has noted, "every large organization has the corporate antibodies to kill any incremental change program."

The Pragmatics of Strategy . . . with Your Head in the Clouds and Your Feet on the Ground

Setting the Stage: How to Be "Strategic" Yet Still Get Stuff Done

Pat Schambach faced significant challenges. As CIO of the Trans-formation Security Administration (TSA), and one of the most effective CIOs in the federal government, he was responsible for rap-idly rolling out and setting up technologies to 429 U.S. airports sup-porting airport administrators, screeners, cargo handlers, and other personnel following the rapid congressional mandate after the ter-rorist attacks on 9/11 to enhance airport security processes. But this roll-out was only the first of his two significant challenges. The sec-ond, as he put it, was "to work with the admirals and other colleagues to make sure we were doing all we could to meet our congressionally created mission statement of 'enhancing our threat perimeter.'" Yet, "How do I do that," he challenged, "when we're running as fast as we can just to stand-up the airports with communications and technol-ogy they need . . . and yet, each of our operations [customs, aviation operations, cargo, shipping], our sister organizations [Department of Homeland Security and the security agencies], and even our IT or-ganization have a different understanding of what *even constitutes* a 'threat'—so how can we *possibly* meet our mission statement?!'"

Philippe faced a similar challenge. As global executive vice pres-ident of global cash and trade for one of the world's largest financial institutions, he was accountable for global products and services, cus-tomer services, and operating centers, handling billions of dollars of financial transactions and settlements every day. Competition in the financial services industry resembles a game of roller-ball—with firms not only close behind but aggressively elbowing for position, exploiting any fast-moving opportunity seen. Philippe's organization, though immensely successful, could not be complacent. "There are always technologies we can and need to exploit," Philippe explained. "But technologies merely help us take advantage of an opportu-nity . . . [and] our fundamental opportunity is to build out the arbi-trage assets of our global base—to see opportunities in Singapore, for example, and within hours, exploit them for our customers in Eastern Europe. That's what our platform, our size, and our assets allow us to do. Our fundamental challenge is to do so consistently and to make sure that all of our people, our processes and our technologies around the global are aligned so we can move quickly to exploit emergent opportunities."

Pat's stated challenge was "how to be strategic" and how to get his big new business to make sense of their mandate consistently so they could execute effectively. Pat's day-to-day worries, however, were different. Using our Blueprinting language, Pat's reality was in Blueprint layers 4 and 3 (infrastructure and applications), and he was running like crazy to create layer 2 capabilities (processes) with only time for a nod to layer 1 (strategy).

Philippe was in an enviable position compared with Pat. His processes, applications, and infrastructure were already established—and running well. Philippe had the luxury of being able strategically to rethink and possibly reposition his cash and trade operation, and their online business approach overall. He could focus on layer 1. His challenges were how to (1) grow in the face of potentially disruptive actors and technologies and given his decision of how to do so, (2) align his global teams around the decisions quickly. Using our Blueprinting language, Philippe's challenge involved driving whatever came out of strategic repositioning throughout the organization, globally and quickly—to convert decisions made at layer 1 into action throughout all four layers.

For both, the challenge was what we sometimes call the Paul Bunyan approach to strategy. Paul Bunyan, an American folk legend, was a giant of a man clearing the way for early American business to grow, and with his closest friend, Babe the Blue Ox, they had the perspective of observation and the power of action to get done what they set out to do. Paul Bunyan had his "head in the clouds and his feet on the ground." Business strategy often starts in the clouds, yet all-too-often ends there too (a colleague, Lee Heindel, refers to this as "where the rubber meets the sky"). Being able, like Paul Bunyan, to work all the way *from the clouds to the ground* is critical in making strategy real and pragmatically useful. An effective strategy needs to be able not only to answer the questions of "what need we do" and "how will we do it" but also anticipate the impacts of those answers throughout the organization, from layers 1 through 4—*from strategy all the way through infrastructure.*

Extent of the Challenge: What You Don't Know *Will* Get You

Philippe had a strategy that he wanted to refine to meet his shifting competitive environment. He needed to test his assumptions then reevaluate his options, creating a new strategy for his business. But, what if you don't have a strategy? What if you're in a similar position to Pat's where he faced a broad mandate but had little or no time to actually formulate, much less act on, his strategy?

Let's think through opposite ends of a strategy continuum: You either have a strategy or you don't. And possibly you have a strategy, but it simply isn't followed. Regardless, an underlying need remains—to execute what you want to do, where you want to do it, and how you need to get it done. Whether this need is packaged in the *Good to Great* insight of doing (1) what you're the best at in the world, (2) having passion for what you're doing, and (3) exploiting your economic fly wheel—for example, focusing relentlessly on what makes you money—or packaged in the language of any of a number of other strategic advice books, the reality is that you need a road map for determining how your business makes its choices—about how it creates value over time.[1] Or stated less formally, you need to do stuff in an effective, focused way that advances your business objectives. Whether you have an effective strategy or not, this need remains, as does the certainty of the uncertain competitive environment.

This last point is key. Uncertainty comes from competition. It comes, also, from structural shifts—large macro-changes—in our competitive environments. A number of such shifts are occurring and will impact many of us, including:

• *Global aging:* Higher costs for social services, pensions, and health care, as well as structural shifts in both labor supply and demand labor shortages resulting from an older labor force, are likely outcomes of the global aging trend, particularly in North America and Europe.[2]

• *Fertility shifts:* In many European countries, fertility rates are now below replacement level (2.1 children per couple). As a result, natural population growth rates are entering periods of declining growth or outright decrease. At the same time, the proportion of elderly dependants continues to grow while the working-age population declines as a share of overall population. Implications are significant of these complementary trends—in aging and fertility shifts—in terms of pension and social insurance liabilities, capabilities to care for the growing elderly population, rising health care costs, immigration policies, and financial assets shifts across family generations, to name just a few.[3]

• *Global labor migrations and immigration policies:* Jean-Pierre Chevenement, the former French interior minister, has claimed that Europe will need 50 million to 75 million immigrants during the next 50 years to fill jobs. In Italy, there were eight workers to every pensioner in the 1950s. There are fewer than four today and, without immigration, that number will dwindle to 1.5 by 2050. Likewise, Germany will need 3 million immigrants a year to maintain the current ratio of workers to pensioners. With numbers like these, and these only in Europe, it is no surprise that the issue of immigration and global labor movement will have implications on business.

• *Back to a bi-, tri-, or n-polar political world:* No doubt the United States is the global political and economic powerhouse today. Yet, the exploding growth of China and the accelerating integration of Europe into an overall European Community is beginning to rebalance the one-sided weight of the Americans. The European Union's (EU) quiet revolution of community building, with a combined population of 455 million far outstrips the U.S. population of 293 million (although far less than the 1.4 billion of the Chinese). The EU is the world's largest trader of goods and services. In 2003, its gross domestic product (GDP) of $10.5 trillion edged out the $10.4 trillion GDP of the United States and is nearly 6.5 times larger than that of China.[4]

• *Reacceleration of mergers and acquisition (M&A) activity:* There was a major surge in M&A activity in the IT services sector last year when tier-one services vendors looked to add scale in the offshore and BPO sectors, and investment groups swooped on cut-price opportunities. *ComputerWire* tracked 262 deals involving IT services vendors in 2004, compared to 191 in 2003, 117 in 2002, and 111 in 2001. The size of these deals has also increased: The top 20 M&As in 2004 had an average value of $550 million, compared to $504 million in 2003, $355 million in 2002, and $316 million in 2001. Five of the 20 largest deals in 2004 involved investment groups acquiring struggling IT services divisions, with a view to turning them around and floating or selling them several years down the line.[5] And this doesn't reflect the exploding growth of M&A activities in other commercial areas globally.

• *Reinvigoration of the debate over climate change:* Increasing confirmation that atmospheric carbon dioxide has already risen to 370 parts per million (PPM) from a preindustrial 275, and on current trends will exceed 500 ppm this century, is leading to accelerating debates over the Kyoto Protocol and mechanisms to cap or allocate emissions globally.[6]

• *Shifts in consumer consumption patterns:* Between 2003 and 2010, according to Donald Hepburn, corporate economist for Unilever, of the $21.6 trillion world consumer spending total, the majority is in the West: $7.8 trillion in the United States and Canada and $6.9 trillion in Europe and Russia. South America accounts for just $1.2 trillion, Africa $1 trillion and Asia $4.7 trillion. By 2010, world's consumption is estimated at roughly $41.2 trillion. The United States and Canada will represent $9.7 trillion, Europe and Russian $9.1 trillion, while Asia will balloon to $15.7 trillion, Africa to $3.3 trillion and South America will settle in at $3.4 trillion. What we see here is increasing recognition of the so-called developing world in the power of consumption, tapping the economic purchasing power of the more than four billion people who constitute what C. K. Prahalad calls the "bottom of the pyramid" but the top of consumer purchasing power in the near-term.[7]

Other shifts are occurring, but these serve to make the point. Big structural "stuff" is happening. We don't know how these will play out over time, but play out they will—with differing impacts in different industries and differing firms that take different actions. There is no business that is immune to uncertainty—whether from one or more of these shifts, or from competition or changing consumer desires. Consequently, a discussion of how to execute on strategy in an uncertain environment remains as relevant as it is urgent. Whether your strategic challenges are more like Pat's or Philippe's, from one perspective they are the same, and they need to be faced.

Pat and Philippe each faced two problems. The first challenge was to figure out *what* strategic adjustments to make. The second challenge was *how* to keep the lights on—the operations going while making those adjustments. Stated slightly differently, given the challenges and shifts faced, how do you "make sense" of those shifts and challenges, and having done that, how do you "take action" on them? *Too often, strategies are conceptually clean and analytically pure, but operationally useless.* Unfortunately, this statement often gets wry grins and aggressive head-nods as people reflect on the number of hours and dollars spent on fine-looking strategy materials that end up collecting dust on a shelf or forgotten on a hard drive. Why? Because too frequently, the "taking action" part of the "make-sense/take action" two-step dance is forgotten, ignored, or not performed well, leaving participants to limp through the implementation phase of many if not most strategy efforts.

So, a key challenge is how to create "executionally aware" strategies—to "make sense" and "take action" in parallel to make sure that what makes sense can be acted on. Having clarity at layer 1 of the Blueprint Framework is far from sufficient. What Pat and Philippe recognized, from their differing starting points, was that to make strategy actionable, they had to be able to go across all four layers as quickly, effectively, and consistently as possible.

Facing the Challenges: "Go Not into Uncertainty Unaware, and Certainly Not Unarmed!"

The reality is that we cannot know what will happen to our competitive environment or to us. Thus, being able both to anticipate and exploit uncertainty—and the opportunities that do emerge from it—becomes one of the most critical capabilities we need to develop. The Conference Board's *CEO Challenge 2004* report reveals that 88 percent of 540 global business leaders from 40 countries interviewed designated speed, flexibility, and adaptability to uncertainty as a top priority for their companies. Some 42 percent of those interviewed considered this an issue "of greatest concern" (the strongest challenge rating).[8] "Developing an agile, adaptable workforce that embraces change and aligns quickly will be tomorrow's competitive differentiator," confirms Carl Steffen, vice president, human capital management, of a cosponsor of the Conference Board report. Added Linda Barrington, director of the report, "CEOs were adamant . . . that adaptability and innovation continue to be the keys to sustainable advantage. This will be all the more so as the world sees emerging markets climbing up the ladder of skill specialization at an unprecedented speed." Adaptable to what? To change, sure; to uncertainty, without doubt. But how do you do that? And how do you do so in a way that goes beyond mere story-telling or trend-watching to action and results? How, in short, do you make your embrace of uncertainty actionable? How do you "make sense" and "take action" of uncertainty?

Characterizing Business Uncertainty

Figure 4.1 is a depiction of uncertainty that we call the *three-arrow picture*. It's a simple but useful way to discuss ranges of potential future business conditions and outcomes in an uncertain environment. Time moves horizontally from left to right in Figure 4.1. The vertical dimension represents the degree of change in business conditions. You are standing at the far left of the figure, looking to the right. The particular path into the future is unknown. All you know

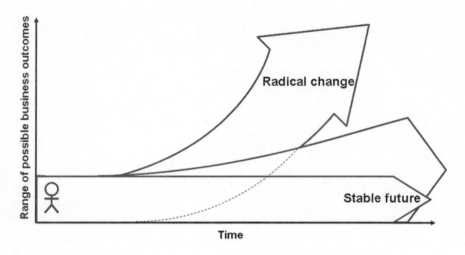

FIGURE 4.1   Uncertainty: The Three-Arrow Picture

for sure is that you can see the path directly in front of you; beyond that, the path is shrouded, with three distinct possibilities for the future.

The bottom arrow represents the stable, reasonably predictable future. Here, little changes as time goes by. In other words, you basically stay in the same business, producing sufficient innovations and adaptation to your products and services while you incrementally increase your customer base or what you sell to your best customers. This is a mature industry model.

The middle arrow that overlaps the first arrow represents a situation where markets are changing, somewhat. Such changes might reflect various things—growth markets, business where new technologies are creating new business channels, consolidation, and so on—generally things that will change your existing business climate but won't make your business obsolete.

The top arrow represents radical change, where the business climate changes in a way that there is little overlap with your existing business. Such disruption results when a significant technology or business model development changes the basic rules of the game.

Which of these areas best reflects your future? Who knows? We don't, and you don't either. What we have found is that business people usually respond to this *not knowing* by assuming the stable future until something indicates otherwise. Their logic is that, since the future is murky and can't be reasonably predicted, they might as well assume a straight line until things become clearer. This tends to be the default strategic assumption for businesses that face inward and focus mainly on operational metrics, as well as for businesses that try to maximize the output of a cash cow. This common assumption is invariably risky and invariably incorrect.

What happens if you plan for a stable future and the future is not stable? The three-arrow picture in Figure 4.2 visually depicts how the story unfolds. Suppose you begin at the left, and move to the right along the bottom arrow. When you reach point A, the radical future scenario may have already begun to take shape, with markets forming represented by the horizontally shaded area to the left of point A. If you are focused down the path of the bottom arrow—if you've made an assumption of future stability—you may miss this

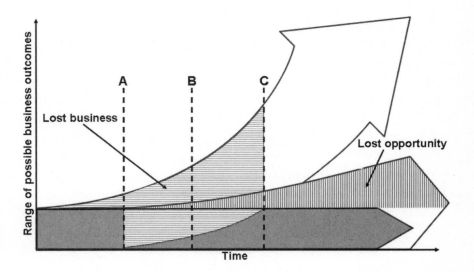

FIGURE 4.2 The Dangers of the Steady-State Assumption

development (after all, at this point there's been no real impact on your going-forward business).

When you reach point B, there are two possibilities, depending on whether the future is unfolding along the middle arrow or along the top arrow. If you have been disrupted and things are radically changing, you are beginning to lose business to the disruption as it emerges from its nurturing niche and starts to invade your markets. This is represented by the horizontally shaded area between A and B. Two different pieces comprise the lost business: *opportunities lost*, which is the shaded area above the bottom arrow, and *cannibalized business* which is the shaded area within the bottom area. However, if the middle arrow future is unfolding, you have not been disrupted but there have been changes that have opened new business opportunities of which you have not taken advantage. The small vertically shaded area between A and B represents this lost business opportunity.

Continuing to move into the future to point C, if you have been disrupted, you are basically out of business: the opportunity has followed the top arrow and left you behind. If instead you have failed to grow into new market opportunities, represented by the area labeled "Lost Opportunity," you might become a target for takeover, or at the very least, miss opportunities for growth.

So what? And given this brief description and uncertain futures, what do you do? Looking at the figures, the kind of choices and the kind of dangers involved in focusing on the wrong strategic plan are pretty clear. What typically happens is that, as you're standing at the left side of that picture looking to the right, most of the right side is shrouded in fog and there's very little to go on other than your gut instincts (possibly supported by data) about what the "probable" future will look like. You need to pay close attention to how you will move into the future in such a way as to insulate yourself from, or be prepared for, the radical change situation. It's not that the radical change scenario is the most likely. By definition, that cannot be known. It's just that preparing for the more radical possibilities puts you in the best position to handle *any* possibility. It is easier to *pull back* and draw from what has already been considered than to attempt to *push into* areas yet anticipated without preparation.

There are significant implications on a company's people, process and technology depending upon the planning approach taken. An assumption of a stable future creates a pervasive culture of stability, instead of creating the agility needed to move into the future quickly. The real challenge is to innovate quickly and cheaply enough that you can respond across the range encompassed by the three arrows while still operating your current business. What is needed, in other words, is an approach that minimizes your degree of planning while maximizing your range of value creation, depending on the type of competitive reality that emerges. Figure 4.3 visually depicts how to expand your range of options in the context of the three-arrow picture.

In Figure 4.3, each star represents a new piece of value for your company, that is, a business opportunity or innovation that a company has created and brought to market. Each star could just as well represent a new product, a new set of customers, access to additional scale, or a change in brand positioning. In Figure 4.3, a company has brought three innovations to market.

The star labeled "1" represents some type of sustaining innovation for your company. This is an innovation—possibly simple,

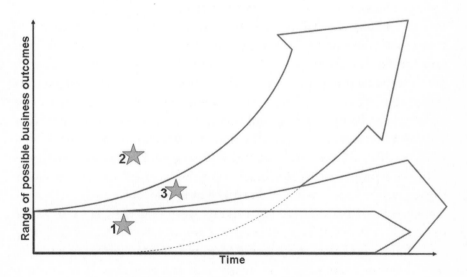

FIGURE 4.3 Expanding Your Options

possibly very radical—that improves your offering to your main-stream customers.

The star labeled "2" represents an innovation that is clearly outside of what you may consider your mainstream business. It represents an experiment and a risk in the sense that it is placed outside of your known sweet spot. However, as it is shown in Figure 4.3, this innovation "sits" in the area defined by the middle arrow and thus is in a newly developing area for your business. If you are the TSA in 2003, this star may represent exploration of an expanded threat perimeter, which could include, for example, security of the global supply chains that end in the United States. Note that star 2 also lies on the path of the top arrow so, by creating this innovation, you are positioning for the possibility of radical change.

Finally, the star labeled "3'"represents an innovation that is outside the known market for your company. It might represent an innovation that in the future will intersect the top arrow. However, from the viewpoint of an established company, it represents an out and out *big bet*. An example of star 3 might be a business process outsourcing (BPO) venture that seeks to create a new business on an internal area of process excellence different from your core business. When Hewlett Packard decided to enter the BPO arena by leveraging its internal world-class finance and adminis-tration (F&A) capabilities, it created a business very far from its technology-provider core and positioned itself to be a leader in this potentially huge market.

In the simplified world of the three-arrow picture, you want to create new stars—new innovations—that cover the range of future outcomes quickly enough that you can move even after the arrow gets there—that is, after the market is revealed—as a very fast fol-lower with a minimum of cost and risk. Figure 4.4 shows this, repre-senting a company that creates several innovations spread out along the possible futures. An effective strategy provides a conceptual framework for prioritizing and choosing among the many different innovations that might be of highest relevance and potential impact.

There are many ways to be responsive to uncertainty, but the core dynamics remain the same. Articulated in terms of the three-arrow picture, the vertical spread of the innovations represents a de-

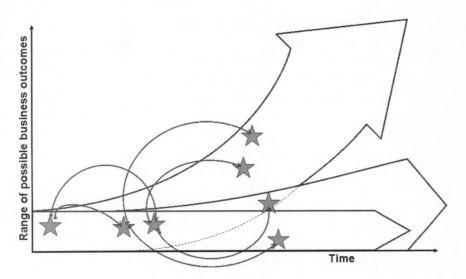

FIGURE 4.4 Expanding Your Strategic Options

parture from the value created in a company's core business, and therefore presumably a departure from the company's core competencies and the competencies of its people.

So what? What do we do with the preceding discussion? And this question is the key question about strategy. *So what* if we craft compelling scenarios, if we figure out what a set of possible stars and innovative products and services should be, if we discern what arrow is likely to emerge and that we are ready for it, strategically? *So what*, in other words, if we *are* able to "make sense" of uncertainty as it develops, and strategically *know* where we're supposed to go next and what we're supposed to do when we get there? How do we get there? How do we take action now having made sense? And, how do we drive the insight, the understanding and the shared semantics of uncertainty and our options throughout the organization. How do we, in short, get the traceability, the alignment, the consistency, and the impact across layers 1 through 4? How do we convert the insight of Figure 4.4 into the operational needs of our execution framework?

Answering the "So What" Question

Here's the reality. Some organizations find it important to continuously refine (if not create) strategy. Some want to justify what they are currently doing operationally in terms *of a strategy*. And some are content to maintain a set of operational plans that drive everyday activities without any pretense of a strategy. Cutting across these options, some organizations struggle merely to figure out what is meant by layer 1 strategy (as in Pat's situation) and others focus on how to drive it deeply (as in Philippe's situation). The challenge remains the same: "making sense" and "taking action." The three-arrow pictures and the semantic stack are means of making sense; the execution framework, with Blueprinting and a process-based continuous improvement regimen like Lean Six Sigma, drives taking action. Separated, we have found them to be useful tools; together, they are powerful.

The "Pragmatics" of Strategy, or Pragmatic Strategy

Next, we look at different ways of using a Paul Bunyon approach to strategy—a pragmatic one—with heads in the clouds with feet on the ground—to go beyond the usual frustration of irrelevant (though fine-looking) strategies.

Creating a New "Outside-In" Strategy

Marcus is CEO of one of Europe's most profitable private banks tucked away on a nondescript street in Zurich, Switzerland. Maintaining his esteemed client base and continuing to drive extraordinary profits year after year had been a steady-state task for Marcus and his management team—until a few years ago. Two structural shifts were set to impact Marcus' quiet but effective position. He saw them coming yet was unsure of what to do about them. The first was a dramatic demographic shift because many of his customers who had been with the bank for over 30 years were set to retire—representative of the enormous cross-generational wealth transfer that is beginning to occur as the baby boomers retire or die off. The second was the exploding usage globally of the World Wide Web as both a communications and transactions platform. Intuitively, Marcus and his executive team were clear that who they supported and how they maintained their customers would be directly impacted by these twin shifts. But they were less clear regarding how to respond to them. Marcus recognized the need for what he called a "strategic reconsideration" of his bank's position, customer base, and means to exploit emerging technologies. He recognized that he potentially faced the upper two arrows; which one he would ultimately experience was unknown, but he was determined to be both strategically and operationally ready for either of them.

Similarly for Philippe; he, too, recognized the need to look beyond what he was currently doing—to create a "strategic challenge" to his already well-established market position to help him adapt to, if not exploit, specific opportunities identified in the course of his strategic initiative.

Both Marcus and Philippe recognized that certain types of disruption were likely; what these disruptions were and specifically how they would play out remained murky. Marcus and Philippe both recognized the criticality of "making sense" of their environment, beyond merely projecting their current position. Yet, they equally recognized that "taking action" was arguably even more important. "It is more appropriate to be directionally correct than accurate," was a mantra used over and over again to goad their respective businesses to continually focus on how to make the strategy and competitive scenarios actionable. Marcus' organization was part of a large global financial services firm, with offices throughout the world. He and his team had endured many strategic sessions throughout the years. He was skeptical of underlying strategy initiatives, having recently worked on one at the board level of his parent company driven by what he called the Scottish strategy firm McKinsey. "They provided brilliant insights into market and financial projects of what could be," Marcus explained. "But we were left with no idea of how to do what we ended up knowing had to be done."

Philippe voiced similar concerns. "We take strategic initiatives very seriously here," Philippe intoned. "It is critical that we create activities that are globally aligned, consistently executed and demonstrably measurable." For such initiatives with global impact,

Philippe's bank draws senior people from around the world out of the line for four to six weeks to foster different perspectives and collaboratively create the shared semantics critical to both "make sense" and "take action."

Our challenge for both Marcus' and Philippe's teams was to ensure that as much attention was focused on layer 1 activities as on how to execute throughout the four layers. We did so by driving what we called an "architecturally informed" strategy process based on the execution framework described in the earlier chapters.

As in any strategy process, we answered the usual questions, (1) what are the trends and "stuff" impacting/disrupting your marketplace, (2) what do you want to focus on, (3) what do you want to be positioned as/be known as/differentiated in the marketplace, (4) what will be your economic fly wheel/where will you make your money, and (5) what will you need to lead with (e.g., how will you focus your resources). But in parallel, we focused as much on what are the portfolios of opportunities, the business cases underlying them, and arguably most distinctively—and equally importantly— what are the underlying "process, application, and infrastructure models" to help you get there. Each of these parts of a Blueprint provides different insights to view the implications of any specific opportunity. Philippe and Marcus needed to fast-start their decisions, and began modeling early to be able to execute quickly. This is the power of an execution framework as a pragmatic complement to the usual strategy activities. Following the execution framework outlined earlier, we focused as much on visibility (on *what needs to be done* where, when, and by whom) as on traceability (and *what will be impacted* by what, where, when, by whom, *and how*).

What we have found over and over again is that overcoming the semantic disconnects between what people "think they said" from "what was heard" and consequently executed on is one of the most fundamental issues to tackle head on. Creating the shared semantics is critical to make execution consistent. Mobilizing senior talent from across the business is a great idea, but only if there are ways to create shared and executable semantics of the different perspectives, personalities, and proclivities into a consistent execution model. Which is why at its core, this execution framework is constructed of models—at all four layers of the organization. For again, as we mentioned in Chapter 2, models are no more than a means to create shared understanding to drive consistent execution.

The next section draws on different examples to illustrate what kinds of models can be used to create those strategically shared semantics. The examples also recognize that we are not all in the situation of Philippe and Marcus where they knew they wanted a strategy based on looking at their organization from the perspective of market shifts and trends. Many of us are in a situation more like Pat's, and do not have such luxury, or focus. Often, strategies are more justifications or packaging up of what we operationally are doing. They tend to be "inside-out," and operationally based strategies. We turn to this situation now.

Justifying an "Inside-Out" Operational Strategy

Scott, the CEO of a mid-sized commercial packaging company out of Minneapolis and two members of his executive team, Donna (senior vice president of operations) and Chuck (CIO), recognized that they had some significant problems. Their market share was slipping badly to lower cost providers who had a broader network of real-time suppliers and consolidators to draw from. They had a large number and broad range of "must do" initiatives all of which (at one time by different sponsors) were considered critical to their success. They were struggling to maintain a balance between a "short-term payback" in any of their initiatives with the longer-term recognition that they had to do something to stop losing market share. And they had to do it quickly.

Debbie is the head of Patient Care Administrative Service in Bill and Carl's hospital system. As we've seen already, they were suffering from inconsistent billing and collections systems across the enterprise, with outstanding bills greater than 70 days to participating insurance companies. They also had to contend with ineffective legacy systems, nonstandard business processes, and IT systems in over a thousand medical centers and clinics. Integrating existing with new applications is cumbersome, costly, and results in cost overruns and poor quality performance. Adding to the urgency to fix these problems, increased shareholder scrutiny has led to enhanced pressure for quick transformation. The need to "keep the lights on" by fixing the hospital's operational problems immediately made any strategy discussion bleed immediately into how to make it real. The question was: How to do so?

Both Scott and Debbie recognized that the challenges they faced were significantly more than ones of operational improvements. They were, at their core, strategic issues. For Scott, the slide in market share reflected a loss of direction and underperformance. For Debbie, the operational complexities were brought into relief because of the attention of the shareholders. Yet, they determined that their strategies needed to be driven out from fixing their operational problems. They both believed that layer 1 discussions *could only be meaningful if the problems of layers 4→3→2 could be fixed.* They both provided direction that their strategies—how they would respond to the marketplace—would emerge from the operational problems resolved.

Both Scott and Debbie recognized that their problems are no one's fault; they were the results of the semantic disconnect that comes from silo-based behavior, miscommunications, misaligned metrics, and disparate behaviors. Remember the Paul Bunyan strategy approach? A fundamental challenge for businesses is how to move from being "hero-based" to "every-guy-based": There just aren't enough Paul Bunyans to go around. Even if there were, that's not the answer: The problem with heroes is that people and organizations become dependent on them; they lose their sense of urgency (because the hero will take care of it) and lose the capability to scale their execution capability to the many.

What was particularly frustrating both to Scott and Debbie was that urgency was felt differently, or not felt at all in some cases, by their executive team members. "I hit my goals," claimed one of Scott's unit presidents at an operating committee meeting, "so *I'm* doing fine. . . . Let me know if I can help you hit yours." Such claims are not uncommon; neither are they helpful. To Scott and Debbie's credit, they both recognized that the key challenge they had to confront was getting a shared understanding that there *was* a problem, one so significant that the next challenge was to get a shared under-standing of how to *start* focusing on the problem, on how to pull on the multiple problematic threads to make sense and have the biggest impact on the core of the problem. Strategically, they both recog-nized that they needed to figure out (1) how to get agreement on what the problem was, (2) where it was, (3) how it impacted them all, (4) how the environment they faced impacted their problems, and (5) what to do about it. Working through this simple-sounding process involved starting with the semantic clarity, with overcoming the se-mantic disconnect of those with their different perspectives, person-alities, and organizational prejudices.

All models, all equations, all marketing campaigns, all docu-mentation, cheat-sheets and notes, all products, all services—in short, all of the activities and "artifacts" that make up things we do and how we do them within organizations—can be considered *gram-mar tools*. But what are grammar tools? They are no more than a means to make sense of what you and others say so that you can un-derstand each other and through that, do stuff together. In our exe-cution framework, they are the tools and methods of Blueprinting and Lean Six Sigma, used to overcome the semantic disconnect that stops people from working together consistently, and effectively. As explained in Chapter 2, even though people may use the same words, what they understand by them often differs. For example, ask an ap-parently simple question—What is a customer?—of a database ad-ministrator, a project manager, the head of marketing, the CIO, and the CEO, and count the number of different "understandings" you get. So, let's go back to the operating unit president who said "*I'm doing fine, how about you?*" regarding her performance. What's the strategic problem here? The company is struggling operationally and strategically, but her response is, "I'm doing fine . . . how about you?" What's this about? If she says this, believes this, and acts ac-cordingly, how do you think her team responds, particularly as they interact with their colleagues from other parts of the business who recognize that there *is* a significant problem to overcome? How can you possibly get stuff done consistently with this response? How do you get the executional consistency across layers 1 through 4 if you cannot get shared understandings of those accountable for layer 1

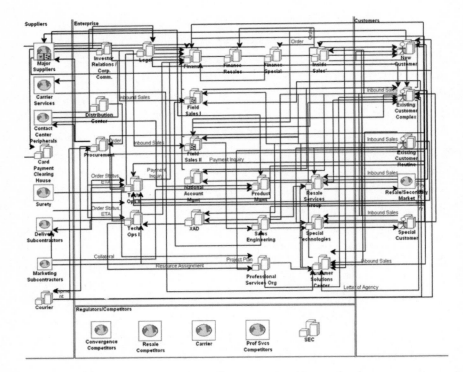

FIGURE 4.5 Understanding Scott's Business Interactions

activities? This was the problem recognized by both Scott and Deb-bie, and the problem they each addressed first.

So, here's a question: How *do* you create such shared semantics? And here's an answer: Through Blueprinting with models that are as meaningful to one person as they are usable by another. Figures 4.5 and 4.6 show two of the types of models used by Scott's and Debbie's team to create that shared understanding.

Creating models that are as meaningful to one person as they are usable to another is a challenge, but necessary to mobilize peo-ple to get stuff done consistently. Scott's executives could quickly see at least one cause of their problems by looking at the business interaction model (BIM) of Figure 4.5—namely, their highly com-plex and redundant processes and organization. Note that we said "looking at," not "understanding." A BIM like Figure 4.5 is too complex to be comprehensible, but it contains the roots of BIMs

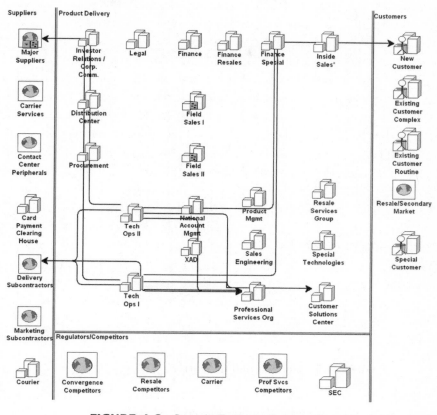

FIGURE 4.6   Scott's Business Interactions

like that shown in Figure 4.6 and serves as a picture of "too much stuff," making a mute case for change that helps shake executives out of complacency. But, we quickly run into the "so what" question—which is where more edifying models like that of Figure 4.6 come in. Teams with different perspectives face a challenge of how to get shared understanding; they are reasonably occupied with the questions "What does it mean *to me*" and "Why should *I* care"? Being able to answer such questions, for different people from different parts of the organization, using the same model creates a simplicity that allows these people to *be able to* answer those questions and to be able to take action on their shared understanding *quickly*. And that's what interaction model Figure 4.6 did—namely, create a simple but shareable means for all of Scott's executive team to say, "Hey, I see how I fit and where what I do impacts what you do, where, how, when, and how much."

We share a humorous image of Marcus, the wealthy, seasoned CEO of one of the world's most profitable private banks arguing with some of his junior IT managers, CIO, marketing director, and comptroller over how to create models similar to those of Figure 4.6. Yet, argue they did, over and over again to create understandings that were meaningful—and actionable—to everyone at this bank. With what result? The creation of shared understanding of the problems and the steps, tangibly and traceably, needed to execute on the strategic decisions quickly and consistently—from layer 1 through layer 4, from strategy through business processes, from processes to applications and from applications to infrastructure deployments. With what impact? Marcus and his team regained their extremely high profitability and high growth capability that they had temporarily lost.

Back to Scott's team. Working through the models (1) resulted in a quick understanding of the core problems with 36 underlying issues; (2) identified 46 opportunities; (3) rationalized 20 competing goals across the organization; and (4) developed 19 business interaction models to create the shared semantics of what impacted what, where, how, when, and how much. The result: a solid foundation of an executable Blueprint for Scott and his team to drive—and all within five weeks. And for Debbie, Business Blueprint models expressed the impacts of the hospital's goals for patient enrollment (layer 1) through its sets of business processes (layer 2), its enabling set of applications and underlying use-cases and functions (layer 3). The result: a redesign of its enrollment systems for consistent use across multiple regions and over a thousand hospitals and clinics.

Philippe and Marcus and Scott and Debbie

Neither Scott nor Debbie started from the perspective of "what market shifts will impact my business." Yet, getting operational clarity on what they had to do could not get done without getting semantic clarity about how to do so. Their strategy became one of "operationally cleaning up their businesses" that had and will continue to have strategic impacts. Yet for Philippe and Marcus and Scott and Debbie, the challenge was ultimately the same: driving strategic execution quickly and effectively—getting the visibility and traceability across layers 1 through 4 in parallel through creating shared strategic understandings that were as meaningful as they were usable. Seeing, and thereby tangibly knowing *what impacts what, where how, when, and how much* is powerful—particularly as a means to understand what really goes on and, most importantly, know what to do about it.

What This Means to You

1. *Why should I care about executing on strategy more effectively? I'm a line manager and corporate strategies and strategy efforts are like political appointees in Washington, DC—they make noise but eventually their term ends, they leave, and I stay and keep the lights on.* There is a Moroccan saying, "The dogs bark but the caravan moves on." While political appointees and corporate strategy efforts might be the barking dogs and the rest of us the caravan, the issue is what direction the caravan is moving in and the amount of goods and services it is carrying to sell profitably along its (hopefully expanding) trade routes. As the routes dry up, eventually so too will the caravan's trade. Putting the analogy aside, think about how nice it would be to see a corporate strategy that made sense, and gave you clarity on what you could do to move that strategy ahead while keeping the lights on. That's what we're talking about in this chapter. At one time or another, all of us have ducked when some new corporate initiative—soon to be forgotten—came our way. We'd be better off if executives made fewer strategic decisions, but the ones they made cut to the core of improving our business. When executives can consistently make sense, and give you the tools to take action, you'll see the difference before the end of the term.

Tipping points—structural shifts—are "out there" that *will* impact what all of us do and how we do so, if they are not already doing so. We discussed some of these shifts earlier and resulting threats, opportunities, and responses taken to them by Marcus, Philippe, Pat, Scott, and Debbie. In short, strategies can no longer be a diversion of resources and effort; nor can they any longer be merely a boon for photocopier businesses. They need to become pragmatically useful—visible, traceable, and flexible depending on the specific dynamics that will and are impacting you, from strategic direction (layer 1) down through processes, applications and infrastructures (layers 2, 3, and 4). They *need* to become *executionally aware*.

2. *I've read a lot about business strategy. What's so different about your approach and why should I pay attention to it?* Effective strategies are those that help you "make sense" and "take action." Many methods exist to help you on the former, including Porter's Five-Forces Framework, Geoffrey Moore's work on core and context, Warren Bennis' focus on strategic leadership, and Robert Kaplan and David Norton's extension of their Balanced Scorecard into Strategy Maps. Yet, too often, disconnects exist between making sense and taking action. From our perspective and experiences, as from those of Marcus, Philippe, Pat, Scott, Debbie, and many others, that disconnect can no longer be ignored. Now, again, recommendations exist to make strategies "real"—from changing metrics to shifting governance, and a whole host of other actions we listed earlier in this chapter. But missing from many of these recommendations is the capability to trace what impacts what, where, how, when, and by how much—tangibly, measurably, visibly.

Taking action is about having in place the execution capabilities that can be drawn on quickly, and in parallel, to support the strategic directions "made sense" of. This is why we strongly believe that an "executionally aware" or "architecturally informed" approach to strategy is not only important, but crucial to make strategic efforts useful, consistent, and effective.

3. *What are the top three lessons to take away from this chapter?* First, recognize that just about any strategy method can be effective at "making sense." It is the "taking action" part that is usually lacking. To get executional consistency and alignment across the business, making sense and taking action must happen in tandem with one another.

Second, recognize that getting such executional consistency depends on bridging the "semantic disconnect" of your colleagues with their differing perspectives, personalities, and organizational focuses.

As explored in Chapter 1, organizations consist of T-Shirts, Turtlenecks, and Suits (operations, marketing, and management people). Each of these groups has very different understandings, often of even the same words, based on what they do. Recall Pat's challenge of getting clarity from his TSA colleagues regarding what their mission-statement means—and what constitutes a "threat" from their various organizational perspectives. Business Blueprinting creates that critical semantic clarity, helping the business to know what impacts what, where, when, how, and how much from layers 1 through 4.

Third, these lessons apply whether your organization has a strategy or not. And, if you have one, they apply whether your strategy is an "outside-the-box"/start-by-looking-from-market-conditions-and-then-see-what-the-impacts-are-inside-here (the *outside-in* approach) or it is a justification of what you are currently doing operationally (the *inside-out* approach). What we have found helpful is the recognition that no matter where you start—whether layer 1, 2, 3, or 4—there are implications on the other areas. Strategies (often) have clear implications "downward"—on processes, how budgets are spent on applications, and so on (on layers 2, 3, and 4). Yet, billing problems and difficulties in bringing in new patients (Debbie's problem at the hospital)—a problem in Blueprint Layers 2 and 3—turned out to have significant layer 1, strategic implications in terms of alliance relationships, health care enrollment criteria, and so on. A challenge many of us have faced is that we have had no visibility as to what happens "over there," in that department. Consequently, we may have felt little accountability for helping them. Yet, nearly every activity has impacts—across all layers of your organization. Becoming sensitive to that, and becoming sensitized to any shifts in markets, in customers, in processes, in resources—in whatever drives your business—is absolutely critical to executing consistently. Being able to see what impacts what, where, when, how, and how much quickly, and strategically, is possible and doable. This third lesson is simple: every activity has strategic impact and every strategy drives activity. Getting the visibility to understand this and the tools to create it are pragmatic starting points for creating pragmatically based, *executionally aware* strategies—for being able *to do* something with your strategies!

Chapter Cheat Sheet

The Issue

Strategies are often conceptually clean and analytically pure, but (usually) operationally useless. They may be great at helping you "make sense" of your competitive environment and challenges. But in terms of "taking action," they are usually woefully inadequate. This is neither good nor necessary. But the challenge remains of how to make your strategies as meaningful as they are actionable.

The Insight

Everything we do has impacts throughout the organization—some more direct and certainly more visible than others. But organizations are no more than accumulations of past results, present activities and future expectations. And these results, activities, and expectations occur at all layers of an organization—those who focus on strategic direction, those who handle the processes, build the applications, and extend the infrastructure. An effective strategy needs not only to answer the classic questions of "what need we do" and "how will we do it" but also anticipate the impacts of those answers throughout the organization. Doing this requires what we call an "executionally aware" or "architecturally informed" approach to strategy—that makes pragmatic and real the conceptual considerations and high level decisions. Like Paul Bunyan with his head in the clouds *and* his feet on the ground, being able to cover *from clouds to ground* is critical in making strategy real, and pragmatically useful.

The Phrases

Executionally-Aware Strategy; Architecturally-Informed Strategy; Reference Architectures; Grammar Tools

The Implications

Knowing *what connects with what, where, when, how, and how much* is vital to being able to getting your strategy to be useful and usable. This principle holds irrespective of the type of strategy you have—whether your strategy is robust or thin, highly analytical and "disruptive-focused" or more of an operational roll-up/justification of what you're currently doing. Focusing on such traceability—from strategy through processes through applications through infrastructure—decreases the risk of your strategy being irrelevant and increases the likelihood of it having real impact. The decision here is straightforward: You can spend your efforts and your dollars either on making pretty pictures and analytically clean recommendations, or on understanding the operational implications of decisions by making visible what is so often invisible. The problem with keeping your head in the clouds is that (1) it's cold and isolated up there and (2) over time, the lack of oxygen starts getting to you and you fall. Besides, *keeping your feet on the ground* will help ensure that your head remains connected with your body—or, no longer using Paul Bunyan's language but that of our execution framework, that all four layers of the blueprinting layers are explicitly understood in terms of the impacts of strategic decisions made, and consequently actions (that need to be) taken.

Business Processes . . . Where Business and Technology Meet

Setting the Stage: All Value Is Built *in* Processes

Jim Dillon has heard the phrase "do more with less" one too many times, to the point where he has banished the phrase from his meetings. As Jim says, "I'm ready to do more with more, and willing to do less with less, but I don't talk about doing 'more with less.'"[1] As CIO of the State of New York, Jim is responsible for the IT underpinnings of a state government that serves more than 10 million citizens. Jim shares a set of challenges with most of his colleagues from other states: shrinking budgets, the continuing shift of program responsibilities from the federal government to the state, and a populace that expects more and more services from its government. Add on top of that the fact that as many as 40 percent of his employees will be retiring within the next five years, taking enormous amounts of institutional knowledge with them, and you understand his point.

Despite Jim's statement on the matter, his situation seems like a recipe for having to do more with less: *more* in the sense of providing increased services, responding to a continual stream of regulations and mandates from the federal government; *less* in the sense of having to provide them within budget constraints (that are undoubtedly unreasonable) but also, as his workforce retires, with less of the human knowledge of how those services are provided. Jim's team has risen to these challenges. He has an outstanding and efficient organization that, over the next few years, is going to have to rise even higher. They will need to be able to provide enhanced services to citizens and execute more globally, with more focus on the needs of the citizenry and less on the traditional boundaries of internal and agency boundaries. And all of this needs to get done while growing the personnel pool more slowly than the growth of the services, all the while watching his most experienced workers retire.

This is, of course, not limited to Jim Dillon in New York, or to public sector agencies. Earlier in the book, we heard Clark Kelso, the CIO of the State of California decry the fact that 42 percent of state and local employees will retire within the next five years, while many of the business processes, systems, and applications they are responsible for are held together largely by the knowledge in their heads. And remember Mike, the SVP in charge of retail banking applications we met in Chapter 2? Mike also has an outstanding and efficient organization that exceeds its performance targets for creating and supporting retail banking applications. In many ways, Mike is in an enviable position compared with Jim. His budget is tied to the performance of the company, and he has a continual influx of a relatively young, stable workforce. That said, Mike has a dog's breakfast of work in front of him as (1) the competitive environment forces constant innovation in the products and services offered by the bank; (2) his bank continues to acquire other banks (and their applications); and (3) he works to maintain, rationalize, and modernize applications while the processes they support continually change to suit new business needs. To make it clear that this discussion is not limited to technology people, remember Bill, the CEO of the major hospital group from Chapter 3? He has top-level business goals for improving the financial performance of his hospital group. And, as we showed in our walk through the layers of a Business Blueprint, those goals are directly tied to the execution of business processes, the applications that support them, and the infrastructure that runs those applications and houses the business information.

Jim, Clark, Mike, and Bill, along with executives in all industries, face a common reality: Their business is changing, and their business processes, with the technology that supports them, need to change, too. They face a common challenge—one often either ignored because it's hard to tackle, or denied because it's hard to see. In fact, this challenge is a near invisible one, but like the tip of an iceberg, it runs deep and is potentially deadly if ignored too much, or denied too strenuously. We met this challenge in Chapter 1—and it is one of the recurring themes throughout the book—the challenge of tacit knowledge, of what we called then the "disappearing or disconnected knowledge."

Business processes are sets of activities people do to get something done. Performing these activities involves talking and walking, writing and typing, analyzing and deciding—using tools and techniques, hard assets (like computers and manuals) and soft assets (like Post-its and cheat-sheets). Each of these activities and "things used" mean something to those who do them and use them; they are help-ful in getting "something" done. Yet, how they are used, and what they are used for often differs, depending on the skill-level, the de-gree of commitment, the clarity of objective, and so on. Few people do the same thing the same way.

Sure, businesses try to standardize processes and procedures, tools and methods. But what happens when new demands and chang-ing requirements outstrip the capability to "keep up to date" with existing infrastructures? Mutations, workarounds, short-cuts, and process improvements result—most if not all of which remain in the heads of the people who create them, or are shared by the teams who exploit them. In short, "stuff that gets done" is much more the re-flection of ever-evolving "organizational wisdom" than it is of "for-malized procedures." And that's the challenge. That was the challenge articulated by Clark Kelso, CIO of California, by the CIO of the retail bank, and by the vice-chair of a global financial institu-tion. They all, using differing terms, bemoaned the same chal-lenge—of how to identify, use, and scale the tacit knowledge, the organizational wisdom, and the embedded rules that live in the heads of the few and so cannot be sufficiently used by the many. And this challenge is crucial. Encroaching demographic shifts, pressures of new technologies, and changing market demands are all putting pressure on ensuring that this invisible stuff, this tacit knowledge, this key to how businesses actually run, gets captured and exploited, used and valued.

Two quick implications arise from this discussion, both of which we'll explore in more detail later. First, all of this "stuff" lives in business processes. After all, business processes are no more than reflections of accumulated activities, experiences, and knowledge that powers them. Yet, everything we said about business processes can be said about technology applications. They too embody inher-ent differences in perspectives, activities, experiences, and knowl-edge. This is why the integration of existing with emerging technologies is so challenging. The very process of attempting to "integrate" different sets of accumulated wisdom that just so happens to be codified in software is like attempting to mix oil with water—they simply separate due to the inability of their respective molecules to bond.

Making explicit this tacit—hidden, embedded, invisible, mutating (take your pick)—knowledge is crucial for both business processes and its supporting technology. And critical to get them to work together more effectively. "Where business meets technology" is in their processes. Making explicit what makes up these processes, and from which to figure out the underlying value and means to scale it—so that what is in the heads of the few can be put into the hands of the many—is the focus of this chapter—and the challenge of Jim, Tom, Clark, and others discussed throughout this chapter.

Second, all of this "stuff" has a competitive "half-life" to it. Because it isn't seen doesn't mean that it has no value. Mark, the COO we encountered earlier, was stunned to find out how much of his Check 21 processing would be based on exception handling. Being able to "see the stuff" that made up 17 percent of his check-processing expenses allowed him to make a decision, for the first time, on what to do with this stuff. His options included cleaning it up, offering it as a service to his customers, or recognizing that it had zero shareholder value so he should get rid of it, somehow. He chose the latter. (He is currently in the process of creating a business process outsourcing business with one of his competitors focused on providing exception-processing capabilities for both institutions.) Mark was only able to make this decision because, for the first time, he had the visibility to see, and understand the implications of, what made up the 17 percent of his "cost bucket" associated with payment processing in sufficient detail that a strategic decision could be made around what to do with it. He determined that the "competitive half-life" of his exception-processing asset was insufficient for him to keep supporting it. So, he decided to get rid of it, to give it to someone else who could exploit it more meaningfully than he could.

Deciding "what to do with something" requires knowing *what* it is you have "to do" something with. It requires making explicit what is implicit, making tangible what is intangible, codifying what is tacit so that decisions of what to do can be based on hard reality rather than presumed intuition. This is an underlying theme of this book. In this chapter, we explore this theme through processes, where business meets technology. From this perspective, then, the issue of "how to optimize business processes" is much broader than the traditional way of thinking about "optimization." Often, optimization means "streamlining" or "making something more efficient." As we'll see through other examples in this chapter, optimizing processes can have different objectives. For us, it means being able to make whatever business decisions are relevant to meet specific objectives. Take Mark's decision to create a shared business utility for his payment processing, as an example. "Optimizing" for him meant something completely different: It meant making explicit an asset—exception processing—and deciding how to exploit it most effectively.

Before we start, let's build on this comment about *business process optimization*. We picked the term to stay clear of other business process phrases that have heavy connotations associated with them, such as *business process reengineering*. We use business process optimization to accent business process solutions that balance the demands of the many people affected by business process. We understand that for some, the word *optimization* might be associated with *maximum efficiency*. This is not our intent. Why not? Because efficiency is just one of many ways to evaluate a business process. Elsewhere, we have shown that in today's business environment, efficiency is often not the most important of those dimensions.[2] Later, we will see an example set of optimization criteria, and the range of different ways of determining the "goodness" or "effectiveness" of a process should become clearer. A study by Accenture on e-government gives a window on how government agencies across North America, Europe, and Asia are "optimizing."[3] Says Steve Rohleder, global CEO of Accenture's government practice, "the mantra we increasingly hear from government executives is, 'Give the people what they want.' As government executives focus on tailoring online services to meet the needs of specific customer segments, just as businesses do, their e-government programs will be more successful and deliver greater returns on the investments." Responding to a question on what factors are "driving development" of online services, the top responses included "improving citizen satisfaction" (93 percent), "customer demands for new and better services" (83 percent), and "government performance targets" (77 percent). Only 51 percent cited "pressure to reduce costs."

In this chapter, we explore processes and "how business and technology meet." We explore how to make this happen effectively—and how to "optimize business processes" to respond to the specific (and frequently surprising) changes that occur continually. We draw on lessons of how people approach this effort to see the larger picture of why business process optimization is important. We again present these lessons in terms of the framework laid out earlier in the book—the Semantic Stack and its operational cousin Business Blueprinting—and how they help in understanding how business processes work, how to change them and the applications that support them as the business changes.

Extent of the Challenge: "Doing More with More"

At the SAP Sapphire '99 Conference in Philadelphia on September 16, 1999, then Governor Tom Ridge of Pennsylvania said: ". . . speed to market often is the single most critical factor in determining which companies succeed and which companies fail. My goal is to make speed an integral component of our economic development strategy. I believe governments that learn to use technology to facilitate speed—those that become *friction-free*—will see their states prosper. And those that hinder it will stagnate."

Recall the first four goals of Lean that we discussed in Chapter 3:

1. *Customer value:* Define customer value from the outside-in, that is, from the perspective of the customer.
2. *Value stream:* Identify all activities used to make a product or provide a service.
3. *Flow:* Create a system where value is continuously added. Clear away obstacles that don't add value or clog the value stream.
4. *Pull:* Initiate work only at the demand and to the specific specifications of the customer.

Without using this terminology, Governor Ridge was clear in articulating Lean principles for the State of Pennsylvania's approach to supporting business. Customers have a particular need in mind when they interact with an organization—whether in person, on the phone, or via computer. They want their needs met fully, quickly, and with a minimum of hassle. The people who work for the business want to be able to make their customers happy. Finally, the business wants all of this to happen as quickly, seamlessly, and as cheaply as possible.

Business process is at the center of all of this. A *business process* is a set of activities that results in some value for some customer. The customers of a business process can be revenue-producing individuals or businesses (e.g., a people or institutions establishing a loan), individuals or businesses requiring service (e.g., a business requesting a license to put a sign on the street), or internal customers (e.g., employees requesting information on their pay stub). These customers just want the value delivered by the process; they don't care how that value is created. Business processes that are focused on the needs of customers inherently cut across organizations, business information, and the technology that supports them. This statement from the Pennsylvania Governor's Office about its Pennsylvania Open for Business web site makes the point well:

> *Businesses will no longer have to approach state government as an array of separate agencies, each concerned foremost with their own administrative needs. Rather, the Commonwealth will use the power of Internet technology to shift the focus back to where it belongs—on the customer—by providing a single face of state government, to any businessperson, anywhere.*[4]

Focusing on customer value—say by providing a "single face of state government"—means re-orienting an enterprise around its processes. This puts pressure on organization structures, from the top-level goals of that organization through to the infrastructure that it runs on. Again, back to Pennsylvania, the new business goals came right from Governor Ridge's "friction-free" initiative announced in 1999 to streamline public services. Said Governor Ridge of the *Pennsylvania Open for Business* web site created specifically to simplify the life of entrepreneurs, "This web site clearly demonstrates the power of the Internet and why Pennsylvania must continue its leadership in electronic commerce. The

Internet is becoming a major conduit for commerce, both for industry and government. We will continue to move state government services onto the Web as a way to better serve our customers and to hold down our costs." And when a popular governor makes a statement like that, his state agencies notice!

How effective is this web site that provides business a single place to register with the Pennsylvania Departments of Labor and Industry, Revenue, and State instead of the multiple phone calls, forms, and visits that used to be required? The *Open for Business* site was launched in October 1999. By March 2000, the site was receiving over 750,000 hits per month. Again, from Governor Ridge, "The immense popularity of the *Open for Business* web site demonstrates the strong public demand for online services." This is the same public demanding online services from private sector organizations as well.

What does this mean in practice? It means that enterprises, whether agencies in New York and Pennsylvania, or Mike's bank customers, are changing how they create value for their customers. Government agencies need to adapt to be more responsive and relevant to their customers—you and me—while recognizing that all of this needs to happen within real world constraints. Commercial enterprises need to make us happy, or else we'll take our business elsewhere.

In New York, one such agency is the New York State Department of Labor (NYSDOL), New York State's primary advocate for creating jobs and developing the workforce. NYSDOL administers approximately $4 billion annually in employer taxes and disbursements to New York State's unemployed, through New York's Unemployment Insurance System, Labor Exchange System, and Welfare-to-Work programs. It also oversees state worker protection programs, including enforcement of safety and health regulations in the public sector, state labor laws and federal statutes related to working conditions, wages and hours, and laws related to Public Work. Finally, NYSDOL serves as the state's principal source for labor-market information; it offers a variety of services designed to help businesses find workers and people find jobs.

By any measure, this state agency is large and complex. To give a sense of its scope (if $4 billion of cash in and out is not sufficient to tell the story), in 2003, NYSDOL hosted more than 3,500 job fairs or recruiting actions involving 27,000 employers and attracting more than 350,000 job seekers. In that year, NYSDOL found over 216,000 jobs for people, reached out to over 10,000 migrant workers, processed over 12,000 Alien Labor Certification requests, handled over 25,000 calls on its Department of Labor Assistance Line, and found over 22,000 jobs for returning veterans and their spouses.[5] Its reach extends further to workplace safety (where it processed over 12,000 asbestos project notifications and performed 3,500 worksite inspections). In addition, it provides research and statistics on the labor markets (including, for example, support for CareerZone, an online career information system that receives about 100,000 visitors a month).

Over the years, NYSDOL has automated large amounts of its business process. Its Unemployment Insurance Division (UID), over the past 30 years, has built up a considerable base of technology to support the business. As you can imagine, the 30-year-old technology base is feeling its age, which impacts UID's capability to provide the sort of service its customers demand. In many cases, new requirements that cannot be met by the aging computer systems are handled manually by UID personnel.

In late 2003, against this backdrop of expanding business goals and aging systems and workforce, UID undertook a modernization of its business processes and the technology that supports them. Their high-level business goals, simply stated, included:

- Improving the effectiveness and efficiency of operations
- Promoting work environments that support excellence
- Improving interactions with their information-sharing partners

UID envisions a future—not too distant—where NYSDOL "knowledge workers" (their term) are more productive—via things like automated workflow capabilities, streamlined business processes, and online decision support—where responses to customers' inquiries are quick and accurate, and where staffing is more flexible. They want employers and employees to be able to manage their own information through an intuitive Internet presence. In short, they want to provide significantly better service, leading to a set of more detailed, and measurable, objectives, such as:

- Reducing the time needed to resolve customer issues
- Enabling customer self-service
- Improving access to information
- Standardizing processes and procedures
- Providing better tools to UID staff
- Matching the organizational structure to the new customer service focus

These are broad goals, with broad impact on several stakeholder groups:

Users: State personnel who perform transactions or retrieve information on behalf of customers

Customers: Employers or benefit recipients doing business with NYSDOL or receiving services

Partners: Other NYSDOL divisions, other NYS agencies, federal agencies, or other external entities with which the UID exchanges information

People from these groups need to be involved in this "modernization" march, to a greater or lesser degree depending on their role. In Chapter 1, we described the T-Shirts, Turtlenecks, and Suits view of an organization, where each group had their own perspectives, priorities, processes, and proclivities. And that was just *within* an organization. UID's stakeholder list goes beyond their own walls, making clear the sheer numbers of people who will be affected, the importance of getting it as right as possible the first time, and the Herculean challenges of doing so.

Facing the Challenge: Mutual Visibility/Useful Action

The UID is a complex organization undertaking a complex change. What are some of the operational challenges that they have to control to hope for success? A detailed listing would be huge, and unnecessary for our discussion now. Six distinct, but not entirely independent, factors comprise *making sense, then taking action* at this scale:

- *Scope:* Controlling the size of the initiative, getting in the things you need, but not letting it grow unmanageably. Maybe most importantly, scope helps you know when you're done.

- *Completeness:* Making sure that you've actually addressed everything in the scope, and that you know when you're done. In complex projects like this, with many stakeholders, convincing people that you understand the problem and the solution in sufficient detail to move to the next step is not as simple as saying, "trust me."

- *People:* The people involved in planning and executing the initiative will include supporters, detractors, people with agendas, obstructionists, and committed zealots; when the time comes to implement the new processes and systems, the people who are affected by the change will include the exact same types.

- *Semantics:* Across this large and diverse organization, and across the layers from business goals to computing infrastructure, different audiences use different language to mean the same thing, use the same language to mean different things, and sometimes speak languages that are mutually incomprehensible.

- *Managing multiple moving parts:* A large transformation project must be broken into smaller pieces of work, and many of those pieces must go forward simultaneously, if the transformation is to be completed in a reasonable time frame. Of course, for the transformation to be completed at all, those multiple pieces of work need to be orchestrated carefully.

- *Getting what you expect:* Where there are many people involved over an extended period of time, it is very easy to get off track as many small individual decisions accumulate into large impacts. Clarity of vision, and good intentions in execution, while necessary, are not sufficient to ensure the desired result.

Tim Garza of CalPERS, another complex organization, sums it up nicely. He recognizes the importance of knowing what would impact what, where, when, by whom, and how much: "We need mutual visibility to get what we all need out of whatever decision we take. Different organizations ha[ve] different ways of understanding what the problem was . . . so, we have to create a shared vocabulary to have meaningful discussions." Our execution framework creates the mutual visibility and shared understanding to get a successful result. Like Tim's group at CalPERS, the UID used Blueprinting needed to make sense of their sprawling, complex business, and to create shared understanding. They started with optimizing their business processes using the process descriptions as the anchor of their business transformation. The Business Blueprint acted as the central repository. We will look in detail at a few of the practices UID focused on, but here's the list of everything in their scope where the Blueprint plays a role:

- Program, Project, and Risk Management
- Creation of the Operational Strategy
- Business Process Optimization
- Organization and Human Capital Design
- Technology Architecture, Design, Implementation, and Test
- Roll Out and Change Management

Process Optimization Leads the Way

Why is Business Process Optimization so important to transformation and agility? Because, in many ways, business processes *are* the business. By optimizing processes, we create a better business, and, crucially, we capture the processes in a Blueprint, making them visible to anyone. If 50 percent of the work done in a business adds no value to the customer, optimizing will eliminate it. When a new release of a vendor application comes out, the Blueprint will show what processes will be affected. Where people in the organization make local modifications to their processes, optimization will make the best of those modifications available everywhere in the organization, and eliminate the worst of them. And as those people walk out the door—through retirement, job change, or layoff—with their head full of "organizational wisdom," the Blueprint keeps that wisdom *in* the business.

Customers are increasingly taking the power of their business into their own hands. In the public sector, citizens and businesses demand better service, aligned with their needs, and businesses increasingly base their decisions on where to locate on the ease of doing business in or with the city or state in question. Tom Ridge understood this in his late 1990s call for the "Friction Free" government, which, according to Governor Ridge, "is based on the simple notion that initiatives that allow the private sector to move quickly are just as valuable—perhaps even more valuable—than all our low-interest loan programs combined."[6] Companies go out of their way to provide a "customer-centric" experience striving (usually mightily) to give the customer a uniform, productive, valuable experience in every interaction with the company.

Back to NYSDOL. Recall that NYSDOL workers were using manual workarounds for some, possibly many, of their citizen services. Quite possibly, these workarounds result in a happy citizen; in that regard, the UID fulfilled its mission. There are, however, two problems with workarounds: first, manual workarounds use expensive people time for nonchallenging tasks and so reduce job satisfaction; second, anything that requires a manual workaround is by definition not available via computer for the self-service capability that citizens (and customers in general) seem to want. When do workarounds become necessary? When there is a breakdown in the relationship between business processes and the computer applications that support them. We said earlier that computer applications in business exist to support some activity or set of activities, but that has not always been the emphasis. And it was certainly not the focus of the programmers of applications 30 years ago when UID's automation process began.

The first commercial computer applications were created to automate specific, repetitive, error prone tasks like tabulating the U.S. census, or printing paychecks. This progressed to the automation of specific business functions such as recording an unemployment claim form. During these early days, it was not unusual for a business process to require a person to interact with two applications that were created separately and not intended to work together: the person would take data provided by one system, for the sake of the example, say the system that has the unemployment claim form, swivel their chair around to another system that, say, prints unemployment checks, and reenter the data.[7] Sure, it sounds primitive today. But the computer applications were providing great value to the business process at the level the technology could support at the time. Over time, companies made enormous investments in computer applications that implement specific, isolated pieces of business functionality. Later still, equally enormous investments in system integration to make those applications work together were made to better support business processes that were themselves becoming more efficient. At the outset, most of the people doing the integrating thought that integrating systems was a stopgap, preparatory to building new applications to do things "the right way." Over time, it became clear that the pressures to automate more and more of the business, coupled with how truly difficult it is to reengineer an application that has existed for a long time and has been modified and enhanced throughout its lifetime, meant that integrated systems would have a long life, and systems integration became the norm.

Now organizations such as UID are at the stage where their trusty legacy systems can no longer be cajoled into supporting business needs that move faster than the old applications can adapt. They have reached the end of their useful life; they need to be replaced. How do enterprises make sure that the replacement applications will be as flexible as the rapidly evolving needs of the customers? And how do they make sure that the organization is agile and flexible enough to be able to respond rapidly, hopefully in anticipation of, new demands by its customers?

The answer, to borrow a phrase, is "it's the process, stupid." Business Blueprinting explicitly separates the business process layer from the application layer because creating an agile organization—one that can take action quickly, effectively, and efficiently—requires keeping business processes and the underlying technology that supports them as independent from one another as possible. A very clean relationship, defined solely on the functional interactions between the two, is necessary, and for a simple reason: Business processes face the customer, and they change as rapidly as the customer needs and the external environment require; although technology needs to support the activities in the business processes, it needs also to change to keep up with the rapidly progressing capabilities of new technologies.

Remember, making sense and taking action requires mobilizing the collective wisdom of all of the people that have something to offer in solving a business problem. Business process people speak a different language from technology people, and while the two groups share the common goals of the business they are in, each group has its own independent agenda. Technology and business process come together specifically in the places where people use application functionality to perform a specific task. The discipline of using the models in a Business Blueprint to distinctly represent business processes, application components, and the specific interactions where business activities use technology functionality helps to ensure the flexibility of process and application that leads to organizational agility. Let's look in more detail at some of the key parts of business process optimization, using the UID to provide examples.

Optimizing for What?

The UID of the New York State Department of Labor started its modernization by modifying its key existing business processes—the "as-is" processes—into a set of improved, "to-be" processes. The "to-be" processes need to run the business, and they need to meet specific additional business goals. Some of the optimization criteria for UID's redesigned processes include:

- Meet, now and into the future, state and federal standards for quality and timeliness
- Raise the overall quality standard of client services provided, improving customer service and making efficient use of staff
- Enforce equality of treatment for both employers and claimants
- Maintain and distribute current information to support, as much as possible, real time processing
- Reduce benefits fraud
- Take maximum advantage of automated workflow capability to improve the timeliness and quality of performance and response
- Eliminate as much as possible manual processes, and reduce the amount of paper-based processing

- Expand the hours of customer service availability
- Shift routine tasks such as data entry to client self-service, and promote client self-service for employers, claimants, and other state and federal agencies
- Impose appropriate and adequate security without inhibiting client and internal staff use
- Recognize revisions to laws and rules and regulations while limiting the need for staff intervention
- Support the collection and analysis of process performance metrics
- Convert paper-based processes and communications to electronic as much as possible
- Provide a choice of channel options for clients to communicate with NYSDOL
- Modify and adjust business rules to address changing dynamics
- Prevent or allow early identification of fraud resulting from identity theft
- Prevent or allow early identification of tax nonpayment and underpayment

Note that the words "increase efficiency and reduce cost" do not actually appear. This is what we meant earlier when we said that process "optimization" does not always mean "push for maximum efficiency." Every business wants its processes to be efficient and low cost, and the UID is no exception. The UID criteria show, however, how to balance efficiency and cost with the broader, and for many businesses today, the more critical goals of providing greater services to clients, partners, and stakeholders.

Optimization of business processes is a good place to start in a business transformation effort because business processes define the scope of the transformation and therefore the supporting technology. What additional business value comes out of process optimization and the resulting Business Blueprint?

Mutual Understanding
Optimizing business processes requires getting all of the people involved in the business problem, with their very different perspectives

and priorities, mobilized into its solution. Process optimization forges the connections, buy in, mutual understanding, and shared semantics needed to create a working team. What we call experiential workshops are used to define, then flesh out business processes; they are intense, facilitated sessions that bring together business and technology stakeholders in a problem-solving setting. By bringing people together using the neutral language of process modeling, the workshops create a nonthreatening, nonpolitical environment that creates an effectively working team. For most participants, the focus on modeling is different enough that it moves them "off center," away from any other agendas they may have. At the same time, participants mutually create the semantics—process names, activity names, what's important, what's peripheral—that stay with them as they move forward to create solutions for their business problems. Participants come away with a shared understanding of the essence and productivity associated with each business process, and of the possibilities and challenges of the technology available to support those processes.

What to Do, Where, and How Much

Process optimization starts with a focus on the top-level interactions between parts of the business, and between the business and the external world. Those interactions are captured in models that we saw in Chapter 3—the business interaction model (BIM) and the top-level business process models.

The BIM in Figure 5.1 is basically a view of UID on one page. It's easily understandable by executives who know the business, and, when created as part of a Business Blueprint, the BIM is a living model that serves as the top-level connection for subsequent business process Swimlane models that get created in experiential workshops. UID used the BIM to scope out the overall effort of their transformation. Tim Garza's team used the CalPERS BIM to play with different alternatives for outsourcing pieces of their business.

Using the BIM, UID executive sponsors were able to perform a simple "in scope, not in scope" walk-through of the organizations and interactions, drawing a clean line around the transformation. For example, executive sponsors could decide that *Collections* is in the

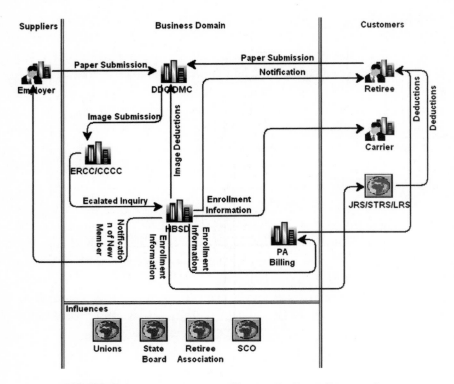

FIGURE 5.1   Insurance Enrollment Business Interactions

scope of the project (we'll assume that it is, and continue through *Collections* with this example). Alternatively, possibly the interaction between *Employers* and *Collections* is mandated by state or federal law, so executives can decide to leave the *Collections/Employer* interaction out of the scope of the project. This "organization on one page" view helps to define what's in and what's out; it's a crucial part of knowing when the process optimization project is complete.

The BIM is sometimes not granular enough to fully determine the scope. For example, while *Collections* might be in scope generally, UID might want to limit scope to only specific functions within Collections. Figure 5.2 shows a top-level view of the activities that occur in one of the organizations in the BIM that are determined to be in scope. This model is linked to the BIM and to any more de-

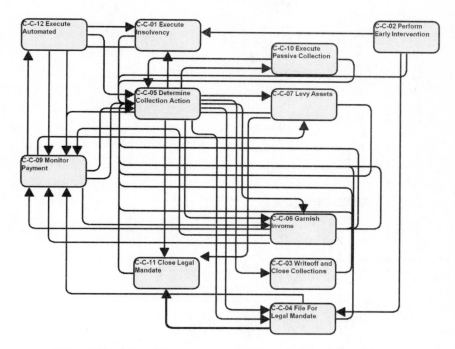

FIGURE 5.2 Drill Down or Top-Level View of Activities

tailed process models that we may create to further detail the business functions shown in the top-level model.

This linkage from top-level models through to detailed process models (and continuing into the technology models that we will not discuss here) has several benefits:

- *Data entered only once:* Everything in the BIM becomes available to the top-level models, everything in the top-level models is available to lower-level models, and so on.
- *No surprises:* Since models are linked together, changes in any one model are reflected in all affected models, so stakeholders are always informed.
- *Iteration:* Since changes are easily handled, it becomes practical to use an iterative approach to solving the business problem.

Shared Vocabulary, Interdependent Actions

Remember Jim Dillon's concern about the graying of his workforce, a concern he shares with Clark Kelso from California, and virtually every other public sector executive? The Blueprint models—the BIMs and the Swimlane models—take the information about how the business runs out of the heads of people and into a form—models—that can be understood by anyone who learns the language of modeling. It's hard to optimize anything if all of the knowledge about it is stored away in a person's head or deeply embedded in computer applications. It is particularly important for government agencies where half of the workers in state and local government in the United States are approaching retirement age. As those workers retire, they will take with them many of the details of how the business "really" works, unless the business can get that information out of their heads and into models, making the knowledge an enterprise resource.

Once business processes are codified into models, other people can begin to work with them. Business architects use business process models, along with input from subject matter experts and business stakeholders, to improve processes by searching out inefficient or incorrect process flows, finding patterns of similar processes in different parts of the business that might be an opportunity to eliminate redundancy and improve service to customers, and looking for opportunities to automate key activities. Technical people use process models to understand the context in which their technology will be used, and of course the process models form a critical link in the chain that connects business needs with technology implementation.

The process models below the top-level model of Figure 5.2 are the Swimlane models we introduced in Chapter 2. Figure 5.3 shows a UID process model that gives the detail for the activity *Monitor Payment* that we saw in Figure 5.2.

This process shows activities that are performed within UID as well as the interactions of those activities with various outside entities such as the debtor or the bankruptcy court.

Each of the horizontal Swimlanes in Figure 5.3 represent a particular role or job function. In Figure 5.3, all of the UID activities are listed in a single Swimlane labeled UID rather than being associated with a particular job function within UID. Why? Because this

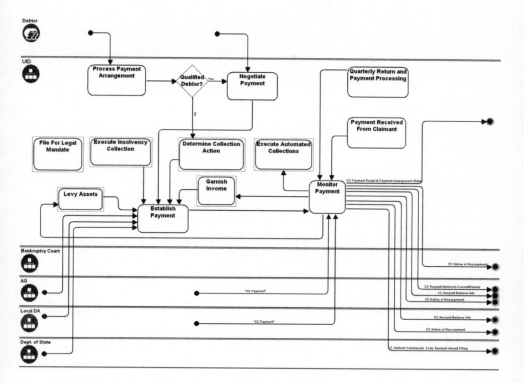

FIGURE 5.3 Making Visible What's Invisible: External Consequences

real-world model was created first to identify the correct process within and outside of UID. Once the process activities are agreed to by stakeholders, through modeling and iteration, business architects can identify specific roles within UID to perform specific process activities. At that point, they would break the UID Swimlane into independent Swimlanes, one for each of the identified roles.

Working with human capital specialists (formally known as human resource experts), the business architects can also use the Swimlane models to determine necessary new roles and changes to the activities performed by an existing role. Process optimization often leads to significant organizational changes and this is where those changes can be mapped out. By moving activities in and out of different Swimlanes, human capital specialists can easily perform "what if" analysis and develop approaches that minimize the resistance to change and identify the training necessary to support employees as they transition to new roles. They can also develop process performance metrics to support service level goals, and measure satisfaction levels of various interested parties—in the case of UID, these include employers, benefit claimants, employees, and other agencies.

Tools to Get Stuff Done

Finally, process optimization identifies all of the business activities that will require support from technology, typically meaning a computer application, that either needs to be purchased or developed. By using Blueprinting to define the scope of the process optimization, we know that all business activities are represented in some Swimlane model. Using the activities listed in the Swimlane models as the basis for determining automation, we ensure that no automation need is missed, and we clearly link automation to the goals of the optimization. This helps further to answer the question, "How do we know when we are done?" Starting from the BIM and down through the activities listed in the Swimlane, we have created interconnected models that make it easy to take into consideration all the activities that will be affected, and equally importantly, make it hard to overlook something. This also helps address Clark's other concern about retiring CIOs taking the knowledge of applications with them. The Blueprint links technology—which may be new development, but it can also be an existing application reused in the new process—to the rest of the Blueprint activities.

These linkages happen through a Use Case, as shown in Figure 5.4, which shows the activity underlying *Execute Automated Collections*. As explained earlier, a Use Case describes how a person performing a business activity will interact with a computer application. It shows a task or a series of tasks that the person will accomplish using the software, and the response of the software. Use Cases are the critical link between business activities above and detailed technology implementation below. Remember that it's important to keep business process and technology as independent as possible; Use Cases fill the formal need to describe a human-computer interaction in a way that is independent of how the computer side of the interaction may be implemented, leaving technologists a lot of room to take advantage of all of the things

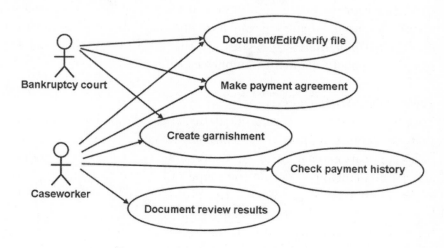

FIGURE 5.4 Bridging-the-Disconnect Use Case

technology has to offer. At the same time, Use Cases are intuitive enough that we have seen C-Level corporate executives argue over them. Finally, Use Cases are descriptive enough that business architects can use them to look for opportunities to reuse application functionality to support multiple business activities. In the models, one Use Case can be used to support multiple business activities, helping to promote efficiencies and reuse.

The Work of Process Optimization

Process optimization can be done via an iterative, inclusive process that:

- Defines the overall scope of processes
- Sets them in relation to business goals
- Codifies processes through facilitated work sessions and modeling

This is shown in Figure 5.5. At the core of this is the experiential workshop, which is no more than a structured means to work/argue-through specific problems—one directly relevant to a person's actual work "experience."

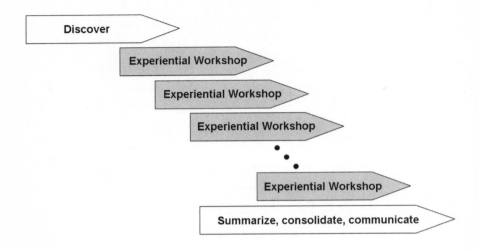

FIGURE 5.5   Excavating the Knowledge

In the Discovery phase of the project—which typically lasts no longer than a week or two—the business architects, key stakeholders, and executive sponsors determine high-level parameters for the optimization project, such as:

- Determining the parts of the business that are in-scope and out-of-scope
- Determining the complexity level of the business functions
- Agreeing on the ground rules for "time-boxing" activities in the project—stakeholders will occasionally fall into the trap of over-optimizing or revisiting settled decisions to the point of diminishing returns; an agreed on rule to time-box any such activity is vital to keeping the process moving
- Finding any existing documentation for the current processes
- Identifying workshop participants and getting their commitment to participate at the required level of commitment—the

experiential workshop approach helps to make efficient use of stakeholder time and permits advance scheduling of activities, but stakeholders must be willing to make themselves reliably available

The experiential workshop is the mechanism used to bring stakeholders together around a specific set of business processes, with the express goal of defining those processes down to the level of activities and the Use Cases that support them.

The participants in a workshop typically include:

- A business architect/facilitator
- A scribe
- One or more modelers
- An external subject matter expert—someone from outside the organization with broad knowledge of the business, to provide "fresh eyes" to the business problem at hand, and a knowledge of what other similar organizations have done
- Business stakeholders—including at least one person who knows the business processes in detail, and at least one person who understands how the business processes fit into the overall context of the business
- A business-aware technologist

Each workshop focuses on a small number of processes, and taken in total they create detailed process flows for the entire part of the business that's in the scope of the business process optimization. Breaking the overall business into bunches of smaller processes has a number of benefits:

- A manageable number of people in the stakeholder community are included, and therefore a manageable number of people are in each workshop.
- A closer focus on fewer processes helps participants concentrate on the small picture, which helps drive productivity and detail.

- Shorter workshops—Because the workshops are very intensive, shorter workshops let the participants work hard for a reasonable amount of time without burning them out.

UID ran parallel workshop tracks for the four major areas of their business—*Tax, Benefits, Collections,* and *Hearings&Appeals*—and workshop activity that spanned six weeks, with any one stakeholder involved in probably 20 percent of the workshop activity. Along the way, the group realized that there was an adjudication process that was essentially the same across these four areas, and so a fifth, short, track was created for that process. Also, the group realized that the *Tax* area of the business included a specialized type of processing—case management—that needed special attention, so they held a workshop just for that.

Figure 5.6 shows the typical activities for a workshop. The business architect and modeler work independently of stakeholders in

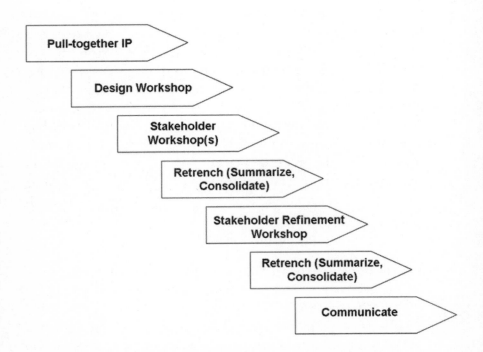

FIGURE 5.6 An Experiential Workshop

designing the workshop. The workshop group meets for the stake-holder workshops and stakeholder refinement activities. The business architect and modeler again work independent of the stakeholders, but in coordination with any other business architects who may be running parallel workshops for other sets of business processes, in the "Retrench" activities. During the Retrench activities, the business architect and modeler do a few important things:

- Complete the modeling from the stakeholder meetings—these meetings move more quickly than modelers can generally keep up with in real time. The business architect facilitates the group, and between the facilitator and the scribe, "everything" is captured. The modeler plays catch-up after the workshop.
- Look for patterns, duplications, inefficiencies, and opportunities for improvement—the business architect uses the models created from this workshop, and models created in other workshops that either he or she is running, or that other business architects are running, to find places where the same activities (possibly with slight variations) are being done in different parts of the business, and to "borrow" good efficient solutions for process problems uncovered in his or her workshop.
- Consolidate the workshop business process with other processes from other workshops—the overall business process optimization effort is broken into smaller pieces to allow for more manageable workshops, and so that multiple workshop streams can proceed in parallel. However, it's still a single business, so all of the processes need to fit together, which requires the business architects to coordinate on things like naming conventions, the style and level of detail of the Swimlane models, and how to handle activities or subprocesses that are common across multiple business processes.

In the workshop itself, the facilitator works with the group to:

- Set the overall context for the workshop with respect to the business goals and other workshops that might be taking place
- Identify and agree on the processes to be improved in the workshop
- Identify and document perceived problems and concerns

- Develop high-level and more detailed process diagrams, within the context of the BIM and other workshops that might be taking place
- Identify key organizations and their interactions
- Identify activities that require automation support, and develop Use Cases

After Optimization

When the process optimization effort is complete, the resulting Business Blueprint will be richly populated with information on the business interactions, processes, and activities of the organization. This information will be used in several ways as the transformation project goes forward. In this section, we briefly discuss a few of them.

Technology

As we saw in Chapter 3, technologists begin with the Use Case model, and extend that model through their activities of analysis, design, construction, and deployment. Technologists have used modeling for many years and are happy that business process audiences have caught up, and are using models to represent the business—it provides for a common language, and reduces miscommunication. Technology implementation is best done with an iterative approach, with functionality created incrementally as iterations proceed. The traceability of a Business Blueprint helps to align the evolving technology with the evolving business process implementation, reducing unpleasant surprises.

Organization Design

Major changes to business processes create changes to the organizational structure of the people who perform those business processes. As we've seen, the Business Blueprint provides tools and information to support the task of human capital specialists in their work. The activities in the business process models created from workshops gives information for task and functional analysis. From this starting point, jobs (job descriptions and job families), can be determined, and the organization can identify new or changed career tracks, leading to an understanding of gaps, the need for change management, and the strategies for migrating from the old organization to new.

Change Management

Organizations that have achieved success in transformation attribute much of their success to the aggressive use of change management in their overall project approach. Change management guides the transition experience, developing commitment to the effort, minimizing resistance, and enabling all impacted audiences to build the necessary competencies to work in the new environment. Repeated studies have shown that implementation failures almost always stem from human factors:

- Between 55 percent and 90 percent of all technology initiatives fail to achieve their objectives because human and organizational problems are not adequately addressed.
- Approximately 90 percent of business process redesign initiatives fail to produce intended breakthrough results.
- About 80 percent of internal quality improvement initiatives fail to achieve tangible results.

Therefore, a focus on change management designed to lead, facilitate, monitor, and support the human workforce transitions caused by process optimization is important. The Business Blueprint, by giving a living, evolving view of the changes resulting from the optimization effort, provides vital information to change management specialists.

Business Case Development

A business case often needs to be developed to justify activities that need to take place to implement the technology and organizational changes that result from process optimization. Executives and operational management often need to measure the level of expenditure and success to obtain funding and maintain high-level support. In the case of public agencies like UID, a business case helps to secure and maintain the support of the legislature for the expenditures. And for any business that uses union labor, the business case is an important part of the overall story of why union membership will be asked to make changes to their work.

What This Means to You

1. *I'm intending to outsource most of my troublesome processes, so I don't have to understand them in the kind of detail you're talking about here. I'll make them someone else's problem.* We discuss business process outsourcing in detail in the next chapter. For now, however, our comment is simply that effective outsourcing requires that either you, or your sourcing partner, need to understand your business processes at a level of detail—and shared understandings—that begs for Business Blueprinting. Here are two quick points on this. First, as Tim Garza of CalPERS knew, the first challenge of outsourcing is working out the new ways that your people, and the outsourced people, need to work together as parts of your business process leave your business. Tim used parts of Blueprinting—the business interaction model specifically—to define the new outsourced environment. He also used simulation of his business processes to refine his understanding of whether outsourcing improved or degraded his performance. Second, the only way you can have a robust, successful outsourcing relationship is if those processes continue to work well in the short term, and improve over the long haul as the outsource vendor improves the processes and replaces the underlying technology supporting them. For this to happen at reasonable cost and without adverse business impact during migration, the vendor needs to understand in great detail how the business processes and technology work together. Too often, organizations—both customer and supplier—"assume" that they know what work gets done and how it gets done. But, as many of us know only too well, much of what actually gets done remains invisible, undocumented, and tacit. Going beyond intuition and "hope" toward rigor and "fact" is critical to make sure that the "gotchas-don't-getch'ya." Making clear, and understandable, what really occurs rather than what you assume does is

as important for outsourcing arrangements as for ongoing inside-the-walls activities.

2. *Does business process optimization help me to take advantage of new options in global sourcing?* Absolutely. The biggest single challenge with a distributed workforce is understanding the flow of work, inventory, and information between your organization and an organization that might be thousands of miles away—geographically, culturally, and linguistically. A Blueprint creates shared semantics among any people who learn the language of modeling, wherever they live and whoever they work for, reducing miscommunication, risk, and rework.

3. *Isn't modeling labor-intensive and expensive?* Modeling for modeling's sake takes a lot of work from talented people—and is a total waste of time. However, modeling to understand something that you are trying to change is just good business hygiene. Our experience is that once the initial costs are out of the way to train or hire business architects and modelers—these skill-sets represent a small fraction of the total workforce—and equip them with the tools they need, creating the Business Blueprint models during a project adds no cost. Any additional project time spent in modeling is recouped, usually with a bonus, in reduced testing, modifications, and rework. Crucially, once the models have been made during the first project they serve as a living representation of the business solution created. Consequently, any subsequent changes you make to the solution go much faster and the pieces of the business solution become available for reuse throughout our organization, making other related projects faster and cheaper also.

4. *Why should I maintain my models after the system is implemented?* See the comments on question 3. Maintaining the models offers the benefits of leverage in subsequent projects. Also, many if not most vendors predict that within three to five years they will be able to create many working computer applications directly from the models; investment in the models to keep them up to date positions you to take advantage of such new technologies.

Chapter Cheat Sheet

The Issue

There's an adage that states that your organization gets what it deserves. That certainly explains the enormous differences among firms—from leaders to laggards, from risk-takers to risk-avoiders. Yet, what is common to most if not all of them is the ongoing challenge of responding, as a commercial firm, to market opportunities and as a public sector one, to changing constituent expectations and demands. Both business and technology sides of the house are certainly willing to make changes, but the nature of what they do makes it hard to do so. Many organizations, over the years, have built up a base of technology—largely computer applications—to support the business. This base frequently feels its age that impacts its capability to change quickly. Organizations do respond, of course. But often, new requirements that cannot be met by the aging computer systems are handled by manual workarounds resulting in mutating and informal activities—effective, perhaps, but often difficult to replicate and nearly impossible to monitor. Yet replicating and monitoring—in short aligning—business activities with underlying technology is critical for ongoing improvement—and certainly for any large-scale change or so-called transformational effort. The question is how do you do so—how do you bridge the inherent mutating and diverse nature of business processes with the need for supporting technology? And of that tacit knowledge that is embedded in both your processes and technology, how do you determine its competitive relevance—and what to do about it? How do you even determine what you have, and how long you're going to have it given the enormous demographic shifts that we are starting to experience?

The Insight

The answer, to borrow a phrase, is "it's the process, stupid." Business process is the place where your business creates the image that your customers see, and the place where technology really adds value. Business Blueprinting gives the process/technology interdependency the attention it deserves, separating the descriptions of business process distinct from descriptions of the applications that support it, because to create an agile organization—one that can take action quickly, effectively, and efficiently—it is important to keep the relationship business process and the technology that supports it as clean as possible, with their interaction defined solely on the functional interactions of the business process.

The Phrases

Process Optimization; Process Model; Business Interaction Model; Experiential Workshop

The Implications

The tacit knowledge in the heads of a few limits the potential of the many to do what needs to get done quickly and effectively. And bottom-line, this is the risk many organizations face with their "organizational wisdom" in the heads of people or embedded in the business rules of underlying applications and systems. Getting this "stuff" in a form that is as understandable as it is usable is critical—and making this happen is where *business meets technology.*

Business process people speak a different language from technology people, and while the two groups share the common goals of the business they are in, each group has its own independent agenda. Technology and business process come together specifically in the places that people use application functionality to perform a specific task. The discipline of using

(Continued)

the models in a Business Blueprint to distinctly represent business processes, application components, and the specific interactions where business activities use technology functionality helps to ensure the flexibility of process and application that leads to organizational agility.

Next Generation Business Process
Outsourcing . . . as Promise and Threat

Setting the Stage: An Industry in the Crunch— beyond the Precipice or into the Chasm

I t was the day before Thanksgiving. Paul Michaels was reviewing a new balance sheet report. As CEO of a large business process outsourcing (BPO) business, Paul frequently created new ways of reviewing his business, from both operational and financial perspectives. As he scanned down the report, he became increasingly alarmed. He knew immediately that he was in trouble, as was one of the world's largest business utilities.[1] The number jumped out at him. Here was €170 million previously unseen, previously unaccounted for, previously unknown. How could this be? How could nearly $220 million of expenses suddenly appear? Paul was shaken. He knew that running one of the first and largest business utilities was a complex challenge. But how would his organization, Advanced Processing Services (APS), survive such findings?[2] How could such a loss occur? How would *he* survive organizationally? As he delved into the details of the report and started making near panic phone calls to his direct reports, a picture began to emerge regarding the causes of the BPO's financial crisis.

APS is a business processing utility used by different organizations to increase operational scale. BPOs are organizations that handle "outsourced" business processes—ranging from credit card processing, human resource operations, mortgage payments, health care claims processing, to any of a broad range of other business processes. APS handles claims processing for a number of the largest insurance companies in Europe. Rather than each of them doing their own processing, they created a separate, jointly owned company, a business process utility (BPU) to handle their claims processing. The main challenge is to process claims as inexpensively but as effectively as possible to maintain sufficiently good customer relationships to get those customers to continue current policies and to purchase new insurance products.

One way to reduce the costs of claims processing is to get sufficient scale across a common infrastructure of business processes, administrative management, and technology enablement. This is a clear and simple logic. But, as Paul painfully experienced, turning that logic into a profitable business was beset by challenges. These challenges stemmed from multiple sources that cascaded into and exacerbated each other creating a tangle of organizational dysfunction and, potentially, financial meltdown. A partial list of the causes of Paul's financial picture included (1) missed or underestimated costs of bringing new business from different insurance companies—with their similar but unique business processes, administrative management, and technology applications—into the common process and technology infrastructure needed to get the benefits of scale; (2) different compensation and severance packages for each new insurance company added to APS; (3) one-off contractual constraints of both participating insurance companies; and (4) involved labor unions. Each of these contributed to the financial shock to APS and to Paul. Why Paul hadn't known of these problems before is a question we'll explore later. But the very complex and very obvious problems APS faced are similar to those faced by BPOs and BPUs all over this very visible industry undergoing significant change.

Extent of the Challenge: At a Tipping Point or Just Plain Tipping Over

Paul is not alone. There are significant challenges occurring throughout the BPO industry. The rationale for BPO seemed—and seems—as inarguable as it is clear: get certain business processes—along with the people who perform them and the technology that supports them—off your balance sheet and thereby drive significant costs out of your organization. Supporting rationales were also clear, and simple:

- For your low-value items, others could (1) do them better, (2) do them cheaper, (3) bring scale, (4) give management attention to areas that were not as important to you; after all, it is *their* business, and (5) deliver investments into their business and hence support continuous improvement.

- For your noncore or noncritical processes, others could deliver multiple goals in parallel, such as (1) do it cheaper, (2) improve service, (3) provide investment to make the process overall more effective, (4) make it their core business and devote their dedicated management time to it, (5) commit to price levels and price improvements, and (6) meet regulatory requirements where applicable.

Gartner Dataquest has identified the following imperatives for organizations taking advantage of BPOs:

- Enterprises around the world are attempting to focus their investments on their core business processes and are increasingly looking at outsourcing noncore business processes.
- The economic downturn and increasing competition is putting cost pressure on enterprises that attempt to optimize their internal operations by reducing the cost of transaction processing in noncore areas.
- In some industries, a shift in regulatory environment is leading enterprises to achieve even higher cost efficiencies in operational management and to focus on their front-end processes. This is true in the financial services, utility, and telecommunications industries.
- Industry consolidation continues to create opportunities for outsourcing as back-office functions become redundant after a merger or an acquisition.
- New technology and media are creating opportunities for outsourcing entire lines of products and services using these new technologies, such as online payroll, online benefits administration, online order management, online transaction processing, and so on.
- Globalization is driving multinational enterprises to outsource business processes to local service providers to gain local process expertise, for instance in finance or human resources (HR) management.

- The high level of competition is making markets more volatile. This makes it more sensible for companies to outsource to third-party service providers to ensure better upward and downward scalability.
- Early adopters of BPO services—primarily large organizations—continue to expand their relationships to include new process areas. For instance, companies that have outsourced their payroll functions begin to outsource other HR or finance and accounting (F&A) functions.
- BPO suppliers are solidifying their market offerings. Both the number of suppliers and the diversity of their offerings are increasing, providing more choice to late adopters, particularly in the mid-market and new vertical industries.
- Both the demand and supply of BPO services are beginning to mature in Western Europe, Asia/Pacific, and Japan.[3]

An exploding market was built on these clear imperatives. Between 1995 and 2003, the BPO marketplace grew an average 30 percent a year. The BPO market continues to show healthy growth, despite outsourcing and BPO getting tangled up politically when CNN's Lou Dobbs and others raised conscientious objections and noise about political constraints on BPO services being delivered "off-shore." Worldwide BPO services are expected to grow from $110 billion in 2002 to $173 billion in 2007, at a 9.5 percent annual growth rate. And the deals are getting larger, on average. The quarterly TPI Index Review, released by Technology Partners International, an advisory firm regarding BPO opportunities, noted that 33 percent of the contracts signed in 2003 had a value greater than $50 million, compared with 22 percent in 2003. Jack Benton, vice president of marketing for TPI, explained the greater contract size as the result of the "BPO concept" having been proven and more and more companies entering the marketplace—particularly as more "traditional conservative European customers" sign BPO deals and as a popular cost-cutting means for companies that have recently merged.[4]

A recent Conference Board report, *CEO Challenge 2004*, based on responses of over 500 global business leaders from 40 countries, stated that outsourcing and BPO involvement will be one of their critical near-term priorities. Sir Martin Sorrell, a trustee of the Conference Board, said, "As a great many European companies have found to their cost, the slightest reluctance to respond to demographic and economic change can prove painfully expensive. This Conference Board research confirms that to many European businesses, off-shoring has become not just desirable but crucial."[5]

Against this backdrop, you might ask why Paul was having any problems at all. But these rosy forecasts are not the whole story. Dark spots on the bright BPO growth horizon remain:

- *BPO losses:* Peter's surprising €170 million loss is not unusual for those involved in BPO activities. The EDS—Navy (NMCI) contract is a "near company-ending event" as Michael Jordan, EDS's CEO and chairman has put it. The landmark mega-project, which was supposed to generate billions of dollars in revenue for EDS, has left EDS with charges and write-downs because of escalating costs and delays. To date, the NMCI contract has cost the BPO provider more than $1 billion, according to most estimates, and has not mustered a single cent of profits for EDS, according to Robert Wright of VARBusiness. Michael Lahman, one of the Navy's Program and Quality Management experts tasked to help salvage the EDS—Navy business commitments, said: "The impact [of this project] on morale, on tax-payer dollars, on both EDS's and our performance is astounding. But the lessons we are all learning out of this mess will help everyone involved in BPOs. And there are a lot of lessons."[6] A study released at the 2003 Gartner Symposium/ITexpo 2003 stated that half of 2003 year's outsourcing projects would fail to deliver on bottom-line promises. Bobby Gill, senior associate of the Technology, Media, and Telecoms group at the law firm, Osborne-Clarke, went further: "Few outsourcing mega deals have been successful in the past 10 years—at least 50 percent fail in the first year and 80 percent don't produce any savings."[7]

- *Differing macro-economic impacts:* 40 percent of Western Europe's 500 largest companies have already begun moving their service operations abroad. Although a core argument of doing so is that wealth can be created for the countries that send jobs offshore and for those that receive them, a new study from the McKinsey Global

Institute finds that this may not be the case in Europe. For example, every euro of corporate spending that German companies send offshore returns just €0.80 of value for Germany's economy. In contrast, the U.S. economy gains more $1.46 in new wealth for every dollar that U.S. companies outsource abroad. Of this $1.46, India (the host outsourcing and BPO country in this study) receives 33 cents through wages paid to local workers, profits earned by service providers and their suppliers, and additional taxes collected by the government. The U.S. economy captures the remaining $1.13 through cost savings to businesses, increased exports to India, repatriated earnings from the offshore providers in which U.S. companies have invested, and the additional economic output created when U.S. workers are reemployed in other jobs.[8] One reason for the increased revenue to U.S. companies results from the outsourced or BPO providers buying many goods and services from the United States. A call center in Bangalore, for instance, might purchase Dell computers, HP printers, Microsoft software, and Siemens telephones. The McKinsey report estimates that for every dollar of U.S. corporate spending that moves to India, U.S. exports to India increase by five cents. This statistic partly explains why exports from the United States to India grew from $3.7 billion in 2000 to $5 billion in 2003. For Europe, the boost in high-tech exports is somewhat smaller because U.S. companies dominate the sector. "For every euro of spending on work outsourced to India or Eastern Europe . . . Germany gains €0.03 from new exports."[9]

• *Return to insourcing:* Scott Abbey, corporate chief technology officer (CTO) for UBS, one of the world's largest financial services organizations, announced their decision to bring back inside UBS all of their outsourcing and BPO processes. He has or is in the process of canceling all of their outsourcing contracts worldwide. By the end of 2006, UBS will have reabsorbed all of their arm's-length processing provided by outside vendors. "We have the scale, we have the competence, and we have the confidence that we can deliver the business benefits better than having outsiders do it. We have learned lots from the experience and we will take advantage of that experience."[10] Additionally, in the fourth quarter of 2004, J.P. Morgan Chase & Co. confirmed that it was canceling the remainder of a seven-year,

$5 billion outsourcing contract with IBM following the $58 billion acquisition of Bank One Corp. in July of that year. J.P. Morgan Chase's CIO Austin Adams justified the return to in-sourcing the following way: "We believe managing our technology infrastructure is best for the long-term growth and success of our company." He added that insourcing what had been outsourced "will give us competitive advantages, accelerate innovation, and enable us to become more streamlined and efficient."[11]

Other examples could be cited. But the point remains the same. There is mega-momentum toward BPO; yet there are some very real—possibly bet-the-business—unanswered concerns underlying the viability and advisability of the BPO business.

There is much noise about the needs of, the requirements for, and the imperative to exploit BPO. Yet, figuring out how to make sense of all this noise, assessing whether and what type of BPO *does* make sense, where, when, how, why, and with whom is becoming an increasingly critical need. We are past the blind infatuation phase of the BPO promise. Trevor Davis is chief implementation officer at Unisys Insurance Services Ltd. (UISL), a U.K.-based company that is one of the world's largest business processing utilities, specializing in processing "closed-book" insurance policies (more on UISL, and on closed-book policies, later). As Trevor puts it, "the maturation of the BPO marketplace is occurring quickly. We are into another wave of BPO . . . we are becoming better informed and learning our lessons that the *BPO-benefits-everyone-equally* promise isn't true. Our transition from an earlier BPO wave to our emerging one is much more complex and requires a deeper understanding to be able to exploit BPOs more effectively."[12] Being able to "make sense" of this transition is becoming acute. And people are asking more informed questions about BPO. They are seeking to "make sense" so they can more effectively "take action."

Tim Garza's management style is an example of the "sense-making" that is occurring over and over again. Tim is chief of the CalPERS Business Solutions Office. California Public Employees' Retirement System (CalPERS) is the largest public pension system in the United States. It manages retirement and health plans for approximately 1.4 million beneficiaries (employees, retirees, and their dependents) from nearly 2,500 government agencies and school districts. Tim is a man of quick intelligence, who always looks aggressively, yet skeptically, to reduce costs while increasing service for CalPERS' constituents. One of his most visible objectives is to improve the efficiency and effectiveness of CalPERS's health benefits program. BPO is definitely one of his considerations. Yet, other options exist as well. "How do I figure out which option will work best for us," Tim asked. "Any option we decide—from reengineering and keeping the work in-house, to BPO the enrollment function, to a modified carrier solution—has pretty big implications on us. There's a lot to be said about each and any of these options—or some combination of them—good and bad. I need a way to help us make our decision and make sure that whichever way we take can be executed by everyone, everywhere." He added, "I know there are lots of transitions occurring within the BPO space, but given all of the losses out there, can we be sure that it is even a viable option for us? I can't just focus on the cost efficiencies of our processes. It is equally important that we focus on servicing our constituents well."[13]

Facing the Challenge: Decisions Made and Decisions to Make

Tim's final two sentences hold a critical key to understanding the BPO transition. "I can't just focus on . . . cost efficiencies . . . ; it is equally important that we focus on servicing our constituents." Cost *and* service effectiveness are *equally* important. Yet, how do you measure cost *and* service effectiveness? One is clear-cut and has been the focus on BPO activities—increasing scale and reducing item or transactions costs. This focus is on decreasing costs not increasing sales or service effectiveness. The metrics, the operations, the sales pitches, the contracts, and the service level agreements (SLAs) tend to be based on reduction-based activities, not enhancement-based ones. *But reducing costs is fundamentally different from enhancing value. Many of the fundamental tensions being faced in the BPO marketplace reflect this shifting focus—from costs to value. More specifically, the BPO marketplace transition reflects the need to figure out* how *to balance these two very different organizational needs.* The transition reflects Tim's needs not only to balance both cost and service needs, but on how to measure them and to make them work effectively together. Yet, neither this balance nor how to clearly measure the value to be realized has been figured out sufficiently. But, we *are* inexorably moving in this direction. The BPO suppliers who figure it out will grab significant market share and add a powerful new tool to their competitive arsenal; their clients will gain a business advantage from a win-win relationship; and *their* customers will benefit from better and more effective service.

The BPO promise was clear. But whether or not the promise has been met is less clear. Certainly, many firms have seen positive returns; value has been created, but much has been lost as well. The countertrends or dark spots highlighted earlier are mere symptoms of an underlying transition. What is clear is that the transition is well underway from a sole focus on cost to a demanding need to provide both cost-based *and* service-driven BPO benefits. Facing the BPO challenge requires figuring out how to juggle these different needs to get the business benefits that the marketplace is demanding.

The Contractual Crunch and the Unintended Consequences of Win-Lose Contracts

Here's how the Gartner Group describes the shifting BPO marketplace:

> *There was activity . . . as some early BPO deals reached their third or fourth years of their contractual life cycle (late 1990s). Renegotiation, including revising the scope of services as original assumptions are disproved or market conditions change, is a sign that the individual contracts and overall BPO contracts are maturing. This restructuring of scope of services and contract terms demonstrates that buyers and providers understand that complex, multiyear contracts have to be revised as business conditions and strategies change. This is a positive indication that buyers and their respective providers are working as long-term partners to ensure contracts continue to drive value for both parties.[14]*

Trevor puts it less formally:

In the early stages of the BPO market, there was lots of fat in the system; it was easy to take out costs from redundant processes and locations, and bloated technology areas. The situation was set for BPO suppliers to exploit and deliver low hanging fruit. That was BPO wave 1. As we entered wave 2 [early 2000s], it became harder to deliver the savings for a couple of reasons. First, the easy fat was cut. Second, customers learned lots about what to do and how to do it. Third, customers learned about SLAs, minimizing change requests from [BPO] providers as they got smarter about how they made money. They learned that they had to get more efficient before they outsourced . . . so they could squeeze the providers harder and get them to work harder on their behalf.

In parallel, aggressive advisors brought organizations seeking to outsource quickly up the learning curve of how to negotiate cost-effective deals. Firms like TPI and the Gartner Group benchmarked BPO deals; they became key advisors for clients looking to outsource parts of their business process, ensuring that their clients created self-advantageous, low-cost BPO deals and low-cost-based contracting commitments. They were able to do so because BPO suppliers saw an exploding marketplace, and they wanted to grab an early market lead.

The industry was set up and still very much runs this way, for the "contractual crunch"—an epidemic of destructive win-lose arrangements between BPO clients and suppliers. In hindsight, this was inevitable. BPOs were conceived and negotiated using cost as the main and, in actuality, the sole criterion. Organizations were looking to get something—their processes—out of their hands because they had neither the scale nor the financial muscle to keep driving unit costs down and thus required new options to do so. Providers wanted to enter this new market with the intent of driving those unit costs down. Clients had gotten clever at driving their costs down. Consequently, they were handing providers, who didn't know nearly as much about the clients' processes as they thought they did, business activities that were already relatively low cost. And with those processes came the challenge of even further and aggressively driving down unit costs. Suppliers took deals that they shouldn't have for the simple reasons that (1) they didn't know what they didn't know other than that (2) they wanted to get into the business. Effective negotiations from the client side around tight cost requirements caused suppliers to make promises that they had no capability to keep. The industry ended up with a win-lose mentality with which it largely runs today.

Sure, the concept of BPO efficiencies-through-scale is clear. But, as Paul found out, the reality is much more complicated, particularly as client needs, expectations, and requirements have and continue to change. In simple terms, suppliers launched into the exploding BPO market with a flawed understanding of the business based on the relative success of technology outsourcing, and entered into strong contracts with ever-smarter clients and aggressive, cost-based advisors.

In many ways, the win-lose contractual crunch was inevitable; the two sides were designed to do battle. "Smart" clients have understood (1) their business drivers and challenges, (2) what the suppliers' low-hanging fruit actions were and consequently did them first, and (3) how to avoid suppliers raising the contract price through change orders. On the one hand, advisors, such as TPI and Gartner, brought their "curve-ball" contracts focusing on (1) tightly constrained commitments and improvements, (2) guaranteed price commitments, (3) embedded investments, (4) required continuous improvement results, and (5) in-built change mechanisms and prices.

On the other hand, BPO suppliers have (1) tended not to understand the complex drivers of costs (or not to understand them as well as the client did!), particularly in new industries and organizations they support; (2) promised the scale and efficiency results without understanding the real investment needed to get those results; (3) committed to multiple, parallel change programs; and (4) treated "business" as projects and failed to put in dedicated or sufficiently qualified management teams and effective improvement plans that could manage the investments or change effectively.

These behaviors led inevitably to what we are calling "the crunch," characterized by:

- One party or both parties are not making money
- Promises are not being delivered
- Investments are made by accident or realized as losses
- Transparency and trust does not exist
- Understanding of the key metrics and drivers is not shared

BPO providers ran into a problem predicted by *The Jericho Principle* and through using insights from the semantic stack: The business process layer is not as well understood as the technology layer, so approaches that are successful with technology outsourcing are not, will not, and cannot be successful with business process outsourcing. And in fairness, neither provider nor client yet understands the implications of the fundamental requirements for mutually-shared success. This is what has given rise to many if not all of the BPO problems, risks, and countertrends currently being experienced by the industry as a whole.

Few organizations start out to create a win-lose situation. Such a start may work in the short term. But the duration and closeness of BPO relationships make a middle-to-longer-term relationship vital. Such durations and closeness need collaboratively based win-win arrangements that share risks and rewards through the many changing requirements that the uncertain business world virtually guarantees. Yet, the inherent dynamics of the contractual process and the lack of understanding of how to service the quickly changing BPO requirements continue to perpetuate the win-lose situation.

Nice New Promises/Same Old Methods

As Paul began to understand the causes of the problems he faced, he began to realize their magnitude as well. He realized how a seemingly simple challenge could quickly spiral out of control. "We had," as he described the situation, "recently won a new contract to bring in another organization and their full book of business, into our [business] utility. What we needed to do was to execute quickly on the contract terms. The reason we won this new business was that we agreed to improve the cost basis [reduce costs] of the policies handled as well as improve the service to our new customers. What we didn't realize was how complex meeting both of the underlying contractual terms to do so would be."[15]

Paul's winning bid for the new business was based on the assumption that he and his team could:

- Dramatically decrease IT operating costs, increase operations efficiency, and improve service levels through a variety of process reengineering work
- Migrate the new organization's book of business onto APS's operations platform for the "two-fer" benefits of reducing the operating costs for the new client while increasing the scale on the APS platform thereby reducing the unit costs for APS's other clients as well
- Modernize the technology platform to improve its cost, maintainability, and performance

None of this was new ground. Paul's team had done these things before—as have many other large BPO service providers such as EDS, IBM, Unisys, Accenture, and ACS among others. They were experienced operational and transformational BPO experts, having migrated several large organizations with their books of business and in the process having created a large insurance business utility. Yet, quickly, things began to unravel and spiral out of control. What happened?

On the "plus side," as Paul puts it, the reengineering work—which was focused on consolidating workflows, relocating people, reducing headcount, and just plain taking out redundant or unnecessary work steps—met its functional and cost targets. However, APS's technology platform had to be enhanced to accept the new client's book of business. This enhancement was necessary to meet both the contracting cost and service requirements. And here is where the seeds of disaster were sown. Delays in getting to "robust and finally agreed to" requirements for the platform enhancements ultimately tripled the cost and time required to complete what Paul called the "basic" functionality to meet both cost and service commitments.

Such delays are not uncommon and, as many of us know, should have been manageable. "Change orders," changes to requirements or other activities that require additional resources, dollars, and time, are how the majority of BPO service providers manage such delays (and on which, not incidentally, significant margins are made). However, in APS's case, there was additional complexity. As an auditor involved in figuring out the causes of the financial implosion described it: "Although the implications of the overrun are clear (i.e., we anticipate [such] overruns) . . . what was not so clear is the impact of this overrun (and more importantly delay) on the remainder of the financials . . . resulting from the inability to get the anticipated realization of efficiencies from the other efforts underway." Stated more bluntly, not having the technology platform capable of supporting the new book of business effectively made it impossible to get either the cost efficiencies or service enhancements committed to in the contract. The result? Commitments had to be pushed out "approximately 3½ years from the end of 2004 to mid-2008." Where Paul's bid projected that technology enhancements and modernization would eliminate large numbers of people and technology costs in 2004, the delays meant that he would not see those savings for over three years. APS had to carry these massive costs on their books even while they overran the budget on modernization. This "triple-whammy," which we describe later in this chapter, is what put the stake through APS.

The final auditing report mentions the triple-whammy obliquely; but it also makes clear that APS's BPO deal suffered as well from the "smart client" effect mentioned earlier. From the report:

(1) even if we had delivered [the technology platform] on time, we would not have achieved the levels of efficiencies projected; (2) we missed significant costs during our Due Diligence; and (3) our proposed price was too low.

It continued with regard to point 1) that the bid model was overly aggressive:

i.e., unrealistic in both absolute efficiency targets and in the timing of the delivery of the improvements . . . only one organization in the industry has exceeded 7,000 policies per full time employee (an industry standard productivity benchmark), and that involves a considerably smaller book and a simpler product mix. However . . . we set overall targets at . . . >8,000 per head.

On point (2), significant costs were missed or underestimated, including finance, HR and facilities manpower costs, severance values, the restaurant and cafeteria that needed to be included in the bid, hardware and software license revisions, relocation expenses, business continuity costs, salary adjustments as people migrated to a shared center, and a host of other items. And, on point (3), since the fixed price contract premised on adding margin to the cost estimates was significantly under estimated (and presuming that changes could be handled through change orders) so too was the proposed, and accepted, price. "In sum, we over estimated the efficiencies we could achieve, under estimated the cost to achieve those efficiencies, and based on these assumptions, priced the bid unrealistically low."

Not a pretty picture. Yet, not an uncommon one either. The EDS Navy contract, the UBS experience serving to justify them pulling all of their outsourcing contracts back in-house, among others, state similar cautions and conclusions. And they all result from similar problems underlying the "contractual crunch" leading to such a win-lose situation.

Explaining the Crunch

The contractual crunch Paul experienced resulted from three factors. At the heart of the triple-whammy crunch lies what we call: (1) the *wedge effect*—also known as "the run-away train," (2) the *bull's-eye effect*, and (3) the *peak effect*.

The Wedge Effect

Clearly, a win-win BPO deal needs to make money for both client and supplier. As in any business situation, the supplier's *revenue* is the client's *cost*, and the supplier's revenue includes the supplier's profit. In Figure 6.1 three lines represent a simplified view of a BPO deal's financials over time. The line in the middle, line 2, is the supplier revenue/client cost line—the negotiated contract price. Note that the line runs downhill, reflecting the BPO's commitment to reducing cost over time. The line on the bottom, line 3, is the

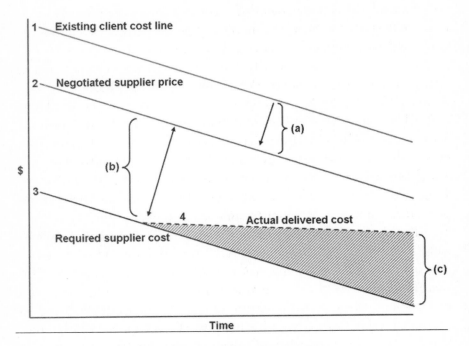

FIGURE 6.1   **The Wedge Effect**

supplier's cost line. Arrow b, the distance between lines 2 and 3, represents the supplier's margin, and clearly the supplier wants this distance to stay the same or increase over the life of the BPO. Finally, the line on the top, line 1, represents the client's existing cost—that is, the cost the client would have if they didn't do the BPO deal. This also runs downhill, because clients are running a business and are trying to drive out costs all the time. BPOs today are premised largely on bringing down the cost line—clients want to bring down the cost from line 1 to line 2 (arrow a), typically for a reduction of 30 percent to 40 percent.

Let's look more closely at line 3. The original client cost must be reduced by a *plus* b to deliver the supplier's margin. Realistically, clients want a 30 percent to 40 percent cost reduction and suppliers want a 20 percent margin. So, in a BPO deal based on cost, the BPO supplier has to reduce the operating cost by as much as 50 percent to 60 percent of the original client cost, ignoring investments.

Consider this number in Paul's context where the proxy for cost is a productivity measure: the number of policies processed per head-count. The new client was currently running at slightly over 4,500 policies per head, substantially less efficient than APS's standard that set the industry benchmark at 7,000 policies per head. However, to get this new client a sustained savings of 55 percent, Paul was forced to commit to processing 8,000 policies per head—substantially outperforming the industry benchmark! This is the first part of the runaway train—the extreme challenge to get sufficient cost reductions that, as we can see, are at best challenging (shown as line 4 in Figure 6.1). Is it any wonder why there is so much effort expended to find low-cost labor to support such operations?

But there's more. Paul was sure that he could hit the productivity goals by further modernizing APS's technology and further improving its processes. This was the deciding factor that put him squarely in the path of the runaway train. The supplier, Paul, agreed to some significant cost reduction objectives for the client, and so must also reduce costs to get his margin. What happens when something delays the supplier's cost takeout? The supplier cost line, line 3, instead of declining, steadily bends up. The distance between line 4 and line 2 decreases, showing reduced margins for the supplier, and the "wedge" (area "c" in Figure 6.1), shows the supplier's revenue shortfall. If line 4 crosses line 2, the client contractually remains on line 2 ("winning") while the supplier's cost stays online 4 ("losing").

Enter the win-lose contract. What causes delays in cost takeout? Paul's case illustrates how the failure to get good requirements delayed their platform modernization effort by three years, but there are many other factors—reengineering, process improvements, salary modifications, union negotiations, location consolidation, offshoring, and so on—that the supplier is counting on to reduce costs and increase productivity. This complicated change program must go off without a hitch for the supplier to keep costs in line. As we will see in the next section, hitting the bull's-eye of change with so many moving parts is something many organizations fail to do.

Suppliers and clients have failed to account for the cause-and-effect reality that missing the benefits of *any* workstream delays realizing the benefits of *other* workstreams. Stated differently, the impact of delayed cost improvement or transformation delivery impacts the contract by the area under the curve—the wedge—not only in the single year or of the specific cost overrun, *but across time and across other efforts.* So, a €10 million cost overrun in a project is the overrun of €10 million *plus* the delay benefits of the process improvement *plus* the delay of the technology improvement *plus* the delay of other efforts resulting in a cost overrun multiple times its initial estimate. The wedge, area c of Figure 6.1, potentially can become very big over time.

Paul and his team achieved a number of operational efficiencies. Quite a few of them resulted from a large number of different, but parallel efforts. Any BPO operation is complex, having to juggle multiple workstreams to drive different results—cost and service. Yet, there were a few workstreams that were singularly problematic. The technology refresh stream, in this case and in particular, hurt the overall business disproportionately to its original projected loss. Paul and his team knew that there were problems with the technology migration. However, they grossly underestimated the rippling effect its delay would have on their other, equally crucial, workstreams. As stated before, not having the technology platform capable of supporting the new book of business effectively made it impossible to get either the cost efficiencies or the service enhancements committed to in the contract—and not only in the first year. As the final auditing report warned darkly, the "wedge effect" pushed out realizing the benefits and the commitments to the clients "approximately 3½ years from the end of 2004 to mid-2008."

The Bull's-Eye Effect

Paul's problem resulted not simply from a technology migration workstream. Actual estimates of the technology overrun was €40 million, but its impact cascaded to other efficiency projects, ballooning the losses to €170 million (the ever-widening wedge of Figure 6.1). But, this *still* understates the problem. Bringing the organization onto the new BPO platform meant that Paul anticipated a profit of €110 million. But the actual projected loss of €170 million resulted in a total revenue swing of €280 million if you add the expected profit to the projected loss. Again, this situation is not unique to Paul and his team. But it is a striking example if only because it is *not* unique. And not surprising.

A significant amount of "stuff" has to occur to outsource a set of a business's processes. The "stuff" ranges from simple things (moving equipment) to hard things (moving and retraining people) with everything in between. Because of aggressive cost-takeout goals, these things have to occur in parallel and work effectively together while in migration. The challenges are daunting. As Trevor puts it, "it's like hitting the bull's-eye with parallel darts thrown with both hands." Figure 6.2 lists the sorts of things that have to be managed in parallel, each "program element" (as they are called here, or workstream, or "stuff that has to be done") unfolds into hundreds if not thousands of specific work items and activities that have to be migrated, managed, and monitored.

Managing large and complex programs is always challenging. But, here again, every outsourcing arrangement includes a large, complex change program, and teams such as Paul's are good at running

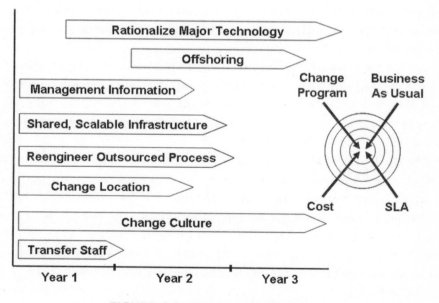

FIGURE 6.2 Hitting the Bull's-Eye

them. What is different here? It's "the crunch" we've been talking about—the BPO focus on cost takeout and the client's aggressive advisors and tough contracts means that the client has a guarantee of the performance of line 2 (Figure 6.1), while the supplier's upside is totally dependent on achieving the costs of line 3. In other words, the supplier is completely dependent on the rapid success of the cost-takeout change program.

Program managers recognize that there are a few things that they *must* keep under close watch in complex programs. Among these are change management and risk management activities. Change management is the discipline of making sure that various parts of the change program actually result in people and systems doing things differently; it's a crucial discipline. What we really need to have addressed, though, is risk management, because the bull's-eye, coupled with the wedge, puts suppliers in an untenable risk situation.

We take a lesson from our personal program management mentor and risk management zen-master Tony Shumskas:[16] "There are essentially four things you can do with risk: transfer it, eliminate it (or reduce it, or mitigate it), accept it (manage it), or take its consequences between the eyes." In a BPO deal such as we describe here, which is very typical of existing BPO deals, the supplier is set up to take risk between the eyes. Why? Because "smart" clients, who are wise to the ways of suppliers who use change orders to transfer risk, have created aggressive contracts that protect their position on line 2 of Figure 6.1. With what result? No place to transfer the risk. And the need for the cost takeout from the change program is woven into the very fabric of the contract, so there's no getting rid of it in the context of cost takeout. Get ready for the impact—right between the eyes, where Paul took it!

The only way to eliminate the risk from the change program, that leads directly to the risk of experiencing the wedge, is to introduce something other than cost into the relationship. As we will soon see, the way out of "the crunch" is to create BPO relationships where the financial return does not depend solely on cost reduction.

The Peak Effect

The concepts of BPO, and BPO generalized to business utilities, are as straightforward as the business propositions are simple. However, putting them into practice requires business, technical, and financial savvy. We've grouped some of the general challenges of BPOs into two categories—the wedge and the bull's-eye. The third effect—the peak effect—stems from the risk/reward tension between the clear need to invest to meet the promises made and the difficulty in assessing the return on that investment. The key question for a BPO is not *if* you're going to invest but *when* to do so.

Figure 6.3 is a conceptual look at the relationship between investment in the BPO, improvements in service levels, and reduction in cost. The dotted line labeled "Transformation Effort and Cost" represents the investment in driving cost out of the BPO. In Paul's case, this is the transformation program needed to get to the productivity levels he needed to make his new BPO client profitable. The solid line labeled "Service Level Improvement" and the dashed line labeled "Planned Cost Savings" are rough complements to one

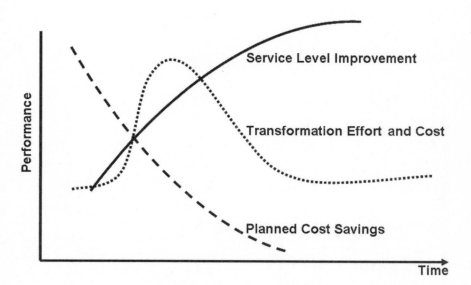

FIGURE 6.3 The Peak Effect

another: Service level improvements come from greater efficiencies which yield cost savings. There are a few interesting things in Figure 6.3 that will find their way into the discussion of Figure 6.4.

First, the cost savings line is not straight, as depicted in Figure 6.1. Also, in Figure 6.1, we explicitly left out the investment part of the relationship between supplier and client. The investment represented by the dotted line is additional cost to the relationship, so line 3 in Figure 6.1 is really made from a combination of the dotted and dashed lines in Figure 6.3.

The second interesting thing is that the investment line peaks in advance of the steadily improving service level line. This illustrates that there is often, if not always, a period of time when the BPO supplier invests more in the relationship than is coming back in cost takeout and margin improvement. Back to the three lines of Figure 6.1, and taking a very simplistic view[17] of how to evaluate an investment, money invested by the supplier reduces the margin during the time of the investment usually to the point where the relationship shows negative cash flow and revenue. Consider Tony's observations on risk: Anything that extends the peak of the investment curve, or delays the onset of the service level improvements, will extend the time it takes for the BPO deal to turn positive for the sup-

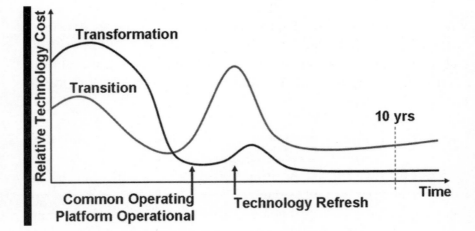

FIGURE 6.4   Options for Investing in Transformation

plier, and thus is risk to the supplier. Either the supplier needs to contractually transfer at least some of the risk back to the client (unlikely in today's contractual environment, but as we discuss this later in the chapter, the focus of adding "service enhancement" into the contractual agreement), or eliminate some if not all of the risk. (Risk people call this *mitigation*, and we will see shortly how the business utility model helps mitigate some of this risk.)

Third, the cost savings line is relatively steep at the beginning; It comes down more rapidly as investment ramps up. This represents the "low-hanging fruit" that BPO providers hope exists in major client inefficiencies that are easily fixed. This is usually a fair assumption, but recall Trevor Davis's characterization of "smarter clients." As clients get smarter, they will have plucked some, if not most of the low-hanging fruit for themselves; they will have driven costs down in their own operation leaving less for the BPO supplier to take. This again throws risk back at the BPO supplier. How so? Because unless "service enhancement" is added to the contract, the investment/return model relies solely on cost takeout as the major return of the investment.

Finally, the fourth thing to notice is that the investment in transformation never goes away. In reality, over time, it turns upward, thanks to things like ongoing modernization and the changing expectations of the BPO client's ultimate customers.

In fact, this last item is important to deciding how much to invest and when to do so. Figure 6.4 essentially shows two flavors of the dotted line of Figure 6.3 giving options for investing in the BPO change program. The one that starts on the bottom is labeled "Transition Program," the other "Transformation Program." Why the two different terms?

First the "Transition" curve: Transition is meant to imply that the BPO supplier's change program focuses on getting a new BPO client up and running, investing only the time, effort, and money needed to make things operational. Particularly significant, on the Transition line, the BPO supplier does not undertake major reengineering of the client's technology; largely for this reason, the bump at the beginning is relatively low. Usually, the intent of the BPO supplier is to improve things over time, so the Transition line in

Figure 6.4 stays relatively substantial into the future. We'll discuss the big bump in the middle shortly.

The Transformation curve shows a significantly higher initial investment because Transformation means sweeping, invasive changes to the client organization—for example, reengineering many of the BPO client's processes, converting them to the BPO supplier's platform, recasting jobs and job functions, and revamping the organization structure. Note that after the peak, the Transformation line drops lower than the Transition line because the client's performance is improved in one "big bang."

What are the bumps at around the five-year mark in both of these curves? They represent a technology refresh cycle, and it's here that the discussion gets more interesting. As Figure 6.4 shows, if the BPO supplier has invested early in transforming the systems that the client runs on, most importantly converting to a single, hopefully modern, technology platform, then the technology refresh cost is relatively low. If, however, the BPO supplier essentially "freeze dried" the client's systems in place during a Transition effort, then the supplier is likely to face many of the challenges during technology refresh that might have been handled at the Transformation phase.

The magnitude of these investments in process and technology reengineering, whether at the beginning of a BPO relationship or somewhere down the road, can be very much affected by the BPO supplier's business model. Let's return to APS, which we called a business utility because there are multiple clients running with common processes atop a common technology platform.

The business utility model certainly lowers the technology refresh hump for any one of the clients because the technology needs to be refreshed only once; that refresh then benefits every client—the risks and costs are spread over a number of client organizations. The business utility model can also reduce the size of the Transformation hump if (1) the supplier's process and technology platform is well-engineered and in place before bringing in a large number of client organizations, and (2) the supplier makes sure that all of the intellectual property related to the BPO and each client's business is accumulated into a Business Blueprint, representing the cumulative organizational wisdom about how to transform and operate new clients and existing clients. A front-loaded investment into the utility's process and technology platform, and the Business Blueprint that describes it, can help mitigate the risk of the surprise investments and unintended costs that will occur as new clients are brought into a utility.

Returning to the Contractual Crunch

The three effects—the wedge, the bull's-eye, and peak performance—underlie the win-lose situations many BPOs find themselves in. For a quick summary:

- The wedge effect results from cascading delays or costs as a result of the slip of any particular effort on those of any others. It is analogous to a small pebble dislodged in the right (wrong) place triggering an avalanche disproportionate to its initial act of being dislodged.
- The bull's-eye effect refers to the massive cascading risk associated with (or the near impossibility of) hitting all of the schedule and functional objectives of the on-boarding change program.
- The peak performance effect refers to the critical timing and impact of the investments in the BPO and resulting performance improvements.

The BPO industry has matured, lessons have been learned, and expectations broadened. This chapter started out with the observation that the BPO industry is changing from a focus exclusively on cost, to focus increasingly on creating new value for BPO clients. From the preceding discussion, we can refine this: The industry is changing from win-lose relationships resulting from a sole focus on reducing cost, to more balanced win-win relationships that balance the investments, risks, and rewards of reducing cost *and* enhancing value. This is the backdrop for the next-generation BPO story—the natural maturation of cost-driven BPO.

Next-Generation BPO—The Search for the Win-Win Contract

Richard is COO of one of Britain's largest financial services institutions and one of the early adopters of BPO insurance services. His institution, along with those of his competitors, faces a significant challenge. Pressures on operating margins are increasing as regulatory shifts impacting privacy rules and enhanced security legislation require greater visibility linking financial flows with customer accounts. Margins have already been squeezed over the past five to six years due to industry consolidation, the European economic downturn, and the continual onslaught of new competitors and technologies. As Richard put it, "we recognize that we cannot continue our way out of our problems to increase our return on equity. We've already been heavily exploiting the cost play of BPO providers." The answer? Complementing the productivity-based cost efforts with efforts to increase return through providing better service. Richard adds, "We are as aggressively focused on strengthening our customer strategy, refining our product strategy, and deepening our channel distribution strategy as we once were on reducing costs."

His focus here is a logical extension of recent analysis he conducted to pinpoint where his organization actually makes its money. Approximately 90 percent of Richard's business results from its existing customer base. Consequently, his challenge is how to get more products to his existing customer base rather than to acquire new customers. The focus on expanding and cross-selling products across Richard's insurance and banking arms, as well as broadening multi-distributor networks reflects how and where his institution needs to focus. Richard's objective is to simplify how his institution interacts with customers, with their distribution networks, with their call centers, and with their administrative centers—to get one view of their customer and provide the opportunity to sell more of the relevant products to that customer.

But shifting from a cost-focus to a balanced cost/value-focus creates two immediate challenges. The first is the language issue—of how to even measure what constitutes value. The second is the visibility issue—of knowing how to align different parts of the organization and different efforts in a manner that is as clear and tangible as it is critical. Solving these two problems is crucial to make the transition to next-generation BPO possible, and successful. They are pretipping tipping points that we can all monitor to see if, when, and how effective the transition will be made.

The Semantics of Value—Why We Need to Care

Measuring costs is clear-cut. There are sets of measures that are well understood, monitored, and reported in addition to forming the basis of BPO service level agreements and performance measures. Benchmarking and clarity regarding what these measures are and their impacts have helped the industry grow and mature quickly. There is significant transparency in the marketplace around what BPO contracts could be, and should be, *based on cost-driven benchmarks.*

The question, however, is how do you measure customer value? What makes up the "value levers" and how do you measure them? And, even assuming you had the language—the semantics—to articulate these levers within *any particular* organization, do these levers hold for different organizations? Are there benchmarks for how to articulate and measure value to be realized? These questions boil down to how do you articulate a value-focus to customers in a BPO marketplace that is currently driven by cost reduction-based SLAs?

The quick answer is, you can't—yet. The industry has not yet matured to the point where it has a benchmark base, and even much less a shared understanding, of what constitutes value consistently. Let's state this point more strongly: *There is no commonly recognized language of customer value; there is a fundamental semantic disconnect between current BPO practices (with its emphasis on cost forming the basis for contractual commitments) and the emerging premise of next-generation BPO on enhancing value to customers* of the outsourcing client. But there are attempts to create such a language. Let's return to Richard.

Richard's challenge, as mentioned earlier, is to retain his customers and to cross-sell more products to them. This is as critical for his closed-book policies as for his open-book policies. Closed-book policies are those that are no longer offered by the insurance provider; they are "closed." Yet, they still need to be serviced since they remain valid financial instruments and remain in effect until the holders either cash in the policy or die off. Consequently, the challenge is to service these contracts as inexpensively but as effectively as possible to maintain sufficiently good customer relationships to get those customers to purchase new or existing ("open") insurance products.

Closed-book products provide no new revenue for Richard's organization (or any finance service provider). However, the customers that have them remain important potential customers for other existing and new organizational products. Richard adds, "Balancing the need to reduce the operating costs of closed-books with providing those customers excellent service so they stay with us [to purchase other products] is what we're after." In the cost-focused BPO world, the key operating metric for Richard's BPO support might be "increase the number of policies per headcount by 15 percent." Richard's caution about the need to balance cost with service illustrates that increasingly, however, this is far from sufficient. Rather than a blunt "cost per policy," (remember that in this industry the "policy-per-headcount" metric is essentially "cost per policy") he recognized that a more effective metric was "cost per policy, *by type* of policy." After all, certain types of insurance products are inherently more valuable and more likely to lead to cross-sell opportunities than are others. Knowing which type of products lead to what types of potential new revenue streams is critical to providing the right amount of service to customers of those products. This makes sense. And this knowledge will *begin* to help Richard assess the relative value of other transactions that are increasingly part of a service-based next-generation BPO platform—for example, the number of customer mailings, number of customer calls into the center, programs to keep distribution agents happy, and so on. Any of these activities *may* be important to retaining customers and selling them more products. But, Richard was still in the dark about what activity was most likely keep his customers with his organization and how to measure it. He was getting closer, but was not yet there.

Here's some of the logic Richard went through—after much modeling, debate, and trial-and-error—to get closer to a value-based measure. If an organization decides that customer retention is *the* key lever for their financial success, and further has determined that the distribution network—the agency network—is *the* key lever for retaining customers, then what is the BPO supplier's role in the client organization's financial success? What does the BPO supplier need to do—financially, operationally, or technologically—to enhance the effectiveness of the agency network? How do the BPO supplier and the BPO client calculate the relative risk and reward for actions leading to such an increase?

What Richard found out is that delivering the agent's commission statements consistently and correctly was one of the most important steps he could take to increase customer retention. (Who would have figured *that* out?) How can Richard and his BPO provider have anticipated this in negotiating the contract? Now, having finally figured this out yet already having a service-level contract, how do you redirect resources from reducing the cost-per-policy to expediting higher quality commission statements? And from a service provider point of view, how do you know that this focus on agency commission statements is as relevant to your other customers? And, if it isn't, how are you going to scale up your operations to support such "value-based" delivery?

Granted, this was not an exhaustive example, but we've asked enough questions for it to be exhausting, and we've only scratched the surface. This example illustrates a simple, but profoundly important yet disquieting point. Namely, the language of cost is well-codified; each industry has its own version of productivity metrics that a BPO supplier can focus on to realize efficiencies through scale and standardized operations. Why is this cost-focus more codified? Because for the past 80 years large institutions have reaped the rewards of mass production and mass marketing, they have finely honed metrics for measuring and improving the efficiency of processes where the impacts of tiny changes are magnified by large volumes. Clear metrics means that SLAs can be established, measured, monitored, and written into contracts. However, *the language of value is messier.* Clear metrics do *not* exist because most companies have only within the past 15 years begun to focus meaningfully on the impact their customers bring to the relationship.

Two implications arise from this discussion. First, BPO suppliers and clients need greater transparency and flexibility so that they can understand their interdependency for servicing customers. Second, the BPO industry needs to figure out a new language—new semantics—for consistently articulating service-enhancement metrics. The cost-side of BPO operational measures is clear. It's the value-side that remains in transition. There are a number of proxy measures used. But what these measures of value are, and how they relate to specific process and technology transformation initiatives, has yet to be codified in any meaningful way. Few organizations understand their *internal* measures and levers of what creates, sustains, and perpetuates value. Given this, there cannot be, and there isn't, any agreement *across* different organizations and industry of how *to articulate* what constitutes "value" and "service" much less *measure* it consistently, and even much less *use* it as a basis of industry-wide or benchmark-based contractual agreement. Yet, as always, large challenges provide huge opportunities—which we'll discuss later. For now, it's sufficient to restate that BPO suppliers and customers will become, and are becoming, partners in figuring out their new, value-based shared semantics underlying next-generation BPO servicing and contracting arrangements.

In sum, focus on value is fundamentally different from one on cost. A cost-focus is a clean one of realizing efficiencies through scale and standardized operations. An over-the-transom relationship is possible because clear metrics and SLAs can be established, measured, and monitored. A value-focus is messier. Clear metrics do not exist. An over-the-transom relationship is not possible. Greater transparency, flexibility, and dependency are necessary between clients and suppliers. And this gives rise to the second requirement for next-generation BPO—that of *mutual visibility*.

Mutual Visibility—Again

Tim Garza, of CalPERS, recognized the need to pull the health carriers and potential BPO providers into the discussion of how to reduce his cost basis *and* improve CalPERS's service for health care enrollment. "We need mutual visibility to get what we all need out of whatever decision we take." The question was how to do so? Tim provided the initial answer: "Different organizations [CalPERS, suppliers, health care providers] had different ways of understanding what the problem was . . . so, we had to create a shared vocabulary to have meaningful discussions." Tim's comment pulls us back toward the first part of this book—and what we called the DNA of executional consistency—that of creating shared semantics.

What connects to what, where, when, how, and how much: This is the basis of knowing what different people in different parts of a business do—maybe one company, maybe a BPO supplier and a client working together—and what you can expect from them, when and how. We have seen, in Chapters 3 through 5, how Business Blueprinting creates this DNA, by extracting the shared semantics, the visibility, and the traceability—from strategy to process, from process to applications, from applications to infrastructure—to pragmatically understanding a business problem. Such understanding is increasingly critical in high-risk but potentially high-reward BPOs and business utilities. Recall, in Blueprint terms, Paul's surprise as he began to understand the runaway train and ripple effect of a poorly managed technology migration (layers 4 and 3) on his business processes, change management efforts, and eventually his strategic capability to grow his business utility (layers 2 and 1). Recall, as well, that Paul's surprise is a surprise to no one. Many have had such surprises. And many more will. This is why the BPO's marketplace evolution toward a balance between cost and customer value enhancement makes the executional consistency challenge even more critical.

Tim's initial model for creating shared semantics across the different constituencies is shown in Figures 6.5 and 6.6. The details—of the business interaction model of Figure 6.5 and the high-level process flow models of Figure 6.6—are less important than the summary of how Tim used them to create his "mutual visibility," so we won't delve into any details of the models here.

Tim used these (and other) models to bound the problem of *enrollment*. They were used to make sure that he and the team (including some of his constituents and participants) understood the processes in sufficient detail to have confidence in the outcome of their analysis. Experiential workshops and the resulting models provided a forum for different organizations to come together and "hash out" different understandings of the health care environment. More importantly, they provided a common means to express what people

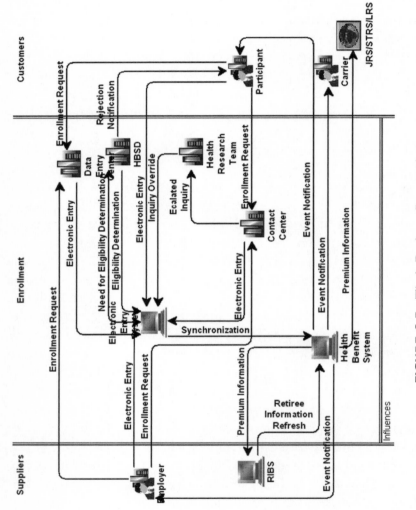

FIGURE 6.5 Tim's Business Interactions

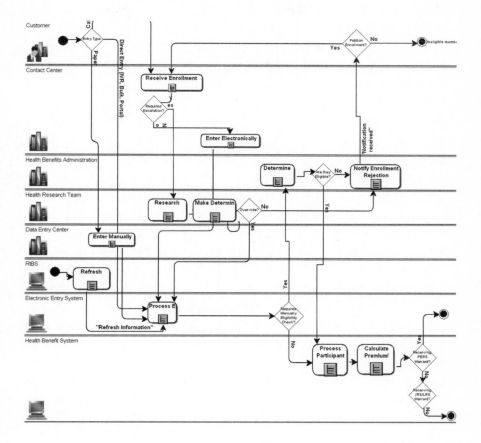

FIGURE 6.6 Drill Down

from different parts of each organization did—business people, technology people, and marketing people. Finally, drilling down into these models provided visibility to all stakeholders on the connections in the organization—the *what impacts what, when, where, how, and how much* issue. It tore off the usual veil of "I-have-no-idea-what-happens-over-there" that too often exists within organizations and thereby further strengthened the shared understandings—the shared semantics—of what had to happen, and how to make it happen.

Tim used these relatively few models in a Business Blueprint to create a shared understanding of his BPO requirements and both cost and service needs. John Conner took his own version of such models even further. As business development director at UISL, the large business processing utility we briefly met earlier in this chapter, John used the visibility provided him by his Business Blueprints to prioritize the workstreams in the considerable change program needed by Abbey Life, one of UISL's major stakeholders and customers, in what they called their "Transformation Outsourcing" effort. The Business Blueprints were used as insight into his cost *and* service metrics, and the connections needed to identify the levers that move those metrics together.

In 2003, Abbey Life realized that it had to move away from a fixed cost structure for its closed-book business. In addition, the organization had to migrate 1.75 million policies from 18 disparate 30-year-old IT systems on to one platform. But costs were not the sole criterion for Abbey Life. For them, it was equally important that John increase its customer service levels by allowing UISL consultants to identify a customer's entire portfolio of policies through using only one system. Further, Abbey Life demanded that its employees moving to John's business be well cared for and, in fact, that the employee turnover rate, a measure of employee satisfaction, decrease from its current level. "We had to reconstruct measurements to be able to compare services and our adding value to benchmark levels. [At the time], they just didn't exist . . . yet we had to be able to align them to specific programs we initiated."

Figure 6.7 depicts a typical BPO "efficiency curve," showing performance improvements mapped to each of the execution framework layers. At Abbey, the new SLAs—with approximately 60 monthly metrics—have been consistently achieved. Niels Tointon, Abbey Life's director of operations, reports that the service levels consistently achieved in excess of 98 percent even where the service level threshold is 95 percent. In addition, the turnover of employees (remember, this was a key requirement) was cut from 18 percent to just 6 percent during the first year of the contract. Commented Niels, "Their [UISL] whole culture is about good service and can-do approaches. . . . We've had other outsourcing experiences in the past where people didn't deliver on their commitments. But they have delivered even more than we thought they would." Aside from

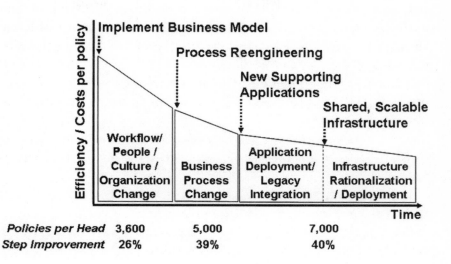

FIGURE 6.7 Example of Benefits

the service enhancements, John notes that productivity increased by 60 percent, from under 3,000 policies per head to more than 5,000. John attributes this capability to balance both service-side effectiveness with cost-side efficiencies to the "Blueprinting approach of looking at all processes and how they were directly impacted by the business strategy"—of knowing what impacts what, when, where, how, and by how much.

Making the Shift to Value

Tying together two parts of the execution framework: Business Blueprints and some form of robust change methods—like Lean Six Sigma—provide a tangible means to make possible the BPO industry transition from cost to value. The industry remains largely in the era of the win-lose contractual "crunch," with many suppliers wary of taking on new deals. Increasingly, however, both clients and suppliers are re-evaluating large-scale enterprise-type BPO deals. A recent Gartner report indicates that the "big-ticket" BPO deals are not dead, but only sleeping. The apparent sleepiness, according to Gartner, reflects that "buyers and providers understand that complex, multiyear contracts have to be revised as business conditions and strategies change. This is a positive indication that *buyers and their respective providers are working as long-term partners to ensure contracts continue to drive value for both parties.*"[18]

But we're not there yet. Current challenges remain. The following list restates some of them:

- The win-lose contractual "crunch" is alive and well—causing both clients and suppliers to reevaluate large-scale enterprise type BPO deals and structures.

- The supplier side remains fraught with huge financial losses—Paul's €170 million loss and EDS's billion dollar loss are two of many possible cautionary tales as the growth in the marketplace continues to heat up, drawing in new providers and leading to an initial round of consolidation among suppliers.[19]

- Clarity over the language of value is becoming clearer on the client side; but this has yet to be translated into understanding between the client and supplier at any scale. The language of cost take-out exists, with agreed-on semantics and established benchmarks. The language of value creation remains largely nascent. But as examples cited throughout this chapter show, such language is potentially understandable and definitely codifiable. In more technical language, the language of value remains unformalized, but based on lessons and insights of our execution framework and semantic stack, not unformalizable.

- Success in next-generation BPO requires juggling lots of "stuff," including cost reduction, service improvement, value enhancement, investment, and timing. Knowing how this "stuff" impacts one another is critical. After all, the wedge, the bull's-eye, and the peak are dangerous effects requiring deft navigation. Knowing what connects with what, when, where, how, and how much—using Business Blueprinting to identify these connections and Lean Six Sigma to measure their impacts and find the levers to push—are crucial sextants for that navigation.

- Next-generation BPO recognizes that the arm's-length relationships of early BPOs cannot work. Increasingly, both client and supplier organizations recognize that their core competency will depend on creating different types of collaborative structures. There is no one-size-fits-all; collaborative structures differ depending on specific business objectives, each with their own time horizon and risk profile. No company can go it alone anymore. Business opportunities move too quickly and the risks of attempting to do it all by yourself are too great. Consequently, the capability to enter into different types of collaborative structures, and to do so effectively and quickly is becoming a vital skill for all organizations. And such "collaborative capabilities" are becoming even more critical given (1) the wide range of business processes being considered for outsourcing, (2) that some of the processes being outsourced include those that are key jewels of a business, such as any customer service or any that create clear value; and (3) that the numbers of options of locations and providers to handle the outsourcing are growing—all of which are broadening the types of outsourcing models and business arrangements that can, if appropriately set up, work.[20]

• Value enhancement remains poorly understood but has rich opportunities with significant implications, for (1) true partnership based on transparency, trust, and win-win deals; (2) alternative goals than simple cost reduction; and (3) consideration of BPO for areas that move closer and closer to the "core value" of a client organization and/or impact the customer areas more directly.

The BPO market continues to grow at a healthy rate, despite its apparent sleepiness. Worldwide BPO services will grow from $110 billion in 2002 to $173 billion in 2007, a 9.5 percent compound annual growth rate.[21] So, this remains an industry in transition. As the Gartner quote emphasizes, and as the examples of Trevor, John, Niels, Tim, and even Paul illustrate, there is much energy moving to push the pre-tipping points over to an sustainable state with win-win contracts, where the focus remains as much on value creation as on cost efficiencies.

What This Means to You

1. *What is the value of BPO versus keeping the work in-house?* Answering this question comes down to a straightforward consideration.

Will the benefits to be gained from using a BPO be greater than the costs and the risks undertaken by doing so? Second, do you have the capabilities and resources to respond quickly to market shifts, or are there collaborative arrangements—ranging from alliances to BPOs— that could quickly be put in place to do so? Third, how can you most effectively make sure your core value to your customers is well supported? Can you outsource its support and be able to maintain your service levels and competitive position? These appear to be clear considerations. They get murkier as you work through the timeframe of the benefits to be gained and the types of underlying risks that need to be managed. For example, is there an immediate need to get certain costs out or service levels up? Asking these questions is easy. Answering them is less so. An easy initial answer, however, is to keep, what Geoffrey Moore calls "core" activities in-house—those important to drive value and differentiation—and outsource everything else.[22] Gartner confirms this stance in a recent report in which they state, "Enterprises around the world are attempting to focus their investments on their core business processes and are increasingly looking at outsourcing noncore business processes."[23] Yet, increasingly, and given the market volatility, from economic downturns to just plain uncertainty, having the flexibility to either scale upward or downward quickly by using third-party providers is becoming an important option—for either core or noncore activities. But again, the decision of what and how much to outsource keeps coming back to the balance among benefits to be gained, in what timeframe, and with what willingness to carry what risk profile.

2. *How will next-generation BPO be achieved? What is it based on? Will the transition to it likely be successful? What are the requirements of making it past the pretipping point tipping point?* Next-generation BPO focuses as much on delivering service-based value as on reducing costs. Admittedly, this sounds like marketing blather. But a sharp distinction emerges between the focus on value and cost when you look at the number and the maturity of the metrics underlying each of these objectives. Reducing costs clearly results from driving inefficiencies out and unit prices down. There are well-established benchmarks and methods to realize such efficiencies and monitor their effectiveness—on the cost side. However, such clarity does not exist

on the value side. Think about it. What *is* value? And what does it mean for your customers and for your organization? Debates rage on this topic, over and over again. Just think about how many meetings, projects, articles, seminars, books, and working sessions are devoted to answering this question. The semantics of value simply are not as codified as they are for cost. Consequently, any next-generation BPO effort based on providing value has to wrestle with creating the "shared semantics of value measurement" across different organizations each with their own understanding of what constitutes value. Only then can the discussion of how to measure that value be had. Compound the difficulty here with creating an industry benchmark and methods to monitor value in a business utility and the difficulty of how to make next-generation BPOs work becomes painfully clear.

Taking this a step further, compound the "lack of language around value metrics" issue with the basic problems we discussed earlier around BPO—the risks of the wedge, the bull's eye, and the peak effects—all of which give rise to the win-lose contractual "crunch." Until win-win relationships actually materialize through operations, rather than are simply promised during negotiations, all of the talk around next-generation BPO remains just that: talk.

3. *What are the trends for the BPO industry?* There are five possible directions for the BPO industry. Any of these is equally likely given where we are in the BPO transition period.

First, the win-lose contractual "crunch" continues. This direction has, after all, a long tail based on previous and many current contractual commitments focused on cost and standard service metrics. The upshot here is that BPO clients will continue to win and suppliers lose in this situation with change control disputes becoming an increasingly bitter battleground. As more BPO deals lose money and as the reasons for those losses become clearer, both clients and suppliers will get smarter and smarter about how to price deals. As this happens, the true costs of BPO operations will become transparent and the structural win-lose situation will start to break down. Currently, in the majority of BPO deals, there is a winner (usually the client) and a loser (usually the supplier). However, commerce cannot continue on a win-lose basis. So, fundamentally, there is no sound business rationale for sustained BPO business as it is currently structured. Having only one party happy with a contractual outcome is no basis for sustained business. New players are aggressively entering the BPO marketplace, exploiting the conflicts and confusions regarding what will happen to the industry. The question is: How long can this situation last? Yet, given the long tail of BPO contracts, it could last awhile.

Second, a rebalancing occurs whereby clients and suppliers look to create win-win situations for existing BPO operations. Rather than a win-lose situation, recognition of the importance of a "partnership" in more than name comes to the fore. In this situation, organizations accept that they cannot go it alone if they want to be sufficiently responsive to fast-moving business opportunities. Consequently, becoming both responsive and competent with respect to different forms of collaborative ventures, including different types of BPO arrangements, becomes critical. Both of these—recognition that organizations can't do everything themselves anymore and that collaboration becomes an important and strategic capability—means that sharing benefits rather than taking advantage of your partner becomes a key focus of your negotiations.

Third, BPO extends into clear value creation models—giving rise (really) to win-win arrangements with new financial models. This extension recognizes that service and price are still key. However, other important areas that drive growth for the client—such as customer retention, are included as well. The promise to focus as much on service enhancement as on cost reduction will be difficult to keep—as discussed earlier. But, as also discussed throughout this chapter, there is solid momentum to overcome the win-lose constraints. New financial models for win-win are included in contracts as well—such as sharing and understanding the drivers of embedded value. Clients and suppliers can then manage cost and ring-fence resources and investments to deliver the value increase.

Fourth, business utilities emerge as a viable option to support multiple client organizations. The business utility concept is the next-generation BPO value proposition on steroids. Here, a service provider operates an operation for a given industry on behalf of several client organizations. Sure, the coexistence of customized services within a utility delivery model sounds like an oxymoron at first. However, focus on (1) standard processing; (2) single and integrated technology; and (3) consistent metrics and metrics management exist as do platforms, processes, and procedures to support them. We've already discussed the existence of codified semantics around costs and the movement toward creating shared semantics around value. We've also provided a number of examples about the execution framework—the Blueprinting layers and Lean Six Sigma—designed to make execution consistent, pragmatic, and measurable. Again, knowing what connects with what, when, where, how, and by how much—across all layers of your organization is crucial in a utility. The problems of semantic disconnects—of how people understand and consequently do stuff differently—is significant in any one organization. Multiply this exponentially in a utility and you end up with an exploding junior high-school "rumor" game with far bigger financial impacts. What is particularly critical about business utilities is the amount and type of investment and management into creating such utility platforms. Up-front investments into such platforms are critical to create the standardization and needed repeatability to drive down the cost equations yet the flexibility to respond to the value-based needs as well.

Fifth, BPO and next-generation BPO decline in relevance. We cannot discount the reality of this possibility. Both BPO and next-generation BPO could decline as customers and/or suppliers fail to make the model work and customers take or are forced to take the contracts back in-house. Scott's decision to take all of their BPO and outsourcing work back into UBS was a shot across the bow to the industry, expressing a concern about the arrangements being able to meet the service and cost expectations while managing risk sufficiently. Other examples of call centers being brought back in-house, the result of customer complaints regarding poor or perhaps uneven service support, provide another shot across the industry's bow. In addition, the very real and very hard problems that give rise to the win-lose situations have not been resolved. Whether they are, and how well they are resolved, will go far to determine if this possibility comes to the foreground or remains a growling option in the background. The EDS-Navy contract example was a hard eye-opener for all suppliers; next time; the supplier might not survive intact from such a dramatic financial loss. If this were to happen, the industry and clients would receive a hard wake-up call.

In Closing

We don't know which of these possibilities will come to pass. There are activities pushing in the direction of all of them. What we do know, however, is that "taking action" *on any* of them requires first being able to "make sense" *of all* of them. There is much noise around BPO and its transition as an industry. We have attempted to cut through the BPO noise, to isolate key issues and constraints, trends and possibilities. We have attempted to do so by showing yet another example of how our "pragmatic execution framework" can help to "make sense" and "take action" of whichever possibility emerges and how you can begin to get more benefit out of your BPO considerations and actions. Knowing *what connects to what, when, where, how, and how much*—part I of our pragmatic execution framework—and knowing which levers to push to measure and monitor their results—part II of our framework—are pragmatic steps to help you assess which of these possibilities are likely to occur. They are equally important to help you get more benefit out of your BPO considerations or actions. As Tim Garza of CalPERS put it, "getting the shared semantics from everyone of what has to get done is where we need to start." It is the DNA of executional consistency and the start of "making sense" and of "taking action" around BPO and its evolution.

Chapter Cheat Sheet

The Issue

The BPO industry is going through a significant transition. There is much noise about the needs of, the requirements for, and the imperatives to exploit BPO and what is being called "next-generation BPO." Yet, how do you "make sense" of all this noise to figure out how to "take action" of BPO, effectively—or do you?

The Insight

Next-generation BPO focuses as much on delivering service-based value as on reducing costs. Admittedly, this sounds like marketing blather. But a sharp distinction emerges between the focus on value and cost when you look at the number and the maturity of the metrics underlying each of these objectives. Reducing costs clearly results from driving inefficiencies out and unit prices down. There are well-established benchmarks and methods to realize such efficiencies and monitor their effectiveness—on the cost side. However, such clarity does not exist on the value side. Think about it. What *is* value? And what does it mean for your customers and for your organization? *The semantics of value simply are not as codified as they are for cost.* Consequently, any next-generation BPO effort based on providing value has to wrestle with creating the "shared semantics of value measurement" across different organizations each with their own understanding of what constitutes value. Only then can the discussion of how to measure that value be had. Compound the difficulty here with creating an industry benchmark and methods to monitor value in a business utility and the difficulty of how to make next-generation BPOs work becomes painfully clear.

(Continued)

The Phrases

Business Process Outsourcing (BPO); Business Utilities; the Contractual Crunch; Wedge Effect; Bull's-eye Effect; Peak Effect

The Implications

Shifting from a cost-focus to a balanced cost/value-focus creates two immediate challenges. The first is the language issue—of how *even to characterize* much less measure what constitutes value. The second is the visibility issue—of knowing how to align different parts of the organization, and different efforts, in a manner that is as clear and tangible as it is critical. Solving these two problems is crucial to make the transition to next-generation BPO possible, and successful.

Neither the balance between how to manage costs *and* enhance service nor how to effectively define what constitutes "value" has been sufficiently figured out. The BPO suppliers that figure it out will grab significant market share and add a powerful new tool to their competitive arsenal; their clients will gain a business advantage from a win-win relationship; and *their* respective customers will benefit from more effective, more relevant, and more useful service.

Secure Global Commerce . . . Managing the Tension between "Assured" and "Agile" Commerce

Setting the Stage: Mutual Visibility and Mutual Dependency

Wal-Mart did it again. In early 2004, Wal-Mart, the giant U.S.-based retailer ($230 billion, 4 percent of the U.S. gross domestic product), made a simple policy statement that would shake the world of commerce. By January 2005, it would expect its top 100 suppliers to use radio frequency identification (RFID) tags on cases and pallets headed for stores in the Dallas/Fort Worth region, with plans to use the technology at 150 stores by the end of 2005, and in all of its stores soon thereafter. Shortly after Wal-Mart's decision to mandate use of RFID, several other large retailers—including Target and Albertson's in the United States, Tesco ($37 billion) and Metro ($48 billion) in Europe—jumped on the bandwagon. The result? IDC estimates that spending on RFID in the retail supply chain in the United States will experience compound annual growth rate of 70 percent over the next five years, from $91.5 million in 2003 to $1.3 billion in 2008.

Why? According to Linda Dillman, Wal-Mart's CIO, "The technology will help us know where inventory is all the time. . . . That will help improve our shelf management, so we can make sure merchandise is available when it's needed. That, in turn, could increase our sales, as well as sales of our suppliers. Cost savings isn't the primary benefit for us of RFID, keeping goods in stock is. We'll see better tracking and moving of inventory, faster receiving and shipping, improved quality inspection, fewer out-of-stock items resulting in improved shopper satisfaction, greater predictability in product demand, and better value for the shopper as efficiencies occur."[1]

The U.S. Transportation Command (USTRANSCOM), headquartered at Scott Air Force Base, Illinois, is another organization that needs to know where its inventory is all the time. USTRANSCOM is tasked with the responsibility of tracing, from origin (depot or vendor) to destination, the identity, status, and location of Department of Defense (DOD) cargo during peace or war. It maintains a capability they call *In Transit Visibility*, (ITV) to fulfill the mission of increasing inventory controls, increasing productivity and operational efficiencies, ensuring timely delivery into the field, and reducing the amount of materiel in the supply chain. ITV extends from "factory to foxhole" tracking the movement of over 300,000 shipments per year in more than 45 countries. This capability is used not only for cargo; it is also used to track passengers, medical patients, and personal property.

In November 2002, the Transportation Security Administration (TSA) provided $28 million in funding for something it called Operation Safe Commerce (OSC), a pilot program with the ultimate goal of improving the security of container shipments. OSC pilots targeted all components of the supply chain, including the three largest container ports of entry in the United States (Los Angeles/Long Beach, New York/New Jersey, and Seattle/Tacoma), overseas suppliers and ports, and the shipping lines used to transport cargo. According to Senator Patty Murray, chair of the Senate Transportation Appropriations Subcommittee, "Securing America's ports is essential for protecting our homeland, which is why I developed Operation Safe Commerce and pushed it through Congress. Container traffic is critical to the health of our economy, but we do not know enough about what is in the more than six million containers that enter our nation each year. This initiative will ensure the security of the containers that will pass through our ports and on to America's highways and railways. TSA and Customs should be commended for taking this important step and I look forward to continuing to work with them on this and other initiatives."

Given politicians' penchant for hyperbole, it's reasonable to be skeptical. How critical, really, is this container traffic? Consider this statement by a senior executive of a Fortune 50 company for the answer: ". . . if an act of terrorism were committed using one of our containers, we believe it would be a company-ending event."[2] One act of terrorism in its supply chain could destroy this 100+-year-old company. Finally, consider this: In early 2004, Italian authorities found a suspected al-Qaeda member inside a sealed container headed for Canada, and in March, following a double suicide attack in which 10 port workers lost their lives, an Israeli security official at the Ashdod Port discovered a secret compartment in an incoming container that had already passed inspection. Israeli security experts suspected that the shipping container was used to smuggle the two suicide bombers into the heavily secured Ashdod Port. This, and many, many other similar examples could be cited in mind-numbing yet shocking detail.

What do all of these things have in common? They involve the global supply chain, the largely unnoticed network by which goods move across the world—from raw materials to finished goods, to wholesalers, retailers, business users, and consumers. Securing the global supply chain is a cause for real concern to all citizens of the world, to countries who find themselves in the crosshairs of terrorist interest, to businesses whose very existence is vulnerable to a single heinous supply chain incident, to companies whose products are counterfeited and sold throughout the world—sometimes costing them money, sometimes costing lives. Creating an agile, transparent supply chain is critical for businesses that need to sustain access to their goods, that need to reduce cost, and that need to know where things are all of the time.

Making sense of this sprawling, pervasive thing requires understanding (1) processes that can stretch from a factory in Karachi, Pakistan, to a rack of shirts at a retailer in Peoria, Illinois; (2) data making these processes work that passes through, on average, 25 different organizations along the way; and the (3) physical goods that are packed, unpacked, repacked, shipped, stored, inspected, and used multiple times by multiple companies.[3] *Taking action* means making strategic, process, and technology changes at potentially every step along the way to build in visibility and security. Most of our examples to this point have been contained within an enterprise (e.g., the unemployment division of Chapter 5 or global cash business of Chapter 4), or the relationships between two enterprises (e.g., the BPO examples of Chapter 6). In contrast, Secure Commerce, also called Visible Commerce, touches workers, families, businesses, and governments on every continent, every air route, every waterway, and every roadway.

The Extent of the Challenge: "Here, There, and Everywhere"

Every year, 80 percent of the world's cargo—5.8 billion tons—moves among the world's top seaports. It is carried aboard 46,000 vessels, filling 200 million sea cargo containers with goods that go in and out of 4,000 global ports. In the United States alone, seven million containers enter ports annually. Making it more granular, 21,000 containers are off-loaded in U.S. ports, every day, bringing in more than $2 billion worth of cargo. In 2002, nearly 202,800 U.S. importers received goods from more than 178,200 foreign exports via liner shipping. There are four million containers in use at any given time throughout the United States. This nearly incomprehensible amount of traffic is predicted to *quadruple* in the next 20 years as imports and exports continue to increase, and as more companies manufacture products and parts offshore.

75 Days, 25 Hands

The world's cargo traffic is big, complex, and touches virtually everything. Figure 7.1 shows a typical import/export transaction based on an actual flow of a retail manufacturing and distribution Fortune 100 company. Note that these goods pass through many hands on their way from first source to final destination.[4] The point here is simple: The goods; the containers the goods are in; and the trucks, trains, airplanes, and ships that may be used to move the containers are open to disruption at every step along the way.

The transaction in Figure 7.1 spans half the globe, five countries, four modes of conveyance, one canal, and three seas:

Day	Action
0	A purchase order for 600 cartons of shirts is cut.
1	The purchase order is received, and the order, containing 75,000 shirts, is filled over the next month by a contract manufacturer.
2–24	Cartons of finished goods are delivered by truck to the consolidation warehouse.

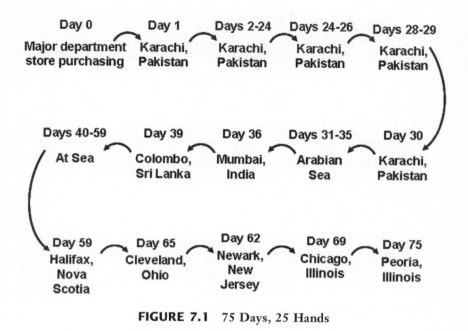

FIGURE 7.1 75 Days, 25 Hands

Day	Action
24–26	The consolidation warehouse loads cartons into a 20-foot container, then seals the container using a barrier seal and indicator tape.
28–29	A container truck picks up the loaded container and transports it to the Qasim International Container Terminal.
30	The container is checked into Port Qasim. There, after being released by customs and terminal authorities, it is loaded on to the "feeder vessel."
31–35	The feeder vessel heads for Sri Lanka by way of Mumbai, India.
36	The vessel arrives at Mumbai Port. After discharging some containers, the vessel then departs for Sri Lanka.
39	Vessel arrives at the Colombo Port in Sri Lanka. There the shipping container is transloaded from the feeder vessel to the "mother vessel" bound for the United States.

Day	Action
40–59	The mother vessel sails 18 to 19 days to Halifax, Nova Scotia, traveling through the Suez Canal, across the Mediterranean, then across the Atlantic.
59	The mother vessel arrives in Nova Scotia. Some of its containers are discharged. The vessel then departs for the final leg of its journey to the United States.
62	The mother vessel arrives at the Port of New York/New Jersey where the container is offloaded. After customs and terminal release, a painstaking process for any container from South Asia, it is then hoisted onto a container truck.
65	The container arrives by truck at the distribution center. Here, officially taking control, the shipper breaks the seal, unloads the container, and updates the warehouse receiving system.
69	Three hundred cartons of shirts arrive by truck at the warehouse of the major department store. The cartons are received and stored, to be shipped when a store requests it.
75	Final store delivery—the shirts are removed from the carton and placed on sale for $24.99, about 11 weeks after they were ordered.

The basic challenges of securing cargo from its foreign export facility to its final destination stem from:

- *Multiple participants and breakpoints:* Securing of physical assets and information flow typically involves 25 different entities. At each point, there are many opportunities for security breaches, not only within each entity, but also during the exchange of both physical assets and information.

- *Isolated security solutions:* Today's infrastructure and solutions have potentially fatal gaps because they are focused on the isolated "nodes"—specific in-transit places—rather than on integrated "in-process places and processes" that have robust, and effective, security demands.

- *Assured process, personnel, and facility security:* Even with a hypothetical "perfect technology solution," ensuring the security of employees, processes, and facilities remains a formidable (and some would argue, fruitless) task.

- *No integrated liability:* No one firm is either responsible or liable for ensuring complete cargo security.
- *Lack of effective cyber security:* Transactional, communication, and data stores remain insecure.

Of the approximately seven million containers that enter U.S. ports annually, only a small percentage are checked. Admiral James Loy, former administrator of the Transportation and Security Administration has said, "Maritime shipments represent about 95 percent of all non-NAFTA commerce in the United States and contribute almost $1 trillion to U.S. gross domestic product. However, they also represent a major vulnerability to domestic security. The millions of un-inspected cargo containers that enter U.S. ports every year represent a gaping hole in border security."[5] We cite these statistics not to be alarmist, but to emphasize that in terms of *making sense*, then *taking action*, securing the global trade lanes is an enormously complex business problem that doesn't admit simple answers. The ports of the United States can't possibly inspect every one of the seven million containers they handle each year, and with 200 million containers shipped globally each year, the ports of the world won't be inspecting 100 percent of their shipments either.[6]

Yet, what happens if security breaks down along the way and an incident happens? Recall the comment of a senior executive of a Fortune 50 company: ". . . if an act of terrorism was committed using one of our containers, we believe it would be a company-ending event . . ." A 2004 study by research company IDC underlines that the most compelling reason for enterprises to adopt safe commerce is that a breach in security at the port can affect their corporate reputation, brand, and bottom line. Says a supply chain manager of a major manufacturer cited in the report, "The more you secure your supply chain for greater velocity, the more you increase your costs. Anything that slows our materials down from coming into the country costs us money." According to the Brookings Institution, a weapon of mass destruction shipped via one of these containers could have a $1 trillion impact on the U.S. economy.[7] Any such incident would send profound ripples throughout the world economy. As evidence, recall the 2002 closing of West Coast seaports in the United States. That labor action is estimated to have cost the U.S. economy $1 billion per day, and its effects were felt throughout the United States and all the way to Shanghai.[8] Here's a breakdown of impacts resulting from the 10-day port closure:

> *Week 1:* Approximately half of the total trade volume from Asia—$200 billion of cargo aboard 200 ships, idles off the West Coast. Supply chains report inventory shortages, leading to plant closures. Just-in-time deliveries are not on time. Air cargo increases, especially for small, light, high-value goods such as electronics.
>
> *Week 2:* Meat-processing facilities across the United States are paralyzed. Twenty-nine thousand metric tons (that's $90 million) of Tyson Foods beef and pork spoils on the docks. One hundred forty-two thousand cartons of Asia-bound Valencia oranges have to be either repackaged, at substantial expense, or juiced for significantly lower value. Another 20,000 cartons of oranges spoil on the docks and must be discarded.
>
> *One month later:* After the ports reopen toward the end of Week 2, there are still 90 ships queued, waiting to be unloaded as the port works off the backlog from a two-week closure.
>
> *Four months later:* Parts shortages prevent the completion of some 18,000 U.S. vehicles, and there are 50,000 fewer Toyotas in the lots of dealers across the United States.

A 10-day closure. Well over $1 billion in losses to the companies and people connected in some way to the goods that were supposed to have moved in and out of the ports. Over $80 million in lost wages to U.S. workers. Over $58 million in higher prices to U.S. consumers. Now, imagine if the closure were due not to action by employers or employees, but rather due to the detonation of a weapon of mass destruction shipped in a container.[9]

The answer to this enormous, complex, critical, high-impact business challenge is not inspection after-the-fact. In the best traditions of Lean thinking, the answer is to understand the processes at work and improve the processes to add in security and visibility at every step. Operation Safe Commerce provides an illustration of what some companies are doing to strengthen the visibility and security of their global supply chains—not as "the" answer, but the start of "an" answer to strengthen their supply chains given the new requirements for more security yet maintaining the need for speed to get to market.

Operation Safe Commerce: Starting Steps of a Long Journey

Operation Safe Commerce has a simple but profound goal: to create global business processes with significantly reduced catastrophic risks—by making it so hard to put the wrong things into the supply chain that the likelihood of being able to introduce a weapon of mass destruction, a terrorist, or, for that matter, counterfeit consumer goods into a shipping container becomes very small. When the processes become that robust, critically supported by technology, the number of inspections occurring at ports will no longer be the sole, critical step of the process. Security will increase, and at the same time, the burden on ports will decrease.

As with any large, thorny problem, this one can't wait for all the detailed analysis to be complete before some parts of a solution go into place (remember the discussion of "many moving parts" of Chapter 6). So, in parallel with launching Operation Safe Commerce, the U.S. government undertook other initiatives that effectively began the work of Process Optimization of this sprawling set of business processes. In January 2002, U.S. Customs launched the Container Security Initiative (CSI) to help prevent global container-ized cargo from being exploited by terrorists. In 2003, the newly formed Customs and Border Patrol (CBP) agency under the Department of Homeland Security (DHS), launched its Customs-Trade Partnership Against Terrorism (C-TPAT) program, a government/business collaboration that specifies import standards for importers and carriers to increase the safety of the global supply chain. Along with the preceding alphabet soup of initiatives, in 2004 the U.S. Food and Drug Administration implemented the Bio-Terrorism Act (but thankfully no new acronym) that requires registration of supply chain partners and prenotification of shipment details. And, in July 2005, the European Union imposed new regulations on the transportation of dangerous goods.

Much of the activity—most notably the actions of government agencies—to make the global supply chain more visible is related to security. As we mentioned earlier, however, there are real economic incentives for businesses. The same IDC study we mentioned earlier gives the top three benefits of visible commerce to enterprises as:

1. Reduced costs
2. Preserved brand integrity
3. Improved supplier relations

Each of these benefits ties directly to the financial performance of the business, so it's no surprise that many enterprises are making progress toward the pieces of Visible Commerce that make sense to them. Some examples include:

- *Slavenburg*, a leading construction organization, is installing a radio frequency identification (RFID) system in the World Trade Center in Amsterdam, the Netherlands. This showcase facility will demonstrate RFID technology for facilities' management creating a "smart building" and have the capability to track assets, people, and maintenance activities.

- The *U.S. Postal Service* has introduced a new wireless technology to USPS operations to increase the productivity of powered equipment, collect data about equipment operation, and control access to only those personnel with appropriate training. It leverages RFID and wireless technology to dynamically manage people and equipment, and will be installed at over 400 USPS locations.

- *General Electric Security* has created a container security solution called CommerceGuard that combines a wireless-enabled Container Security Device with a global information network to notify interested parties when a container has been secured using the Container Security Device, when an authorized person disarms or rearms the Container Security Device, and when an unauthorized person opens a container. This is an important step to a so-called "smart" container, considered a crucial link in streamlining the flow of goods through the ports by providing a so-called "green lane" of expedited processing for containers that meet certain stringent criteria for visibility from the beginning of the chain to the port. In a speech given on March 3, 2004, CBP Commissioner Robert Bonner stressed that "the smart container must make the transition from novelty item to industry best practice. This is the only way that we will be able to offer a true 'green lane' for secure trade into the United States."

• *Motorola*, which ships approximately 250 million kilos of components and finished goods per year with an estimated sales value of $36 billion, is closely analyzing its supply chain.[10] Says Janice Webb, senior vice president, "We realize that we need to take the cost out of it if we want to be more competitive and beat our peers in the industry. . . . That's the way companies are going to have wars going forward. It's going to be my supply chain against your supply chain. If you could have real-time data coming in and being filtered into your supply chain systems, such as sophisticated warehouse management systems and ERP (enterprise resource planning) systems, I think companies would be surprised what a competitive weapon that could become for them."

Corporations will be significantly impacted by the demands for more visibility and security in the supply chain. Each constituent group along the supply chain will feel the effects, especially those doing business with the Global 2000 importers of consumer products, retail, and life sciences, the "Top 20" global ports, and various government agencies such as the U.S. Transportation Security Administration (TSA) in the United States, and various Ministries of Transportation/Customs in other countries. Some probable impacts include:

- A significant increase (from 2 percent to 8 percent) in physical inspections for "nongreen-lane" goods moving through ports. Full compliance with regulations and standards to achieve "green lane" status significantly reduces the probability of physical inspections.

- An expanded requirement for source manufacturers, logistics providers, carriers, and service providers to create, document, and report on security policies and procedures, and to verify— possibly indemnify—that the trade and security information they provide is accurate.

- Increased security and encryption requirements for the information flow that parallels the physical cargo flow.
- More timely and accurate documentation of goods and shipping information.

Facing the Challenge: Turning the Tension into Harmony

Experts agree that technology is just one piece of the puzzle. "The types of solutions that have to be applied to global commerce are very complex in that they require a reconfiguration of the way technology is applied to process," says Linda Cohen, managing vice president of The Gartner Group. "It's really reinventing the processes behind the whole value chain so that you not only optimize that value chain but you secure it and you're in compliance."

So, yet again, "it's the process, stupid." In Chapters 4, 5, and 6, we saw examples of enterprises transforming themselves using our pragmatic methods to make sense and take action, often breaking down organizational silos in the process. The BPO examples in Chapter 6 added the complication of putting a business partner—a separate enterprise altogether—into the middle of a company's business processes. As that chapter explored, adding a partner adds much more complexity as the two enterprises negotiate the shared responsibilities, risks, and rewards needed to make the partnership work. Chapter 6 also makes the point that companies continue to struggle mightily (though not profitably) to make BPO work, largely because of the complexity of creating such workable agreements.

Visibility through Blueprinting

Now consider the global supply chain of a company—say the U.S.-based "SuperWidgets" company importing goods from the country of *FarAway*. (Companies are understandably wary of exposing the details of how their supply chains work, so we couch this example in terms of a generic consumer-goods company. The example is real, based on work from Operation Safe Commerce, but scrubbed to make it less personal.) As we saw earlier in the Karachi-to-Peoria supply chain, consumer goods go through many hands before making it to the retail shelves. Figure 7.2 illustrates a typical SuperWidgets supply chain—as applicable to shirts made in Pakistan, as it is to coffee beans from Brazil, or electronic parts from Taiwan.

This so-called *communication* model is a cousin of the Business Interaction Models (BIMs) we've seen earlier in the book. It's a high level abstraction, showing the different entities—for example, organizations—involved in the overall supply chain. Interactions among each of these entities are shown in BIMs and workflow models that

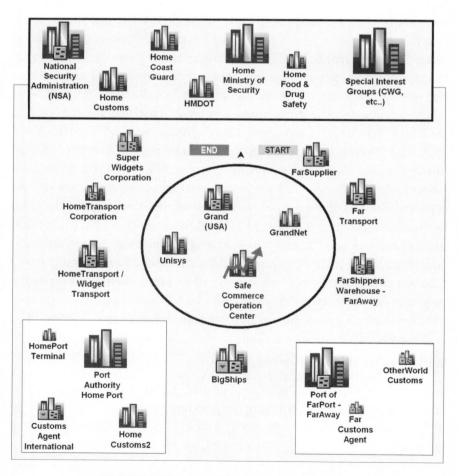

FIGURE 7.2   SuperWidgets Supply Chain

we will see soon. But at this highest level, SuperWidgets is trying to figure out how to *make sense* of Secure Commerce so it can *take action* in the best way. Especially in a complex web of interactions like the global supply chain, an "in the context of everything else" picture like Figure 7.2 shows the pieces that connect—typically via events and/or deliverables—with the chain starting in the "one o'clock" position with Far-Supplier and ending in the "eleven o'clock" position at the SuperWidgets factory. The entities in the ellipse are the things in the spotlight for SuperWidgets' concerns over securing their supply chain.

SuperWidgets knows that it needs to add visibility to its supply chain even though the regulatory details are still emerging and will continue to change into the future. Figure 7.2 is not a page in a document that SuperWidgets will put on a shelf to collect dust. It's a model, meant to be useful now and evolve with the business to be as useful in the future. It tells SuperWidget that there are things that must sit outside of any one piece of the supply chain and overlook all of the handoffs that happen clockwise around the outside. Today, those things may be the types of systems that Gerald McNerney, a senior research analyst and supply chain specialist with AMR Research, explains that many companies use, or are considering using, to provide inventory visibility and track the location of goods in the supply chain as part of their secure supply chain solution.[11] As new regulations come into play, this model, with its "supply chain on a page" perspective, lets SuperWidgets focus on those parts that will be impacted. How? Before we delve deeper into one part of this supply chain, we need to explain a critical element of the complexity of the SuperWidgets' supply chain overall and how Business Blueprinting helps us cope with this complexity.

A company like SuperWidgets might have hundreds or even thousands of supply chains due to its large product line and many different suppliers. Each of these supply chains is as similar in many ways as it is unique in others. For example, the supply chain shown in Figure 7.2 starts in *FarAway*, and comes through *Home Port*. If *FarAway* represents a high-risk country like Pakistan (this is from a U.S. perspective; remember that we said SuperWidgets is a U.S. company with their own specific perspectives and understandings of what makes up high risk), then its containers will have to meet some stringent conditions to get the green-lane status explained earlier. If *FarAway* represents a country that is considered less risky, like Germany, the conditions for green-lane status are likely to be less stringent. Similarly, *Home Port* could represent the Port of New York/New Jersey or the port of Long Beach. Each of these ports has its own unique ways of processing cargo—though, of course, they share many similarities as well. We could make the same observation for every one of the nine entities around the supply chain of Figure 7.2.

The communication model in Figure 7.2 is one of approximately 50 models—including BIMs, process models, organization models, and workflow models—that capture this supply chain. According to Hari Chaturvedi, the senior business architect who led the modeling effort for the Operation Safe Commerce pilot projects,[12] Blueprinting the Visible Commerce solution for this first supply chain was an 8-week effort including site visits to *FarAway*, *Home Port*, and *FarPort*, interviews with key stakeholders at those locations, and work by a Blueprinting team to model the entire supply chain. However, Hari's team then went on to Blueprint three other supply chains for Operation Safe Commerce—one more for "SuperWidgets," and two others for two different U.S.-based companies—that moved different goods through different ports. Hari reports that Blueprinting Operation Safe Commerce took five weeks for the second supply chain, three weeks for the third, and only two weeks for the fourth. Each subsequent Blueprint was easier to create because it leveraged the commonalities from the Blueprints created earlier. Hari estimates that, in Blueprinting two different SuperWidgets supply chains, his team captured more than 80 percent of the variations in SuperWidgets, so it would be a manageable effort to extend the Blueprints to cover all of the SuperWidgets supply chains.

To what end? To codify the processes—the flow of goods, but also, critically, the flow of information—so that making sense of inevitable future changes can be easily evaluated in the Business Blueprint. So too, then, can the scope and impact of taking action become much easier to both anticipate and manage. Also, critically from the perspective of SuperWidgets, but also for the overall security of the supply chain, having a clear picture of who does what, where, when, and how, where changes need to occur, and *who will bear the cost* becomes a critical part of cutting through the noise and obfuscation—okay, the crap—that too often surrounds these conversations and limits what actually gets done.

Not surprisingly, that last piece, "who will bear the cost," is an obstacle to global implementation of supply chain security measures. "Who will bear the cost" is a question for any new initiative. It is a question creating significant tension, according to Gerald Woolever, a 35-year veteran of the U.S. Coast Guard, now senior vice president for homeland security operations at Innovative Logistics Techniques, "between the people in the ports, the carriers, and the transporters, who don't necessarily want to bear the expense of buying the technology and putting these procedures in place, and the government, which is trying to pass the cost down to the people in the supply chain."[13]

How the costs of securing the supply chain will be spread remains unclear at this point. What is clear, however, is that companies can gain business benefits from making their supply chains generally more visible. Recent estimates have found that companies with the most effective supply chains realize a compound annual growth rate in their market capitalization between 7 percent and 28 percent higher than their industry averages.[14] This is nothing to sneeze at. Yet, this was also prior to the introduction of new security requirements that add friction to the supply chain. The need for both speed *and* security in the supply chain creates an inherent tension that businesses and the agencies that regulate them must manage. By implementing Visible Commerce solutions, and by creating Business Blueprints of those solutions, companies will be able to manage the tension more effectively, for a simple reason: They will gain the insights into what really occurs, and where and how it really does so. Such visibility is critical to meet both the security requirements and minimize the risks of not knowing what is done, where it is done, and how it is done.

Recall the import/export transaction of Figure 7.1? The cargo was supposedly "at sea" from days 40 through 59. What happened during this time? According to corporate executives of this chain, not much. After all, it takes a long time to get from Colombo and Halifax, from one ocean to another. But Hari found something that stunned everyone: The ship actually docked in the Maldives—not for long, but for long enough to pick up some additional cargo from smaller ships passing through. It's common enough for a ship to make a quick stop like this, reflecting the "you scratch my back and I'll scratch yours" attitude of the sea-faring fraternity. But *common enough* does not equate to *secure enough*. And it certainly does not meet the requirements of a Fortune 50 company attempting to optimize and secure its supply chain. This insight into what "really happens" certainly motivated the company to recognize and embrace Visible Commerce to manage the inherent tension between optimized processes and security initiatives.

Visible Commerce and Connectivity

Making visible what is far too often invisible is critical to these supply chain processes; the risks of the unknowns are far too great not to tackle head on. Optimizing through digging and challenging, through understanding and changing is hard, sure, but it's the only way of finding those extra stops in the Maldives. Knowing *what connects with what, when, where, how, and how much* builds the shared and executable understandings needed for visibility; it increases the likelihood of managing the tension between what you *will* do to meet security requirements, and what you *must* do for competitive speed.

Blueprinting your processes—codifying that tacit knowledge that runs rampant throughout organizations—makes implementing the changes needed, at the scale needed, more manageable. For example, consider the BIM in Figure 7.3. It shows the interactions among the eight entities involved in port operations, only one of which is SuperWidgets. This gets to the heart of Linda Cohen's earlier observation: "It's really reinventing the processes behind the whole value chain, so that you not only optimize that value chain, but you secure it and you're in compliance." Secure Commerce is going to change these processes.

Figure 7.4 shows the same port operations but with a conceptual safe commerce solution installed, coordinating the information flow as envisioned by emerging regulations. The extra interactions are clear, easily modified to track changes in regulations, and there's something to point to when arguing about who should pay for it!

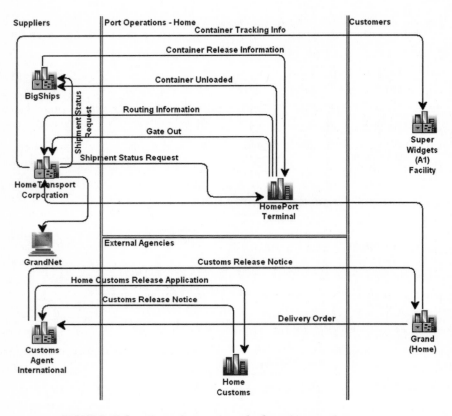

FIGURE 7.3 Port Operations before Secure Commerce

Making your supply chain visible requires optimizing processes within your business and across your entire supply chain. Regulations affecting the supply chain and the technology used to implement it will continue to be moving targets and consequently will have differing impacts at different times. Visibility will be a competitive strength in helping you not only anticipate but also respond to these moving targets. As with many examples in this book, the supply chain has to stay up and running all of the time, even while you're modernizing it. Besides, details of your supply chain are of interest not only to you but to others as well: regulators of your government, possibly other governments in countries where you do business, your suppliers, and, of course, your customers. All of this

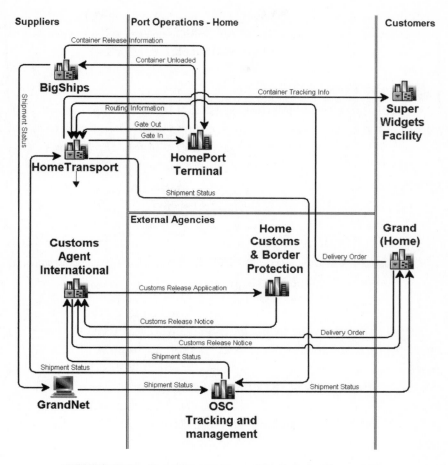

FIGURE 7.4 Port Operations after Secure Commerce

makes it doubly important to use Blueprinting. Not only will such codification help to make your business/technology interactions more effective (for reasons we've covered elsewhere) but the resulting visibility required by the security initiatives will make it easier to navigate the inevitable regulatory thickets that will only get thicker.

For all the reasons we've seen, Visible Commerce is particularly challenging for business processes and information flows. Blueprinting helps make sense of these processes and flows and complex interactions and from there to take action. Specific business benefits result:

- *In-transit visibility:* Visible Commerce starts with tracking and tracing—the ability to know what's where at all times and where it has been—and virtual warehousing, which extends visibility beyond organizational walls and allows near real-time in-transit inventory allocation.

- *Anticounterfeiting:* Prevention (stopping counterfeiting before it happens), detection (finding counterfeits already introduced into the supply chain), and response (triggers and actions when threats are detected or suspected).

- *Secure supply chain:* New processes and technologies for in-transit shipment security, perimeter security, facility access and border crossings, port security, worker and visitor "credentialization," identity management, and data integrity and sharing.

- *Compliance management:* Changing regulations for international trade management and security.

Some of the most critical of these flows concern the physical security of the containers from the time they are stuffed until the time that they are unloaded by a trusted person at SuperWidgets. In remarks made at a meeting with officials from the Ports of Tacoma and Seattle on the results of the Operation Safe Commerce pilots, Senator Patty Murray made a special point of the importance of container integrity and how it needs to be built into the process rather than tacked on through after-the-fact inspections:

> . . . *it's not possible to physically inspect every container. And, simply placing a seal or a lock on each container was no guarantee that we knew what was inside when it arrived—we had to work smarter, not just harder. We needed a coordinated approach between federal agencies, the ports, shippers, operators, and shipping companies.*
>
> . . . *In many cases it was discovered that the origination point lacked access control and general security. So, now we know that cameras, biometric identification technology, and third-party inspection are necessary to ensure the product's integrity before it is loaded into a container. In other cases, it was found that the integrity of container seals wasn't verified at each point in the supply chain. If the seal has been compromised when it arrives here, it is too late. So several technologies were recommended to ensure that we know if a seal has been broken, or a container has been opened.*[15]

Stuffing a container is a relatively simple business process:

- The transport company brings an empty container to the warehouse.
- The warehouse validates the driver and the container.
- The container is weighed, then stuffed.
- The contents are verified.
- The container is weighed and sealed with a customs seal.
- Documents are generated, and off goes the container.

Figure 7.5 shows the process used by the provider in *FarAway* to stuff a container today. In this scenario, how the warehouse and transporter get a container stuffed is not something that SuperWidgets much cares about as long as the right amount of the right goods get into the container through the ports and into the SuperWidgets factory. No one else much cares either as long as the customs requirements are met.

In the world of secure commerce, however, the extra requirement of end-to-end security means that more people are paying attention to the process by which the container gets delivered, validated (along with its driver), stuffed, verified, sealed, and documented. As an example of the importance of one such additional check, the TSA has been piloting a program called Transportation Worker Identification Credential (TWIC). Admiral James Loy, the former administrator of the TSA, claimed, "[this pilot] will provide valuable information used to guide future business process and technology selection decisions." Once the pilot is complete, TWIC will issue identification—cards that contain security features such as biometrics—to government workers, contractors, and private-sector employees, such as truck drivers, who need access to secure ports and other transportation facilities. Driver verification is an important part of a system of business processes that ensure that a container remains secure from the time the empty is delivered until the driver drops it off at the port.

Extra process steps, extra people (or at least additional roles), and special skills are needed at various places along the way. Figure 7.6 shows the new process at the supplier's location with the types of

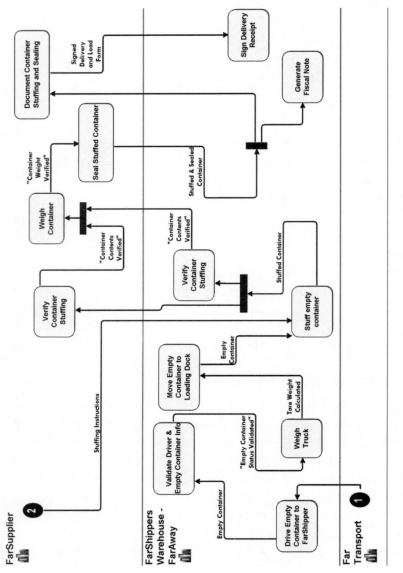

FIGURE 7.5 Stuffing Containers before Secure Commerce

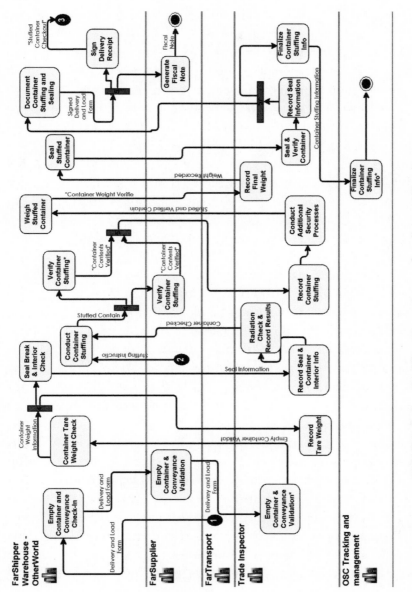

FIGURE 7.6 Stuffing Containers after Secure Commerce

241

additional activities required by the requirements of Safe Commerce. Note that there are many new activities, some performed by new roles, and substantial additional information flow. There are two new Swimlanes representing the roles of "Trade Inspector" and "OSC Tracking and Management." The trade inspector is a trusted person who checks the empty container (including an explicit check for radiation) and also seals and verifies the container seal.

The OSC Tracking and Management role is responsible for managing the information required by Secure Commerce. Who's going to actually perform this management task? The Swimlane in Figure 7.6 just calls it out as a role that needs to be performed. Recall the discussion earlier about the need to figure out who will pay for what in the new world of Secure Commerce? This is a perfect case in point, where the process models create a clear, neutral picture of what needs to be done providing the information needed for people to make business decisions.

Another additional activity in this new process flow is one conducted by the trade inspector, "Conduct Additional Security Processes." What sorts of additional security processes? Recall GE's CommerceGuard system that included a Container Security Device that we saw earlier. The additional security process might include arming a device like this to detect intrusion. The activities of the trade inspector and new technologies like CommerceGuard will require defining new job functions and training personnel to perform those functions.

From the perspective of the Secure Commerce initiative, this is a "human capital requirement" (jargon indicating a focus on "who does what") much like the one we saw in the Department of Labor example in Chapter 5. The difference is that, instead of the human capital requirements applying *within* an enterprise, Secure Commerce basically puts requirements on *external* organizations—in this example, the *FarAway* supplier's warehouse, but in general, all of the processes along the supply chain whose "to be" processes show additional Swimlanes or activities. Secure commerce must be unambiguous, which implies that its requirements will be prescriptive. The organization model in Figure 7.7 shows the "as is" organization at the *FarAway* supplier's company.

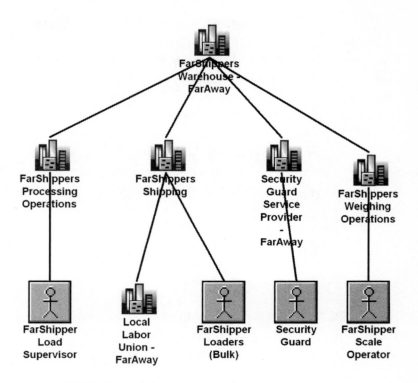

FIGURE 7.7   Impact on Warehouse Workers

Based on the new processes, there are new activities that some of these people will need to perform, and, based on the new roles, there may need for new jobs to be created. Based on the organization models, "human capital specialists" with the OSC project can devise templates for work routines and training plans to be used by suppliers generally. These can then be customized by the *FarAway* supplier. Blueprints allow the human capital people to see what the general process looks like, generally what the training will need to look like, and also to zero in on the specifics for any one supplier and thus what that supplier's training needs to look like.

Finally, there's something that might seem at first blush to be a side issue, but is actually central to the reality of SuperWidgets' business environment. Figure 7.8 shows a BIM that you get when you sum up the nine individual BIMs that describe the major operations of the SuperWidgets global supply chain:

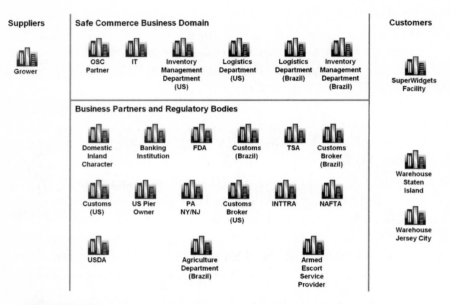

FIGURE 7.8   Making Visible What's Invisible: "Silent Partners"

- Demand for empty container
- Container stuffing
- Inland dray
- Port operations—OtherWorld
- Vessel/container movement
- Port operations—home
- Final destination home transport
- Final destination SuperWidgets' facility

What's the use of this BIM that doesn't show interactions? Taken one by one, the various interactions that a SuperWidgets import has with regulatory agencies seems small. Looking at it in this rolled-up view, we can see that regulatory agencies are a big—maybe the biggest—influence on SuperWidgets. When SuperWidgets needs something like, say, coffee beans to package with its premier coffeemaker product, it gets them from a grower in Brazil via an import/export path like the one we saw earlier between Karachi and Peoria. Before SuperWidgets can roast those beans and get them into customers homes, it may be affected by policies and regulations by U.S. agencies, like the TSA and FDA, and also by regulations from Brazilian government agencies.

Many government and quasi-government organizations exist in SuperWidgets' business environment as seen in the BIM in Figure 7.8. In the interest of *making sense*, SuperWidgets needs to know that it has these "partners" just as it needs to pay attention to what regulations they are creating and how they might affect SuperWidgets' business. Depending on how critically involved these entities are in its business, SuperWidgets might decide to create, perhaps, an "office of OSC policy," and model its direct interactions with these agencies. For example, if the TSA decides that changing the threat level from yellow to orange will change the rules used to process containers through ports, we might see SuperWidgets creating a direct interaction with the TSA to get timely notification so they can respond more quickly.

It *Is* a Small World after All

Never has global trade been more pervasive or more critical to life as we now know it. Never have economies been more interdependent or smoother functioning—at their best, seemingly flawless in their capability to deliver goods on time with extraordinary efficiency. Yet precisely because they are so tied together, supply systems—and the companies and global economies that depend on them—have never been more fragile or exposed to disruption. The speed of events and news also means that relatively local national events can quickly become global events, if not chains of events, connected in ways that even a few years ago would have seemed impossible.

This is the burden—or responsibility—of globalization. The modern supply chain is one of the great inventions in wealth-creation. However, as we saw during the 2002 West Coast port strike, the system is as fragile as it is critical, and the greater the degree of globalization, the more vulnerable the entire system is to the forces of disorganization, discontinuity, and disruption. In *The World Is Flat*, Thomas Friedman argues that the issue of "globalization versus nonglobalization" is ultimately moot: the world is "already flat"—in terms of a competitive playing field across the world.[16] A bit of a hyperbole, sure. But his point remains trenchant: the world is flat and getting flatter through an ongoing, dramatic, and fundamental transformation. Any fundamental transition entails bumps and risks; it contains as many challenges as opportunities. Knowing how to manage those bumps and risks while taking advantage of uncertainties and opportunities becomes increasingly key for those dependent on the global supply chain.

Friedman's flat world is an extraordinarily interdependent one with exacerbated risks and returns, and the global supply chain is one of its major components. The demands of Secure Commerce for "assurance" in the supply chain conflict with the ongoing business requirements of "agility" exacerbating the tension in the very core of the flat world. How a company balances this tension will impact its competitive relevance and capability to take advantage of global commerce. While multiple ways exist to balance these tensions, they all rest on the single, and stark, necessity of sharp and deep visibility of what it is that you do, where you do it, and how it gets done.

What This Means to You

1. *I don't have global supply chains, so why do I care?* Thomas Friedman's characterization of today's and tomorrow's commerce is that the "world is flat"—meaning that today's competition is based on individuals collaborating in ways that they never could before, from anyplace, anytime. The lever for this, as he points out, ". . . is not horsepower, and not hardware, but software—all sorts of new applications—in conjunction with the creation of a global fiber-optic network that has made us all next-door neighbors. Individuals must, and can, now ask, 'Where do *I* fit into the global competition and opportunities of the day, and how can *I*, on my own, collaborate with others globally?'"[17] Two points stem from this: First, we all compete within an environment; it just so happens that our competitive environment has gotten much larger, very quickly. Consequently, that

you might not have a global supply chain—with your specific suppliers providing you materials from lands far from you—does not mean that you don't face Flat World competition. Understanding *your* global—your Flat World—environment means that our discussion here on global supply chains is as relevant to globally based as well as to purely locally based organizations. Second, even if you don't buy the first argument, you probably have processes that span multiple companies, and you have relationships with government organizations. Supply chains are those that entail *any* activity beyond your specific organizational walls. The minute you go outside these walls, the pressures and risks, opportunities, and demands—that we discussed throughout this chapter—become relevant.

2. *Why is this important to me?* Disruptions matter. We all know that. That's why continuity planning in terms of what to do if, and more likely, when something traumatic happens to your business is increasing in relevance. And just think about the ever-increasing pressure on your margins. What's driving that? Technology changes, sure. Optimized processes, of course. Yet another factor is the radically shifting expectations of business buyers and the consumers who drive them. Just as consumers now expect perfect products, they, like the companies that support them, expect pinpoint predictability when it comes to managing store shelves and delivery schedules. Whether as cause or consequence, the reality is that we are all attempting to streamline, buff-down, and optimize to meet the competitive and margin pressures we are constantly under. Yet, stuff happens: disruptions occur, regulations change, competition heats up, customers demand more—all requiring us to respond quickly. Being able to do so requires us really knowing what we do (the visibility thing) and having the capability to respond quickly and effectively (the execution thing).

Now, let's answer this question from another perspective. Borrowing from Sandler and Travis, a consultancy focused on global supply chain issues, Without an architect, a rule maker, or authorized decision maker, welding the parts and parties to a global supply chain together to create a secure global network is a daunting task. On the other hand, the governments, companies, and organizations involved are not starting from scratch. All parties to the supply chain are and have been concerned with issues of cargo theft, pilferage, contraband and smuggling, trafficking in arms and ammunition, and narcotics smuggling for decades. Many government and nongovernmental agencies, multinational companies, carriers and consortiums are working on these issues. Yet, recall again the metaphor of the T-Shirts, Turtlenecks, and Suits used throughout the book—of the very different people with their (appropriately and necessarily) different perspectives, priorities, and processes to get stuff done—within your organization. And, recall the inherent semantic disconnects that often result leading to morale destroying behaviors and organizational arthritis. Now, multiply these disconnects, dysfunctions, and dyspeptic behaviors across dozens if not hundreds of people/places/organizations and we end up with what we have all experienced: big morale problems, management mistrust, dysfunctional organizational behavior and sclerotic decision making, just simply on a broader scale.

But it need not be so. As we've argued, given examples of, witnessed, midwifed, driven, and experienced, it is possible to get done what needs to get done—to drive executional consistency. How? By manipulating the DNA of executional consistency—building the shared semantics that are as meaningful as they are actionable to the T-Shirts, Turtlenecks, and Suits—both within one and across many organizations.

Getting the visibility needed is critical. Not having such "true" and tangible visibility means merely doing more of the same. Doing what you're currently doing—only "running harder" to do it, like the Red Queen from *Alice in Wonderland* who runs faster and faster merely to catch up—is ultimately a losing race. Running differently means having the visibility into what connects with what, when, where, how and how much and being to do something about it. That's what visible commerce does. And *that's* why it's important to you, to your suppliers, and to your customers.

3. *Explain a bit more about the tension between "agile" and "assured" commerce.* Earlier, we cited a report that found that companies with the most effective supply chains achieved a compound annual growth rate in their market capitalization that was between 7 percent and 28 percent higher than the industry averages.

This is no surprise. The past 20 years have witnessed an explosion in attention, focus, and results of Lean Manufacturing, just-in-time, Six Sigma, and other means to drive costs out of and build responsiveness into supply chains for a simple reason: the world economy and ever-increasing interdependency take us much closer to the global arbitration of costs and optimal allocation of resources that classical economics have been propounding for well over a century. Yet, the ever-increasing demands and pressures for more visibility and wringing out productivity costs globally are running straight into the requirements and imperatives for increased security and regulatory adherence to counter terrorism and other disruptive forces. Thus, global supply chains are faced with the "battle of the visibilities": visibility to drive productivity and visibility to ensure security—and these are most definitely not the same. As mentioned earlier, there are inherent tensions between an "agile" and an "assured" supply chain. To those who manage these tensions well will come the competitive returns. It's a new game now. The flat world is here, as are the increasing risks and opportunities of sailing in it.

4. *What are the costs of compliance?* It is difficult to calculate. The number of security initiatives, and their costs of compliance, change frequently. Some of these costs and estimates are cited either in the text or Notes to this chapter. Another way to think about this topic is to ask what is the cost of *not complying*. Ask yourself the benefits of being on the customs "fast-track" list into the United States or of other countries complying to specific security initiatives. It's pretty easy to quantify those benefits of faster-to-market, or the costs of delays of not getting your goods to market on a timely basis.

To look at this yet another way, again recalling Sandler and Travis, the reality is that we are increasingly interdependent. Global trade has increased significantly over the past several decades. The growth of global trade has not been concentrated among a select group of nations. Rather, it has increasingly become a significant contributor to national economies across the globe. Look at the data: In 1975, trade contributed to over 60 percent of the GDP in 29 percent of the world's countries. By 2001, 45 percent of countries reported trade as contributing over 60 percent of their GDP. The global trade club has become more inclusive as trade value has grown and the number of countries participating in the game has increased. As trade has become increasingly important for nations' independent economies, countries have become increasingly interdependent which in turn perpetuates the positive growth trend. The delicate balance of trade sustained through this growth points to a system where numerous parties rely on each other to serve as suppliers and customers. As trade becomes more critical to countries' GDP, the resulting growth in their economy leads to an increase in consumerism—which makes them even more entrenched in the trade system and increases the interdependency.

Yet, precisely because they are so tied together, supply systems—and the companies and global economies that depend on them—have never been more fragile or exposed to disruption. The speed of events and news also means that relatively local national events can quickly become global events, if not chains of events, all connected in ways that, even a few years ago, would have seemed impossible. This also explains why economies, reputations, and even governments can fall faster and farther than ever when events seriously disrupt the world's cherished routines.

This is the burden of globalization. There is another take on this—the "political risk" of the world economy—estimated by Aon Trade Credit's chief economist, Dr. Michel Leonard, at $800 billion in 2003 that could balloon to $1 trillion in 2005. Dr. Leonard's team calculates that uncertainty surrounding political risk cost the world economy more than $800 billion in reduced corporate spending, investments, and growth in 2003. That's compared to an estimated $200 billion prior to the September 11, 2001, terrorist attack. Leonard argues that uncertainty surrounding political risk has contributed to the global economic slowdown and imposed the equivalent of a 0.25 percent "geo-political tax" on global GDP growth. The combination of terrorism and traditional political risks—such as general strikes in Nigeria, political insurgence in Venezuela, and the war in Iraq—substantially decreased the risk tolerance of investments, exporters, and bankers, thus negatively impacting global trade and investment.[18]

Increasingly, the economic effects of the new global terrorism are becoming apparent. There are "demand" shocks—the result of weakening consumer confidence. Increasing emphasis on security will result in higher "transaction costs" that have a direct bearing on international trade. The collapse of the Twin Towers and the damage done to the Pentagon destroyed a substantial amount of real capital. Estimates suggest that the direct damage caused amounted to 0.1 percent of total national assets. The amount of capital destroyed in the earthquake in Kobe in 1995 (of 2.5 percent of national capital assets), hurricane Andrew in 1992 (at 1 percent), and the initial estimates at well over $100 billion as a result of hurricane Katrina suggests that this figure is not so high.[19] But, the indirect effects are even more substantial. These include impacts on:

- *Transaction costs around the world:* The various negative feedback effects via different markets and countries, the negative demand shocks, and the increase in economic risks and uncertainties, and the fiscal impact caused by the attacks.[20]

- *Security measures:* They imply higher costs. Legal provisions in the immediate aftermath of the attacks; transaction costs in transport, tourism, and international trade rose significantly—estimating at 1 percent of the value of internationally traded goods; and there was a decline in labor productivity by 1.12 percent and in total productivity of 0.63 percent. This is equivalent to a loss of around $70 billion per year in U.S. GDP.

- *Financial markets:* Investors have been forced to adjust their portfolios to the new risk structures; at the same time, the return on various forms of equity has changed because capital has moved toward safer forms of financial investment.

- *Demand shocks:* Consumer confidence has been shaken, which we discussed earlier.

- *Insurance markets:* Insurance providers have changed what they have to offer, how to offer them, and how to price them.[21]

- *World trade:* New global terrorism imposes higher transaction costs. A 1 percent increase in transport costs reduces interregional goods trade by 3 percent. Calculations show that one-day delays in border controls generates costs of 0.5

percent of the value of the goods. This increase in transaction costs has a particular impact on agricultural products, textiles, nonmetal minerals, and machinery because for these goods, the relative value to weight is particularly low, making them particularly vulnerable to any increase in transaction costs.

Others could, of course, be cited. Our point, however, is simple: All of these require understanding and exploiting one of our recurring mantras of *what impacts what, when, where, how, and how much—* the key lesson of this book.

Chapter Cheat Sheet

The Issue

Never has global trade been more pervasive or more critical to life as we now know it. Never have economies been more interdependent or smoother functioning—at their best, seemingly flawless in their capability to deliver goods on time with extraordinary efficiency. Yet, precisely because they are so tied together, supply systems—and the companies and global economies that depend on them—have never been more fragile or exposed to disruption. Attempts to strengthen this fragility to minimize the threats of disruption highlight the criticality of making supply chains more visible and the risks of not doing so. "Secure commerce" is an increasingly important initiative of governments, and increasingly, businesses around the world—with significant impacts and implications on how supply chains are set up, run, monitored, and increasingly protected.

The Insight

With enhanced security comes additional responsibilities adding costs and time—precisely those things that supply chains are designed to eliminate. The result? Increasing tension between "agility" and "assurance," between the need for speed (for agile supply chains) yet the requirement for assurance (for security and visibility). How a company balances these tensions will impact its competitive relevance and capability to take advantage of global commerce.

The Phrases

Visible Commerce; Secure Commerce; Operation Safe Commerce; Global Supply Chain

(Continued)

The Implications

The ever-increasing demands and pressures for more visibility and wringing out productivity costs globally are running straight into the requirements and imperatives for increased security and regulatory adherence to counter terrorism and other disruptive forces. Thus, global supply chains are faced with the "battle of the visibilities": visibility to drive productivity and visibility to ensure security—and these are not the same. There are inherent tensions between an "agile" and an "assured" supply chain. To those who manage these tensions well will come the competitive returns. It's a new game now. The flat world, as Thomas Friedman calls it, is here, as are the increasing risks and opportunities of sailing in it.

Pragmatic Execution . . . in the Context of Everything Else

Setting the Stage: From Being Compelling to Being Useful

Albert Bressand is the chief scenario strategist for the Royal Dutch Shell Company. A quiet man of sharp intellect, Albert's responsibility is to work with Shell's executive team to anticipate future market trends that might impact Shell's investments, operations and consequently, competitive future. He does so by creating scenarios of different time frames, and using those scenarios to challenge, test, and refine the 1-to-3-year, 3-to-5-year, 5-to-10-year strategies of each major business unit and geography. As a global energy supplier, political and economic trends, market disruptions and shifts, demographic patterns and migrations, individual consumption patterns and preferences all play heavily into what they need to do and how they need to do it. Scenarios are means to sensitize them to emergent opportunities and potential threats. Shell has been using scenarios to help them "make sense" and "take action" for over 30 years now, to help them be able both to anticipate and to respond to specific challenges and opportunities.

Jim Dillon, CIO of New York whom we met before, was facing a significant challenge that if not addressed, would mean high visibility in the press and further stress on his budget. Jim was attempting to install a new application that would handle all of the state's unemployment insurance enrollment and benefit disbursements. The existing system was cumbersome, expensive to maintain, and incapable of keeping up with the changing needs of New York's citizens. Worse, he was six months behind the schedule that he wanted to be on, delaying other projects important to him and the department. The pressure was on.

Significant pressures lay heavily on both Albert and Jim. They worked within very different time horizons: Albert's time horizon was a cascading one from 1 to 10 years; Jim's focus was six months ago! They had different focuses as well: Albert had to help refine a set of operationally relevant strategies that could predict and adapt to shifting market conditions; Jim had to implement a large application that had significant impacts on millions of citizens, and dozens if not hundreds of other applications throughout the state. They also had very different constituents, or customers: Albert worked within the executive team of Shell—the CEOs, COOs, and CFOs of each of its business units; Jim had to ensure adherence to state legislature mandates, the various CIOs and IT directors throughout other state agencies who would be impacted by his initiative as well as the many vendors and their tool-sets, applications and systems that were critical to perform the rip-and-replace of his critical applications. In terms of our Business Blueprint, Albert's focus was layer 1; Jim, layers 2, 3, and 4.

What is common to them, however, is more important than their differences. Both had to execute, and do so consistently and effectively. Both had challenges in doing so. Scenarios are compelling stories of what could be. As such, they are useful tools to challenge existing strategies and priorities. However, being compelling is not necessarily compatible with being useful. And, too often, scenarios are brushed aside as being the former rather than the latter. Albert's challenge, and the challenge of scenario work in general, is how to "ground them," to make them operationally useful, to understand their potential impacts not only within layer 1, but to know what needs to happen at layers 2, 3, and 4—of processes, applications, and infrastructure—to be able to respond to whatever market conditions emerge.[1] Jim's challenge, as we described in some detail in Chapter 5, was to get his different constituencies, vendors, and work teams—each with their own ways of doing what they did and understanding what should be done to get done what was supposed to be done—to work together effectively. Both needed to create *shared semantics*—shared understanding of what had to be done in a way that could be executed on consistently, quickly, and effectively.

Facing the Challenge: Managing the Impossible Decision

Making a Scramble Not a Scramble

These, and any of the examples throughout this book, could have been replaced by countless other examples. There is much written about execution and executing. In Bossidy and Charan's book, *Execution*, they stress the importance of following through, and in *Confronting Reality*, the importance of facing the hard choices that have to be made.[2] In both, they discuss the criticality of establishing what they call a "culture of execution." In neither, however, do they discuss the pragmatics of how to make it happen at scale, and at all layers of the business. In both, they speak to the executives, to those responsible for layer 1 activities and leadership. What often happens, however, is that a significant gap exists between what executives say they need to get done, how to make it happen, and then how it actually does happen. Cultures of execution, by themselves, will *get things done*. However, though they may have identical business outcomes in the end, there is an enormous difference between a smoothly executed initiative and a harried death march. A significant gap exists between exhorting the "culture of execution" and making it happen pragmatically, consistently, and effectively. From this perspective, our books dovetail nicely. Our focus has been on the pragmatics of execution, critical to bringing any "execution culture" to life.

We all have to scramble everyday—to meet deadlines, respond to opportunities, tackle problems. The question is how to do so effectively—an answer beyond the lists and wishes of making it so. How to scramble without making it a scramble—so that the efforts conducted are done consistently and effectively—across teams with their differing perspectives, personalities, and priorities is the basis of our execution framework, of *pragmatic execution*.

Creating Information Advantage

Ketan Patel is chief strategist at Goldman Sachs. His responsibility is to anticipate market shifts and thereby create an information advantage for Goldman traders. Financial markets, and indeed all markets, strive to create more and more efficiencies in them: The greater the efficiencies, the faster things move through them and the more responsive they are to changes in their environment. Just think about how quickly financial markets move up or down triggered by either positive or negative news. What drives market responsiveness is transparency, or using the term from our book, *visibility* among the people who want to sell stuff, the people who want to buy that stuff, and the stuff itself. Such visibility and responsiveness reduce the risk of bad information in the marketplace. Complementing visibility is the traceability—or linkage—between certain pieces of news with particular market shifts. A decision by OPEC to raise the price of oil may lower the share price of a particular large oil company but increase that of another one that has significant investments and revenue from alternate fuel sources, while having little to no impact on for example, the share price of software companies (except for those who supply specialized energy applications). Ketan's challenge is to know *what* information triggers *what* opportunities so he can exploit them all quickly. Having this insight of *what impacts what, when, where, how, and how much* provides *information advantage* to those who have it and to those able to use it. And, having such knowledge reduces the risk of not being able to take advantage of any specific opportunity.

Albert's scenarios are no more than attempts to create an information advantage of what could be. Stated differently, they are means to reduce the risk of not knowing what might happen. It is not possible to know what will occur in the future. However, Albert's team prunes the uncertainty back by identifying different possibilities of what might occur, increasing Shell's capabilities both to anticipate and to respond to whatever possibilities *do* occur. And that's what scenarios are—structured means to suggest possible directions of *what might occur*. From this perspective, Albert and Ketan do a similar thing: *create information advantage* that they use to respond quickly to whatever they need to do—for Ketan, it is making corporate transactions and trades and for Albert, prioritizing energy investments around the world. And they do this by creating visibility into their markets—by creating shared understanding of what might happen, figuring out what needs to be done, and executing consistently on these.

Nirin, Scott, Patty, Trevor, Tim, Pat, Philippe, Marcus, and all of the other examples we used throughout this book face the same challenges: how to execute consistently and respond quickly to specific opportunities—how to, in short, "make sense" and "take action" quickly, effectively, and consistently. It requires having the visibility and traceability across strategies, processes, applications, and infrastructure, and having them in a way that you can use them. Each challenge highlighted in the book stemmed from a lack of knowing *what connects with what, when, where, how, and how much*—and what to do about it even when it was known. Pat Schambach, former TSA CIO, put it well: "We don't even know what we don't know . . . [because] each of us assumes that we already know what we have to do . . . the problem is that we don't know how what each of us is doing impacts the rest of us." Tim Garza, of CalPERS, summarized what needs to happen to execute consistently: ". . . until we get a shared understanding of how to even think about our problem, there's no way we'll be able to make a good decision much less implement it well. But if we could, we'll have insight that provides us with an advantage over our competitors." *Visibility and traceability create information advantage.* If you know what the implications are—of what connects with what, where, when, how, and how much—you can better anticipate the implications of decisions; you can respond more effective to specific opportunities; you can, in short, execute more consistently and effectively.

Making sense and taking action. It sounds so simple. And conceptually it is. But pragmatically, we all know it isn't. As we started out this conclusion, having a "culture of execution" is no doubt important. But the "science" of how to do so is equally important—to go beyond the promises of such a culture to making it real. That's what both parts of our execution framework accomplish: helping you make sense *and* take action. The Business Blueprints—part I of this framework—create the visibility of what connects with what, where, when, how and how much. Lean Six Sigma—part II of this framework—provide the measurement discipline to understand the impacts of decisions made and actions taken. Together, they create pragmatic execution capabilities, based on bridging the gap between executive promises and field reality, on helping us all both make sense and in parallel, take action.

What This Means to You

1. *Hasn't there been enough discussed and written about execution? What is different about what you're talking about here? Why do we need yet another discussion about execution?* No doubt, much has been written on execution. However, much of what has been written has been targeted toward senior executives, those responsible for creating what Bossidy and Charan call the "culture of execution." Culture, as commonly defined, is a set of norms, values, and expectations to guide behavior. Each of these cultural attributes is a guideline for what actions to do, not how to do them. A culture of execution requires a complementary framework of action—which we provide here. Much of the discussion on execution is wrapped around what effective execution would look like; or it is geared toward the senior executives creating the boundaries of such an execution-oriented culture.

We take a different tack. Rather than offering lists of recommendations of how to operate more effectively, we look at the so-called root causes of the challenges—the DNA of what we call pragmatic execution. Given this, we complement discussions of the "culture of execution" by focusing on its "science"—on the pragmatic and underlying ways to drive execution consistently and effectively. *What connects with what, where, when, how, and how much* expresses a need we all have. Too often, our actions are separated from those of others, and their impacts remain invisible and unknown (and as too often described, unknowable). It is no surprise then that decisions made cannot be implemented quickly and effectively. Having little to no visibility into *what impacts what, where, when, how, and how much* makes it nearly impossible to respond effectively. And having no means to monitor, to measure, and to manipulate the impacts of your activities make it nearly impossible to understand the implications of your decisions. Consequently, we often face a double-constraint in our attempts to get stuff done: We seldom know either what impacts we create or how extensive those impacts are. These constraints are seldom malicious or intended. They merely reflect that the T-Shirts, the Turtlenecks, and the Suits that make up where we work—ourselves—often use the same language but understand them very differently. It is no wonder that we seldom get the executional consistency needed. At its core, then, a semantic disconnect exists throughout our organizations.

Happily, if we pose the executional challenge this way, then the issue of how to overcome the challenge becomes clear: Create and apply tools and methods to overcome the semantic disconnect and thereby provide means to get the executional consistency needed. And that's precisely what our pragmatic framework is about—providing means to develop "shared semantics" that can be both understood and acted on equally and consistently by the T-Shirts, the Turtlenecks, and the Suits throughout our organizations. Having a culture of execution requires the methods of bringing such a culture to life. And that's precisely what our execution framework does—again and again.

2. *Making sense and taking action sound pretty simplistic. Isn't that what all managers have to do—to get anything done? So, what's different here?* Sure it's simple. All managers certainly have to make sense and take action, and many of them are very good at it. But, it's one thing to know *what* to do, quite another to know *how* to do it, and still another to know how to make hundreds or thousands of others do it *consistently, at scale.* One of our favorite aphorisms about software development is, "the reason there are so many designers is that circles (graphics) don't crash." It is much easier to *say what to do*—to design a solution to a problem—than it is *to* actually *do it.* Not, of course, that it *is* easy to make sense. In fact, as in the examples of Pat (of TSA), Marcus (of the private bank), Ketan (of Goldman Sachs), Tim (CalPERS), and others highlighted here, getting a shared understanding of "what to make sense of" is as critical—and as difficult—as taking action on that shared understanding. Getting the visibility of what connects with what, when, where, how and how much across strategy, processes, applications, and infrastructure—layers 1, 2, 3, and 4—and *expressing* them in a way to allows us to trace the impacts of any activity everywhere in the business has been a dream of business for years. Yet, that the quest has been a difficult one does not mean that it is an impossible one. Overcoming the semantic disconnect—by *creating the possibility of finally being able to express differences in a way that both makes sense and can lead directly to action is powerful.*

And it is also what is significantly different from mere attempts of making it happen.

3. *There was lots of discussion about shared semantics and the semantic disconnect as the fundamental issue to overcome to get pragmatic execution. Is this really a useful way to characterize execution-based problems? Or stated slightly differently, does it really make sense to characterize overcoming semantic disconnects as the DNA of pragmatic execution?* Ask yourself a question: How many times have you heard a colleague explain their understanding of a particular challenge your organization is facing, you nodded, walked away, then said to yourself, "I have no idea what she said?" As addressed in Chapters 1 and 2, each layer of the blueprint has its own set of people with its own language, its own sets of activities, its own metrics, and so on. Yet, such semantic disconnects occur not only *between* the different organizational layers but *within* them as well. As we have all experienced, with such disconnects come political infighting—and finger-pointing. Through dozens and dozens of workshops, we have found that neutralizing such political infighting is crucial to air out the room. A terrifically easy yet powerful way to do so is to characterize the disconnects as just that—semantic disconnects. Having characterized the problem this way, it's relatively easy to get people with their very different perspectives and priorities to acknowledge that what is needed is a new "method of communicating"—a new set of grammar tools—a new way of expressing the particular business problem to tackle so that a shared understanding can be created, and action taken. Creating shared semantics in a way that is meaningful to everyone is the first step to making it as meaningful as it is actionable. And this is why we say that "making sense" and "taking action" can and do occur in parallel—they just naturally result from creating a shared semantics.

Shared semantics—a shared understanding of what it is that has to be done—is absolutely crucial to being able to execute consistently. This is why we say that the DNA of executional consistency is overcoming the semantic disconnect. And helping people to acknowledge that a semantic disconnect *is* a critical issue to overcome becomes a politically neutral way to have people leave their politics at the door as they engage in a manner that is as meaningful as it is actionable.

Afterword

Ron Strout

The Pragmatics of Getting Work Done: A Perspective from State Street

I enjoy restoring my house—taking things apart and putting them back together—tearing off parts of the house and rebuilding them—making them in keeping with what I and my family need. In the process of doing this, I get to know my house well—how it's put together, what works, and what still needs work—from its foundation through its flooring to its siding to the roof. After years of doing this restoration work, I still marvel at the craftsmanship of all the different things that have to come together for our family home to be as comfortable and usable as it is.

Perhaps not a perfect metaphor, but our business at State Street Corporation, and any business, requires constant "restoration," continual renewal, and knowing its foundation, how it's put together and how it works. Sure, I have the luxury, on my home, to work on it when I want and when I can. With businesses, we don't have such luxury. Potential disruptions and threats, new competitors and opportunities, market shifts and emerging technologies continually coalesce into new waves of concerns, and opportunities. And being ever more sensitive to the rippling effects of global markets makes all of us even more aware and attentive to the needs of our business. This sensitivity also makes the importance of our knowing our business inside and out, of what actually occurs throughout our businesses, even more important so we can be sufficiently responsive to the competitive changes that do and will continuously impact us.

We all know this. And, interestingly enough, many of us have been saying if not experiencing, this same thing for years. But, knowing our businesses, and being sufficiently responsive, has continued to remain a challenge for many of us. Knowing that there were parts of our businesses that were "invisible" to us—or that we weren't clear on (to use Ralph and Vince's simple but spot-on phrase) "what connects with what, where, when, how, and how much" throughout our organization was okay Many of us had sufficient market presence, differentiated products, or sufficiently strong operational skills to compensate for the lack of visibility, organizational alignment, and consistent execution throughout the organization. No longer. Not having what Ralph and Vince call the "visibility" throughout your organization and strengthening your executional capabilities (or using their terms, "getting done what has to get done") will lead only to continual margin pressures and nibbling away of competitive advantage.

Much has been written about these pressures and how to deal with them. But Ralph and Vince offer a different and actionable insight into what can be done about them and how to strengthen capabilities to "get the stuff done that needs to get done." They approach it from a "pragmatic" perspective—rather than a purely theoretical one that lets you understand your pressures and problems differently and do something about them pragmatically. There were a number of times reading this book where I circled, or wrote, or challenged, or got insight into what we were doing and could do differently. I'll talk about some of this later, but first I want to step back and provide some information on some of the specific issues that we, as a leading global corporation, are facing and that makes "getting stuff done" and strengthening what I've been calling "our revolution for better execution" so critical.

State Street is one of the world's top financial service providers, with $9.5 trillion in assets under custody and $1.4 trillion under management. We are the number 1 servicer of U.S. mutual funds, the number 1 servicer of U.S. pension plans, the number 1 investment manager of U.S. pension assets, a leading pension manager globally, and the number 1 provider of foreign exchange services worldwide, the largest offshore fund service provider worldwide and the eighth largest investment manager worldwide. In short, we do a lot of things in a lot of places with a lot of people, globally.

Essentially, we are a microcosm of the competitive environment. We are extremely sensitive to market conditions—both financial markets and the competitive market overall; after all, our clients are corporate clients so we experience the effects that they either cause or feel. We are involved in global sourcing, always looking to find the most productive and efficient places to do different types of work; we are heavily involved in outsourcing—both information technology outsourcing (ITO) and business processing outsourcing (BPO) activities; we collaborate extensively, again driven by our relationships with our corporate clients and their ever-changing needs with their customers; and we are also continually working to better manage what Ralph and Vince call the "impossible decision" between controlling costs while fostering innovation. Each of these challenges is difficult alone; together, they create a continuing flux of juggling priorities, resources, operational commitments, and market opportunities—all while making sure that we maintain our operational excellence for which we are known.

However, challenges exist in our juggling as well as in executing on those things that are being juggled. There's a three-part trade-off we consider, or balance we need to maintain, for all the projects we need to execute. We attempt an effective balance among (1) *time spent*—for example, how quickly to get the project done to get to market; (2) *money allocated*—for example, how much money and resources will be spent in getting it done; and (3) *standards maintained*, for example, how much consistency to ensure and leverage or re-use of what was done for subsequent efforts. At times, we don't maintain an effective balance; It is tempting, and sometimes we get seduced by it, to keep pumping in money over and over again to get a project completed quickly—while sacrificing the consistency and adherence to standards which impacts being able to re-use what was built for other market needs. The good thing about this imbalance is that a product or service can be delivered quickly; the bad thing about this is that, over time, the overall cost of development gets higher and higher since we don't have sufficient re-use of the process or the product elsewhere because we didn't sufficiently drive consistency or standards effectively. Furthermore, we've faced challenges of products or services developed not meeting what the customer—our corporate client—actually wanted. They may have "signed off" on what the requirements were but when actually presented with the new product or service said that they it didn't meet their specific needs. There was a breakdown in communications and understanding between what was needed and what was delivered.

These challenges all highlight the need for better execution between what we know has to get done and how we get it done. I've been calling for a "revolution in execution" at State Street for the past year—a reconsideration of how we maintain an effective balance between time, money and standards and a strengthening of our capabilities to do so. I've been arguing that a key means to do so is to go ensure that we have the effective "language" among our different constituents—to make sure that what they want is what we delivery and that the alignments across our globally diverse workforce and organizational service are strengthened. Key to this is more effective governance—to set, monitor and evaluate what gets done. Equally important is solid project management—to ensure that how stuff gets done gets done well, consistently. And of course, underlying both of these is capability to execute better and better all the time. A global firm requires exploiting standards consistently to get the leverage, the reuse, and the productivity needed—as well as reducing the risks of projects delays and the increasing the likelihood of them getting done well. Boil this all down and our fundamental challenge is continually getting better at executing on our model. It is not in modifying our model, just making it work better. And that's where Ralph's and Vince's book comes in.

As they mention, there has been much written and discussed on how to execute more effectively. But their focus on what they call the *underlying DNA of execution*, and of going beyond the theory to pragmatic insights of what to do to strengthen your execution capabilities is provocative, insightful, and, most important, useful. It's provocative in that in that they've tackled an old problem in a new way. It's insightful in their use of multiple and real examples and lessons from different sized firms in different industries from different parts of the world. It's useful in that they suggest specific tools and techniques that can be applied right away to, using their words, "manipulate the DNA for effective execution." It is refreshing to find a book that is as provocative as it is intuitively simple and immediately useful. Also, their focus on the "underlying DNA" for execution means that the lessons and tools that they describe are useful no matter what the executional challenge is—as their various chapters describe.

I've often talked with our clients and our project teams about the importance of "language," of governance, of consistency of standards, and the necessity of re-use. For us, being better at these things is critical to making our "revolution for better execution" successful. In *Get It Done!* Ralph and Vince show how we, and you, can move beyond the demands and the wishes for getting stuff done more effectively, to making them a reality.

Notes

Introduction: Making Sense and Taking Action

1. Jim Collins, *Good to Great: Why Some Companies Make the Leap . . . And Others Don't* (New York: HarperBusiness, 2001).

2. Ralph Welborn and Vince Kasten, *The Jericho Principle: How Companies Use Strategic Collaboration to Find New Sources of Value* (Hoboken, NJ: John Wiley & Sons, 2003).

3. Rosamund Stone Zander and Benjamin Zander, *The Art of Possibility: Transforming Professional and Personal Life* (New York: Penguin Books, 2000).

4. Citation from *The Gods Must Be Crazy*, Jensen Farley Pictures (1980).

Chapter 1: The DNA of Consistent Execution

1. Unisys Corporation Agility Study: A Global Survey of Senior Business and IT Executives and Industry Analysts (2003), http://3d-ve.unisys.com/C3/3DVE%20Literature/Document%20Library%20for%20Research/The%20Agile%20Corporation.pdf.

2. Geoffrey Moore, *Living on the Fault Line: Managing for Shareholder Value in Any Economy* (New York: HarperBusiness, 2002). Also, *Crossing the Chasm* (New York: HarperBusiness, 2002).

3. Business Blueprint Video. Interview for Unisys video production (June 13, 2003).

4. Personal conversation with Don Redlinger, former senior vice president of human resources, Allied Signal (June 2004).

5. See also Ralph Welborn and Vince Kasten, *The Jericho Principle: How Companies Use Strategic Collaboration to Find New Sources of Value* (Hoboken, NJ: John Wiley & Sons, 2003), Chapters 3 and 6 for a more

271

detailed description of specific operational implications enabling organizational agility, with a specific focus on emerging collaborative models. Also, see Ralph Welborn and Vince Kasten, "The DNA of Organizational Agility," in *The Agile Enterprise*, Nirmal Pal, Ed. (New York: Walter Kluwer, 2005).

6. What is it about this process, this dynamic, that makes it so important, and so essential to explain competitive pressures? Tacit knowledge has potentially high value and high margin. It is not scalable. It resides in a few heads and is subject to multiple interpretations hence fragmented uses and possible conflicting standards. Tacit knowledge, then, by design and structure has inherent scaling limits. Let's think about this through an example. Many of us have been involved or subjected to corporate strategy projects or proclamations. Yet, what many of us have come away with from such involvement is the recognition that strategy is only conceptually clean and analytically pure, but operationally useless. Why? Because there is frequently a significant "execution" gap between strategic proclamation and operational reality, a result often due to the development of the strategy by a few without thinking through how to scale the shared assumptions, expectations, and objectives to many of us who need to execute on that strategy. However, it is certainly understandable why there is such difficulty doing so. Strategy formulation is inherently a messy process, heavily reliant on tacit knowledge—on a few people with their own set of assumptions, beliefs, and perspectives attempting to create some shared sets of overall objectives. Even with some agreement of shared objectives and strategic formulation, there are no consistent sets of standards, frameworks, or process to drive strategic thinking into everyday operational execution. Chapter 4 describes means to develop more "executionally aware" and usable strategies.

7. See note 5, Welborn and Kasten, *The Jericho Principle*, for multiple examples of using the stack for competitive insight and collaborative options.

8. Interestingly enough but not surprisingly so, the codification into executable standards has significant implications on the competitive environment. Stated differently, as activities become more codified, the very nature of competition shifts. This tacit-to-codified market transformation process well characterized the 1960s and 1970s with respect to network connectivity, the 1980s, and throughout the 1990s with respect to standard technical architectures and platforms (resulting in

today's emerging acceptance of either J2EE or .NET as architectural standards) and well characterizes today's battlefield among enterprise application providers and those attempting to create more standards around business processes. For a quick example, not until Internet Protocols were clearly codified into a set of executable global standards could we witness the rise of Cisco Systems and other (once) network-dominant enterprises, nor could we have a reliable network environment enabling the "plug-and-play" of TCP/IP-enabled devices. With global acceptance of the TCP/IP standards, the competitive battlefield among network competitors shifted. Rather than battling over which protocols would underlie global connectivity and "lock in" the network environment, competitors jousted over what architectural platforms, what applications, and how to accelerate the speed of those protocols. Thus, what was once a high-value, high-margin business—defining the TCP/IP standards—became a commoditized, highly scalable, codified business shifting the competitive battleground. It is this competitive logic that we see over and over again and that underlies the bases of the power of codification to respond quickly to fast-moving business opportunities.

9. Business Blueprint Video. Interview for Unisys video production (June 13, 2003).

Chapter 2: Maps, Models, and Action—Blueprinting Your Business

1. As many of us have experienced, and as we discuss in Chapter 4, strategies are often conceptually clean and analytically pure, but operationally vacuous. It is for this reason that we have developed what we call an "architecturally informed" strategy that moves from the elegance of concept to the pragmatics of execution around making strategy "stuff" real, usable, and pragmatically actionable. Much more on this in Chapter 4.

2. Mark Monmonier, *Rhumb Lines and Map Wars: A Social History of the Mercator Projection* (Chicago: University of Chicago Press, 2004).

3. In Chapter 4, one of our examples highlights the entertaining process and huge impact that wrestling over the noun-verb naming as well as even using Use Cases had for one of Europe's leading private banks. The wrestling occurred among the bank's CEO, IT director, and marketing manager and led to entertaining

stories but much more importantly, significant break-throughs in understanding and performance for the CEO and his team in accomplishing what they had to get done.

Chapter 3: Measurements, Gauges, and Graphs— Doing What's Important

1. Michael George, *Lean Six Sigma for Services* (New York: McGraw-Hill, 2004).

2. Ralph Welborn and Vince Kasten, *The Jericho Principle: How Companies Use Strategic Collaboration to Find New Sources of Value* (Hoboken, NJ: John Wiley & Sons, 2003). As we stated earlier, competition results from different companies attempting to exploit a sufficiently attractive market opportunity. Initial market opportunities are usually high-margin and/or high-revenue opportunities, the results of their underlying value propositions being novel, consequently relatively unexploited or difficult to replicate, and largely embedded in the heads of relatively few people. Over time, these margins tend to get arbitraged away or shrunk as new competitors, recognizing the potential of those market opportunities, enter the competitive fray. What shrinks those margins are processes, technologies, and other activities that bring down their operational costs and allows them to become more scalable, hence executable by many. The means of driving such scalable activities is the enabling codification of those activities—of the tacit knowledge, the knowledge in the heads of few—into frameworks, into standards, into executable and repeatable activities.

3. Shoshana Zuboff and James Maxmin, *The Support Economy: Why Corporations Are Failing Individuals and the Next Episode of Capitalism* (New York: Viking, 2002).

4. James Champy, *X-Engineering the Corporation: The Next Frontier of Business Performance* (New York: Warner Books, 2002).

5. Kara Romanow, "RFID in 2005: The What Is More Important Than the When with Wal-Mart Edict," *AMR Research* (August 27, 2003), http://www.amrresearch.com/content/view.asp?pmillid=16539.

6. See note 4.

7. James Womack, *The Machine That Changed the World* (New York: HarperPerennial, 1991).

8. Lean Aerospace Initiative, http://lean.mit.edu.

9. Automation World, "From Warring Camps to Optimized Processes" (December 7, 2004).

10. Martin Michael Joyce and Bettina Schechter, "The Lean Enterprise: A Management Philosophy at Lockheed," *Defense Acquisition Review Journal* (August/November 2004), http://www.dau.mil/pubs/arq/2004arq /arq2004.asp#Aug-Nov.

11. According to the Department of Transportation's Bureau of Transportation Statistics, in the first Quarter of 2004, there were over 127 billion passenger-miles flown.

12. See note 3.

13. Michael George et al., *The Lean Six Sigma Pocket Toolbook: Reference Guide to 70 Tools for Improving Quality and Speed* (New York: McGraw-Hill, 2004); Alastair Muir, *Lean Sigma Statistics* (New York: McGraw-Hill, 2005); Juran Institute, *Juran Institute's Six Sigma Breakthrough and Beyond: Quality Performance Breakthrough Methods* (New York: McGraw-Hill, 2003); also, the *Defense Acquisition Review Journal* (August/November 2004) issue is dedicated to Lean examples and lessons.

14. It does by the way: Each of the main suspension cables is made up of 27,572 individual wires, 80,000 miles of them in all. Also, the anchorages required removal of 3.25 million cubic feet of dirt, which is 5.6 billion cubic inches, or 120,000 cubic yards, pick the units that seem the most impressive. Big engineering projects create mind-boggling statistics, and Lean Six Sigma projects at big companies generate breathtaking results.

15. Subrata N. Chakravarty and Naazneen Karmali, "Fast Food," *Forbes Global* (August 10, 1998).

Chapter 4: The Pragmatics of Strategy . . . with Your Head in the Clouds and Your Feet on the Ground

1. Jim Collins, *Good to Great: Why Some Companies Make the Leap . . . And Others Don't* (New York: HarperBusiness, 2001). See also, Ralph Welborn and Vince Kasten, *The Jericho Principle: How Companies Use Strategic Collaboration to Find New Sources of Value* (Hoboken, NJ: John Wiley & Sons, 2003), p. 23.

2. AARP Global Aging Program and Wirthlin Worldwide, AARP International Opinion Leader Study on Global Aging (November, 2004).

3. Jonathan Grant et al., *Low Fertility and Population Aging: Causes, Consequences, and Policy Options* (New York: Rand Europe, 2004).

4. T. R. Reid, *The United States of Europe: The New Superpower and the End of American Supremacy* (New York: Penguin Press, 2004). Also, Jeremy Rifkin, *The European Dream: How Europe's Vision of the Future Is Quietly Eclipsing the American Dream* (New York: Jeremy Tarcher, 2004).

5. http://www.cbronline.com/article_news.asp?guid=C915CDC9-FAC0-469A-943F-FE0A68DD25CF.

6. Greg Price, "No Place for Kyoto in Asia," *Asian Wall Street Journal* (January 14, 2005), p. A7. Jeffrey Ball, "Kyoto Pact's Ratification Heralds New Market: Investment Funds Form as Trading Heats Up in Global-Warming Permits," *Wall Street Journal* (November 8, 2004), p. A2.

7. C. K. Prahalad, *The Fortune at the Bottom of the Pyramid: Eradicating Poverty through Profits* (Philadelphia: Wharton School Publishing, 2004).

8. Esther Rudis et al., *CEO Challenge 2004: Perspectives and Analysis—Report 1353, The Conference Board* (Philadelphia, Conference Board, November 2004).

Chapter 5: Business Processes . . . Where Business and Technology Meet

1. From a Panel discussion at the 2005 *Out Execute to Win* conference in Orlando.

2. Ralph Welborn and Vince Kasten, *The Jericho Principle: How Companies Use Strategic Collaboration to Find New Sources of Value* (Hoboken, NJ: John Wiley & Sons, 2003).

3. "eGovernment Leadership: Engaging the Customer," Government Executive Series, *Accenture* (April 2003).

4. "PA Open For Business Executive Policy Information," *Technology Bulletin*, Commonwealth of Pennsylvania, Governor's Office of Administration/Office for Information Technology (August 30, 2000).

5. New York State Department of Labor, *Annual Report* (2003).

6. From an interview with Tom Ridge, Victor Rivero, "A Ridge to the Twenty-First Century," *Government Technology* (December, 1999).

7. This particular example is hypothetical but so-called "swivel chair automation" was very common at places like the telephone companies of the 1960s where they had embraced automation very early for highly technical tasks.

Chapter 6: Next Generation Business Process Outsourcing . . . as Promise and Threat

1. Closed-book policies are those that are no longer offered for sale yet require servicing to maintain until the life of the policy is over.

2. We have changed the name of this organization for privacy purposes.

3. "BPO Market to Grow to $173 Billion in 2007," Gartner Focus Report (July 7, 2003). Additional Gartner reports were used for some of this information, including: "Business Impact of the BPO Market in 2005," *Gartner Research Note* (December 17, 2004); "Market Focus: BPO Demand Overview, Asia/Pacific, 2004," *Gartner Focus Report* (December 22, 2004); "Market Focus: BPO in Financial Services, Western Europe, to 2007," *Gartner Focus Report* (July 22, 2004); and "Market Trends: Business Process Outsourcing, North American, 2004," *Gartner Market Trends Report* (January 18, 2005).

4. TPI Index Review, Technology Partners International. Some people have said that the mega-BPO deals are declining. Jack Benton disagrees for a simple reason: About 40 percent of the deals contain a sizable offshore component. Of that 40 percent, 38 percent of the total contract value is performed offshore. Because work performed offshore can be handled at less cost than work done onshore, the appearance of flat growth hides the actual growth that is occurring. Another reason that outsourcing may be growing even faster than the numbers indicate is that in some cases, organizations are retaining responsibility for capital expenditures. "The service provider doesn't have to lay out the cash, and the equipment financing doesn't have to be factored into their pricing," said Benton. "It's more effective for the clients to manage that, and the service providers are quite happy not to do the capital outlay. It makes their deals look more attractive."

5. Esther Rudis et al., *CEO Challenge 2004: Perspectives and Analysis—Report 1353, The Conference Board* (Philadelphia, Conference Board, November 2004).

6. Personal discussion with Michael Lahman, August 2004, San Diego, CA.

7. Bobby Gill, "Outsourcing Losses and Write-Offs," *Banker* (March 1, 2003).

8. Diana Farrell, "How Germany Can Win from Offshoring," *McKinsey Quarterly* (No. 4, 2004), pp. 114–123.

9. See note 8, p. 118.

10. Discussion, December 2004, New York City.

11. Stacy Cowley, "J.P. Morgan Scraps $5B IT Deal with IBM," *Computerworld*, September 20, 2004, http://www.computerworld.com /managementtopics/outsourcing/story/0,10801,96015,00.html. See also, http://www.scudderpublishing.com/featured columnists/borska.php.

12. Personal discussion, February 2005, London, England.

13. Personal discussion, November 2004 and March 2005, Sacramento, CA.

14. "Business Impact of the BPO Market in 2005," Gartner Group (December 17, 2004). See also note 3.

15. Personal discussion, February, 2005, London, England.

16. Dr. Anthony Shumskas, personal discussion, August 2005. Tony is a gifted engineer, practical program manager, and scholar, with enormous experience in the sorts of sprawling, multifaceted programs that until recently only the government could afford. We had the opportunity to work with and learn from Tony (for two years) about large-scale systems integration, and while he may never have said exactly these words in one sentence at one time, this is a fair representation of his pithy take on program risk. See also the IT Services CMM from the European community, based on the SEI model, which defines new processes for services, such as Billing and Resource Management from ashumskas@comcast.net.

17. This is not a finance book, we are primarily concerned with operational issues. That said, outsourcing in general, and BPO in particular, is a business that depends intensely on financial engineering. The investment expense in Figure 6.3 might be expensed, capitalized, securitized (with financial partners or business partners in the transformation effort), syndicated (with a team of financial partners), or shared with the client. Each of these options has different implications on revenue recognition, taxes, and the overall financial performance of the deal. However, for the purposes of this discussion, we

want simply to call attention to the fact that there is a period of time when the supplier is investing, with the expectation of return somewhere down the road.

18. See note 3.

19. In 2004, the BPO market consolidated and several major BPO mergers were announced. Synergy HR Technologies and Mercer Human Resource Consulting, and Hewitt Associates' acquired Exult. In addition, Computer Sciences Corporation and Aon, and Hewitt and CapGemini formed major alliances, among others. In November 2004, two venture-capital firms bought General Electric's captive center, GECIS, that includes services for finance and accounting, supply chain management, customer service and support, software development, data modeling, and analytics activities. Venture capital firms are aggressively looking to roll-up BPO providers recognizing the opportunity to invest aggressively to create the utility scale necessary to ease the transition of many organizations to standardized platforms and processes—something easier done for VCs than it is for profit-strapped BPO providers.

20. Ralph Welborn and Vince Kasten, *The Jericho Principle: How Companies Use Strategic Collaboration to Find New Sources of Value* (Hoboken, NJ: John Wiley & Sons, 2003). See particularly Chapter 2 where we discuss different collaborative structures based on different types of business objectives.

21. See note 3.

22. Geoffrey Moore, *Living on the Fault Line: Managing for Shareholder Value in Any Economy* (New York: HarperBusiness, 2002).

23. See note 3.

Chapter 7: Secure Global Commerce . . . Managing the Tension between "Assured" and "Agile" Commerce

1. Excerpts from conversation between Linda Dillman and *BusinessWeek Online* reporter Olga Kharif, reported in "Talking RFID with Wal-Mart's CIO," *Hewlett-Packard Enterprise Solutions* (January 29, 2005).

2. Personal conversation with the CEO of a consumer product company, who asked that his name be withheld due to sensitivity of the topic. Throughout this chapter, we use examples from this company.

3. Ralph Welborn, Vince Kasten, and Bruce Duffy, *Your New World: A Visual Guide to Global Commerce* (Unisys Corporation Research Monograph, 2004).

4. See also OECD, Directorate for Science, Technology, and Industry, Security in Maritime Transport: Risk Factors and Economic Impact, July 2003, for a similar analysis of a generic manufacturing supply chain. As they put it, "The vast ranges of goods of various origins and descriptions are today transported from the point of manufacturer by land and sea, transshipped at different ports before arriving at the final point of consumption by mean of door-to-door delivery. This entire process involves approximately 25 different actors, generated 20 to 40 documents and is usually handled at as many as 12 to 15 locations."

5. Secure Supply Chain Initiatives: Risks and Opportunities (Unisys Research Monograph, February 2004).

6. The situation gets even more alarming when we consider the number and makeup of the world's shipping fleet. By the middle of 2003, the world fleet of ships of 1,000 gross tons or greater totaled more than 28,000; at least half of these were Flags of Convenience (FOC) vessels, registered in places such as Cyprus, Malta, Liberia, Bahamas, Panama, and other small nations. All of these countries provide ship-owners cost-cutting havens where they can register their vessels without having to meet the manning, maintenance, safety, pollution, and seaworthiness laws and regulations in the developed world, including lack of adherence to proper training and accreditation. The result of such poor adherence is that they tend to become "pariah vessels . . . or coffin ships— aging, badly maintained, polluting hulks . . . the 50 percent of the world fleet that flew flags of convenience in 2000 accounted for 75 percent of the gross tonnage lost." Richard Pollak, The Colombo Bay (New York: Simon & Schuster, 2003), pp. 61–62. See also William Langewiesche's excellent book, The Outlaw Sea: A World of Freedom, Chaos, and Crime (New York: North Point Press, 2004).

7. Michael E. O'Hanlon, Peter R. Orszag, Ivo H. Daalder, I. M. Destler, David Gunter, Robert E. Litan, and James Steinberg, *Protecting the American Homeland: One Year On* (Washington DC: Brookings Institution Press, 2002).

8. A variety of different reports and articles covered different parts of port closure implications—ranging from port and shipping lane logjams, to jobs lost in the United States as well as in China, to revisions of Wall Street estimates, to the Russian cargo airline Anotov taking advantage of market opportunities to dramatically increase its cargo shipments. For a sample of these, see, Anderson Economic Group, LLC, Working Paper 2002-10, http://www.airfoyle.co.uk/news/heavy-lift-news.asp?NewsID=37, http://www.bdpinternational.com/news_events/al_200301131500.html, http://www.bdpinternational.com/news_events/al_200211270800.html, http://www.eagletribune.com/news/stories/20021008/FP_004.htm.

9. During the nine days that the Colombo Bay, a container ship, was stalled in Seattle because of the port closing, the operations meter continued to tick, at a cost to the owner of between $25,000 to $30,000 a day. More importantly, "the clogged pipeline meant that the containers aboard could not be circulated back into the system for unpacking and then repacking of new paying cargo. And once the ship had lost two or three days, she could not catch up to her original schedule without dropping ports, which ultimately leads to canceled voyages and more revenue loss," Richard Pollak, *The Colombo Bay* (New York: Simon & Schuster, 2003), p. 78.

10. Terry Maenza, "Supply Chain Visibility Exposes Weak Links, Hidden Costs," *Unisys Transportation Insights*, 2005, http://www.unisys.com /transportation/insights/articles/articles.htm?insightsID=97844.

11. Andrew K. Reese, "Building the Secure Supply Chain," *Supply & Demand-Chain Executive*, http://sdcexec.com/article_arch.asp?article_id=5287.

12. Personal communication, June, 2004.

13. See note 11. An OECD study estimates the initial ISPS code compliance burden on ship operators to be at least U.S. $1,279 million and U.S.$730 million thereafter as annual expenditure. This study reported that there were 43,291 vessels trading internationally in 2000. So, this is $29,544 as initial costs and $16,863 per ship annually to meet the ISPS code requirements. Similarly, ports facilities are also expected to comply with ISPS code rules. The estimated costs of such adherence amounts of $963 million and $509 million annually thereafter. The U.S. Coast Guard estimates that there are 226 ports and 4,365 port facilities in the United States. Assuming that all of the 266 ports are involved in international trade, average costs to be borne by each port will be 4.26 million for

initial cost and $2.25 million as annual expenditure. See also, Wong Hin Wei monograph, *Economic Impacts and Implications of Trade and Maritime Security Initiatives on Malaysia* (August, 2003). http://www.mima.gov.my/mima/htmls/papers/pdf/whw/whw_econ-impact.pdf.

14. "Connecting with the Bottom Line: A Global Study of Supply Chain Leadership and Its Contribution to the High-Performance Business" Accenture (2003), http://www.accenture.com/xd/xd.asp?it=enweb&xd +services%5Cscm%5Cscm_thought_fp.xml.

15. Operation Safe Commerce: An Early Picture of Success. Press release from the office of Senator Patty Murray, September 2, 2004.

16. Thomas Friedman, The World Is Flat: A Brief History of the Twenty-First Century (New York: Farrar, Straus and Giroux, 2005).

17. See note 16, p. 10.

18. See http://www.vanguardngr.com/articles/2002/business/b418022004 .html. Also, see Aon's 2004 Political and economic risk map rating the economic, currency, and political risks of doing business in more than 200 territories worldwide.

19. See note 18.

20. http://www.diw.de/english/produkte/publikationen/bulletin/docs /eb02/n02_10okt_1.html. This list results from an economic conference on the economic consequences of the new global terrorism in Berlin (October, 2002).

21. Kyle L. Brandon and Frank A. Fernandez, *Terrorist Risk: Insurance Market Failures and Capital Market Solutions* (Securities Industry Association, January 31, 2004). Demand for terrorist insurance exists, but it is not being supplied in sufficient amount at a reasonable price. This apparent market failure results primarily from two factors: the reinsurance industry not fully recapitalizing after losses stemming from a series of extraordinary, catastrophic events and the difficulties inherent in evaluating or "pricing" terrorist risk. Whether the temporary Terrorism Risk Insurance Act of 2002 needs to be supplemented, modified, or just allowed to expire at end of 2005, work is needed on longer term responses to terrorist risk. Capital market instruments may provide an alternative in the current public debate on reinsurance issues. The following is drawn from Brandon's report, pp. 3 and 4:

A series of extraordinary events hit the global insurance and reinsurance industry in recent years. In 1992, Hurricane Andrew produced losses of $20 billion in 2002 dollars and in 1994 the Northridge earthquake caused losses of $17 billion in 2002 dollars. And then September 11, 2001, hit. Estimates of the insurance losses arising from 9/11 remain imprecise, ranging from $40 billion by $75 billion. Yet even at a conservative $50 billion, it represents the single largest loss by the global insurance and reinsurance industry. Various types of insurance losses are represented in these totals, including: business interruption, commercial property, workers' compensation, life, health, disability, aviation liability, aircraft hull, and other liabilities. . . .

The insurance industry suffered substantial capital erosion due to these extreme events, as well as the poor investment environment—stock market losses and a low interest rate environment—in recent years. The insurance industry experienced $200 billion in capital losses since 9/11 and the global insurance capacity has shrunk by 21 percent compared to early 2000. Attempts to increase capital have not been fully successful, with only an estimated $30 billion having been raised. . . .

The industry's difficulties led to a reportedly severe shortage in terrorist catastrophe insurance and reinsurance. Premiums rose 10 percent to 15 percent for January 2003 renewals, the third annual increase in a row. According to a Conference Board survey, "insurance costs have risen a median 33 percent since 2001, while insurance costs of 20 percent of companies have doubled. . . . More than half of the companies surveyed said they had faced difficulties getting insurance for city offices." Terrorist risk insurance also suffered limited availability. Insurers were wary of extending coverage for terrorist risk. Pre-9/11 terrorist risk insurance was essentially free and included in many policies. Post 9/11 most policies exclude terrorist risk because there was no reinsurance available. . . .

Since 9/11, reinsurers have withdrawn from providing terrorist risk reinsurance due to massive losses, which has deprived the insurance industry of a method of laying off risk. In turn, insurance companies have been unwilling to offer anywhere near the amount of coverage previously offered. Pricing for terrorist risk coverage, which used to be included in general commercial property and casualty insurance, was so limited and priced at such a high level as to put it out of reach for some large commercial properties. In other words, commercial entities are operating with little or no terrorist risk insurance, leaving the companies carrying the risk themselves and causing the economy to be more broadly vulnerable to the economic consequences of a possible future terrorist attack.

And we are only now starting to estimate both the primary and secondary financial and business impacts of Hurricanes Katrina and Rita on businesses and public expenditures, to say nothing of the horrific earthquakes in Pakistan in October 2005.

Chapter 8: Pragmatic Execution . . . in the Context of Everything Else

1. See our work on scenarios and scenariolettes for how to do this.
2. Larry Bossidy and Ram Charan, *Execution: The Discipline of Getting Things Done* (New York: Crown Books, 2002); and *Confronting Reality: Doing What Matters to Get Things Right* (New York: Crown Books, 2004).

Index

A

Abbey, Scott, 178. *See also* UBS
Abbey Life, 206
Account/customer, semantics of, 15, 30
Adams, Austin, 179
Advanced Processing Services (APS), 173–174, 185–186, 189. *See also* Michaels, Paul
Agile vs. assured commerce, tension between, 248–249
Aging, 110, 156
Albertson's, 219
Allied Signal, 17, 90
Amadeus (movie), 29
Analysis classes, 70, 71
Antibodies to change, 86–99, 103
Applications layer, 21, 26–27, 49, 52–54, 150

B

Balanced Scorecard, 130
Banking examples:
Marcus, 120–123, 128–130, 260–261, 263
Mark, 39–41, 44, 45, 48, 50, 53, 54, 66, 140, 141
Mike, 3–7, 22–24, 28, 138, 144
Richard, 198–201
training, 9
Bank One Corp., 179
Barrington, Linda, 113
Bell curve, 89
Benton, Jack, 176, 277
Bio-Terrorism Act, 227
Blueprint. *See* Business Blueprinting
Bonner, Robert, 229
Bossidy, Larry, 16–17, 92, 259, 262
Brain drain, 10
Bressand, Albert, 257–258, 260
Bull's-eye effect, 190–192, 197
Bunyan (Paul) approach to strategy, 108–109, 124
Business Architects, 156, 160
Business Blueprinting, 37–76
defined, 49–50
examples, 39–41, 55, 205, 206
execution framework, 261

Business Blueprinting
(*Continued*)
icon for, 49
issue/insight, 75–76
layers, 51–54, 98, 108, 131,
150, 203, 213
applications, 52–53, 54,
150
infrastructure, 53
process, 52, 54, 150
strategy, 51–52
Lean Six Sigma and, 85, 91,
98, 99, 261
maps-as-models, 45–73
meaning/relevance, 73–74,
76
Red Queen challenge, 42–45
semantic stack and, 25, 30, 33,
40
value/benefits of, 33, 41, 69,
131, 164, 206, 261
Visible Commerce solution,
233
"What's Waldo Doing" in
your organization, 51–54
"Where's Waldo" of your
organization, 48–51
Business case development,
165–166
Business Interaction Model
(BIM), 43–44, 126–127,
153–158, 164, 169, 204,
231, 233, 235, 243, 244
Business Process. *See*
Process(es), business
Business Process Execution
Language (BPEL), 26

Business Process Modeling
Language (BPML), 26
Business Process Outsourcing
(BPO), 171–216
bull's-eye effect, 190–192, 197
complexity of global
partnerships, 221, 230
contractual crunch, win-lose,
173–184, 187–190, 197,
211–212, 216
decisions, challenge of,
180–209
efficiency curve, 206, 207
growth, 177–178, 209
industry, 173–180, 211
losses, 177
M&A activity, 111, 208, 279
meaning/relevance, 166,
209–214, 216
next generation, 198–199,
208–222
opportunities/uncertainty, 118
peak effect, 193–197
pragmatic execution and, 267
promise and premises of,
174–181
semantics of value, xxvi–xxvii,
180–181, 199–202,
207–209, 210–211,
215–216
tipping point, 174–180
trends and scenarios for,
211–214
visibility, 202–207
wedge effect, 187–190, 197
win-win contract, search for,
198–199

Business Process Reengineering, 141

Business process utility (BPU), 173

Business uncertainty, characterizing, 113–119

Business utilities, 212–213

C

California CIO (Clark Kelso), 10, 28, 137–140, 156

CalPERS (Tim Garza), 147–148, 153, 166, 179–180, 202–205, 209, 214, 261, 263

Cannibalized business, 116

Cargo traffic, complexity of, 222–227. *See also* Secure global commerce

Cases, Use, 66–70, 158, 159, 273

Chakravarty, Subrata N., 100

Champy, James, 84, 85, 92, 103

Change:
  corporate antibodies to, 86–99, 103
  management, 165

Charan, Ram, 16, 33, 92, 259, 262

Chaturvedi, Hari, 233, 234–235

Check 21, 39–41, 44, 45, 48, 50, 53, 54, 66, 140, 141

Chevenement, Jean-Pierre, 110

China, 110–111

Cisco Systems, 273

Climate change, reinvigoration of debate over, 111

Codification, 5, 19, 20, 22, 25, 27, 31–33, 43, 50–51. *See also* Execution and Semantic stack

Cohen, Linda, 230, 235

Collaborative Imperative, 42–43, 83–84

Colony, George, 11

CommerceGuard, 228, 242. *See also* Secure global commerce

Communication, excess, 30–31

Communication model, 231

Competitive half-life, 10–11, 140

Compliance costs, security initiatives, 249–250

Computer programs/databases, codifying, 31

Connections/connectivity, xxiii–xxiv, 18, 21, 23, 235

Conner, John, 206, 207, 209

Consequences, unintended, 69, 181–184

Consumer consumption patterns, shifts in, 111–112

Container Security Device, 228, 242

Container Security Initiative (CSI), 227

Contractual crunch, win-lose, 173–184, 187–190, 197, 211–212, 216

Core/context, 11, 130, 210
Cost(s):
   benchmarks driven by, 199
   compliance, security
      initiatives, 249–250
   focus on, versus value, 202,
      216
   of poor quality, 94
Cultures of execution, 259
Customer/account, defining,
   15, 30, 125
Customers-Trade Partnership
   Against Terrorism
   (C-TPAT), 227
Customer value:
   focus on, 142, 143, 149
   Lean principle, 86, 142
Customized services within
   utility delivery model,
   212–213
Customs and Border Patrol
   (CBP), 227

D

Davis, Trevor, 179, 182, 191,
   195, 209, 260
Defects per Million
   Opportunities, 89
Deliver-to-cash, 89
Demand shock, 251
Deming, W. Edwards, 47
Demographic transformation,
   Europe and Latin America,
   10

Department of Homeland
   Security (DHS), 227
Dillman, Linda, 219
Dillon, Jim, 3, 137–138, 140,
   156, 257–258
Distribution, normal (bell
   curve), 89
DMAIC (Lean Six Sigma, key
   steps: Define, Measure,
   Analyze, Improve, and
   Control), 93–98
DNA of consistent execution.
   See Execution, DNA of

E

EDS-Navy contract, 177, 187,
   208, 213–214
Einstein, Albert, 62
Entity-Boundary-Controller,
   70–71
Europe, 8, 10, 110–111,
   177–178, 227
Examples:
   Bill/Carl/Debbie (hospital
      group), 55–73, 123–126,
      128–130, 138
   John/Mary interactions
      (semantic disconnect,
      business operations, and
      technology), 13–16, 17,
      23, 28
   Marcus (Swiss bank),
      120–123, 128–130,
      260–261, 263

Mark (Check 21), 40, 44, 45, 48, 50, 53, 54, 66, 140, 141

Mike (retail banking applications), 3–7, 22–24, 28, 138, 144

Pat (TSA), 107–108, 112, 129–131, 220, 225, 229

Paul (claims processing BPO), 173–174, 184–187

Philippe (Global Cash & Trade), 21–22, 107–109, 112, 120–123, 128–130, 260

Reginald (IPSL), 79–80, 98–100

Richard (British financial services institution), 198–201

Rick (electronic subassemblies), 87–89, 100

Scott (packaging company), 121, 123, 124, 126, 128–130, 213, 260–261

SuperWidgets (secure commerce), 230–245

Tim (CalPERS), 179–180, 202–206, 214

Execution:
consistency in, 7, 19, 51, 82
difficulty of, 7–12
disconnected, or disappearing intellectual assets, 9–11
integrating existing with emerging technologies, 8–9

mobilizing diverse teams (T-Shirts, Turtlenecks, and Suits), 11–12
reducing cycle time, 8
DNA of, xxiv, xxv, 1–35, 54–55, 85–86, 214, 248, 262, 264, 268–269
framework, xxiii–xxiv, 120, 207, 213, 214, 261
gap, 13
issue/insight, 34–35
meaning/relevance, 35, 262–264
pragmatic, 255–264
semantic disconnect and, 12–29, 262–264
semantic stack, 29–33
Execution: The Discipline of Getting Things Done (Bossidy and Charan), 16, 92, 259, 262
Executionally aware companies/ strategy, xxiii, 112, 131
Experiential Workshops, 74, 153, 159–164, 169, 203
eXtended/eXtensible Markup Language (XML), 26, 27

F

Fertility shifts, European countries, 110
Financial markets, 251
Flat world, the (Friedman), 245–247, 249, 254

Food & Drug Administration (FDA), 227, 245
Framework, execution, xxiii–xxiv, 120, 207, 213, 214, 261
Friction-Free initiative, 143–144, 149
Friedman, L. Thomas (the flat world), 245–247, 249, 254

G

Galvin, Bob, 89, 90. *See also* Motorola
Gartner Group, 175–176, 181, 182, 210, 230
Garza, Tim (CalPERS), 147–148, 153, 166, 179–180, 202–205, 209, 214, 261, 263
General Electric, 90, 92, 228, 242, 279
Gill, Bobby, 177
Global Cash & Trade (Philippe), 21–22, 107–109, 112, 120–123, 128–130, 260
Global issues:
  burden/responsibility of globalization, 245–246, 250
  commerce (*see* Secure global commerce)
  labor migrations and immigration policies, 110

political realities, back to a bi-; a tri-; or an n-polar political world, 110–111
  sourcing, new options in, 167
  supply chain, 221, 254
Golden Gate Bridge, 100, 275
Goldman Sachs, 259
Good-to-Great insight, 109
Grammar tools, 19–20, 125
Graying of workface, 156
Green Belts, 92, 93
Green lane and secure commerce, 228
Group-think, versus diversity of perspectives, 29

H

Half-life, competitive, 10–11, 140
Heindel, Lee, 108
Hewlett Packard, 118
Hospital group (Bill and Carl), 55–73, 138
Hurricanes, 251, 283, 284
HyperText Markup Language (HTML), 27

I

IBM, 179
Improvement, continuous, 85

India, 100–101, 178
Information advantage, 259–261
Information technology, 8–9,
    33, 111
Infrastructure, 21, 49, 53
ING Insurance, 11
Innovative companies, 82–83
Inside-out versus outside-in
    approach, 131
  inside-out strategy, 124–129
  outside-in strategy, 120–123
Insurance, 11, 154, 179,
    199–200, 206, 251
  NYSDOL Unemployment
    Insurance Division
    (UID), 144–153,
    156–157, 162, 165, 221
  terrorism, 282–283
Intellectual asset issue, 10–11
Interface codification, 27–28
Internet, 22, 27
In Transit Visibility (ITV),
    220
IPSL, 79–80, 98–100

J

Japanese carmakers, 81–82, 86
Jericho Principle, The, 17, 42–43,
    83, 184
John/Mary interactions (semantic
    disconnect, business
    operations, and technology),
    13–16, 17, 23, 28

Jordan, Michael (EDS CEO),
    177
J.P. Morgan Chase & Co.,
    178–179
Just-in-time, 249

K

Karmali, Naazneen, 100
Kelso, Clark, 10, 28, 137–140,
    156

L

Lahman, Michael, 177
Language:
  as grammer tool, 19–20, 125,
    169–170, 264
  through semantic stack,
    20–33
  of value, 201, 208, 211 (*see also*
    Business Process
    Outsourcing, semantics
    of value)
Languages, business process
    modeling, 26
Leadership, 17, 33
Lean Aerospace Initiative
    (LAI), 86–87
Lean Manufacturing, 81–82, 86,
    142, 226, 249

Lean Six Sigma, 85–101
  DMAIC steps (Define,
    Measure, Analyze,
    Improve, and Control),
    93–98
  execution framework, 120,
    207, 213, 261
  history of Lean concept, 86
  issues project charter will
    address, 93–94
  meaning/relevance, 99–101
  Six Sigma Belts, 88, 92–93,
    94, 95, 97
Legacy carriers, 26
Leonard, Michel, 250
Lockheed Martin, 80, 87, 90,
  91, 93, 100
Loy, James, 225, 239

M

Mantra (codified/executable/
  scalable), 20, 31
Maps-as-models, 45–73
Maxmin, James, 83
McGrath, Joseph, 95
Mercator map development,
  62–63
Mergers and acquisitions
  (M&A) activity, 111
Metrics, 21, 201–202
Michaels, Paul, 173–174,
  184–186, 189, 190, 192,
  203, 208, 209

Mirror, semantic stack as, 24,
  29
Models, 45–73, 76, 167
  Analysis Classes, 70, 71
  definition, 47
  Deming on, 47
  labor-intensive and
    expensive, 167
  maintaining after
    system implementation,
    167
  maps as, 45–48
  swimlane, 60–65, 156, 157,
    242
Monmonier, Mark, 62–63
Moore, Geoffrey, 11, 130,
  210
Motorola, 89–90, 229
Mozart, 29
Murray, Patty, 220, 238

N

Nagaraj, C. R., 92
New York State (Jim Dillon),
  3, 137–138, 140, 156,
  257–258
New York State Department
  of Labor (NYSDOL),
  Unemployment
  Insurance Division
  (UID), 144–153,
  156–157, 162, 165, 221

O

Object Oriented Design
(OOD), 27, 70
Operation Safe Commerce, 220,
226–230, 254
Optimization, business process,
141, 148–151, 159–166, 169
Organization/organizational:
constancy of change, 32
design, 164–165
lore, 25
will, 92
Outside-in versus inside-out
approach, 131
inside-out strategy,
124–129
outside-in strategy,
120–123
Outsourcing. *See* Business
Process Outsourcing
(BPO)

P

Parris, Andrew N., 91
Patel, Ketan, 259, 260, 263
Paul Bunyan approach to
strategy, 108–109, 124
Peak effect, 193–197, 216
Pennsylvania Open for Business
web site, 143–144
Postal Service, U.S., 228

Pragmatics. *See* Execution;
Strategy
Prahalad, C. K., 112
Process(es), business, 135–170
codifying, 25–26
defined, 138, 143
extent of the challenge,
142–146
issue/insight, 168–169
meaning/relevance, 166–167
modeling, 21, 49, 52, 54, 63,
150 (*see also* Business
Blueprinting; Semantic
stack)
optimization, 141, 148–151,
159–164, 169
outsourcing (*see* Business
Process Outsourcing
(BPO))
value and, 137–142
Process variability, 89, 102

R

Radio Frequency Identifiers
(RFID), 84–85, 219, 228
Rational Unified Process, 3
Red Queen challenge, 42–45,
248
Regulatory environment, 81, 84
Ridge, Tom, 140, 142–144, 149
Right-sizing, 9
Risk mitigation, 195
Rohleder, Steve, 142

S

Salieri, 29
Sarbanes Oxley, 84
Scale, 19, 20, 31, 43
Schambach, Pat (TSA),
    107–108, 112, 120, 129,
    130, 131, 220, 225, 229,
    239, 245, 260, 261, 263
Scope, 147
Secure global commerce,
    217–254
  burden/responsibility of
    globalization, 234,
    245–246
  complexity of typical import/
    export transaction,
    222–227
  example (SuperWidgets),
    230–245
  extent of the challenge,
    222–230
  facing the challenge,230–246
  issue/insight, 253–254
  managing tension between
    assured and agile, 221,
    230–235, 248–249, 253
  meaning/relevance,246–252
  mutual visibility and
    dependency, 219–221
  Operation Safe Commerce,
    220, 226–230, 254
  visibility through
    blueprinting, 230–235
  visible commerce and
    connectivity, 235–245

Secure Supply Chain initiatives,
    U.S. government, 84
Security assertion markup
    language (SAML), 27
Semantic disconnect, 12–29, 54,
    130–131, 263, 264. *See also*
    Semantic stack
  bridging the semantic
    disconnect for
    executional consistency,
    xxv–xxvii, 12–20, 29–32,
    34, 75–76, 102–103, 131,
    262–264 (*see also*
    Execution)
  as key challenge to execution,
    xxv–xxvii, 12–29, 54,
    107–108, 130–131, 139,
    166, 247–248 (*see also*
    Semantics of value)
Semantics, 147
  shared, xxiii–xxiv, 126, 263,
    264
  of value, xxviii–xxix, 180–181,
    190–202, 207–209,
    210–211, 215–216
Semantic stack, 20–33
  detailing, 25–28
  DNA analogy, 31–32
  graphical representation as
    simple grid, 21
  meaning/relevance, 29–33
  as mirror, 24, 29
  "walking up and across,"
    23–24
Service level agreements (SLAs),
    99, 180–181, 199, 201, 206
Shell, 257–258

Shipping fleet, world's, 280
Shumskas, Tony, 192, 194, 278
Six Degrees of Separation principle, 94
Six Sigma. *See* Lean Six Sigma
Slavenburg, 228
Sorrell, Martin, 177
Stack. *See* Semantic stack
Standards/standardization, 32, 33, 267
State Street Corporation, 265–269
Steffen, Carl, 113
Strategy, 105–133
   executionally aware, xxiii, 112, 131, 132–133
   extent of the challenge, 109–112
   facing the challenge, 113–123
   inside-out, 124–129
   issue/insight, 132
   justifying an inside-out operational strategy, 123–129
   layer in Business Blueprint, 49, 51–52
   meaning/relevance, 129–131, 132–133
   outside-in, 120–123
   Paul Bunyan approach to, 108–109, 124
   pragmatics of, 120–123
Strout, Ron, 265–269
Suits, T-shirts, Turtlenecks, and, 11–12

SuperWidgets (generic consumer goods company), 230–245
   impact on warehouse workers, 243
   port operations after, 237
   port operations before, 236
   stuffing containers after, 241
   stuffing contains before, 240
Supply chains, 84, 221, 254
Swimlane models, 63–65, 156, 157, 242

T

Tacit knowledge, xxviii, 12–29, 34–35, 75–76, 102, 107, 130–131, 139, 168–169, 235. *See also* Semantic stack
TCP/IP, 273
Technology:
   business processes and, 169
   computer programs/ databases, codifying, 31
   information, 8–9, 33, 111
   integrating existing with emerging, 8–9
   Internet, 22, 27
   optimization and, 164
   outsourcing, 267
   secure commerce, 230

Technology Partners
  International (TPI), 176,
  182
Terrorism, 220–221, 250–252,
  282–283
Tesco, 219
Third-party logistics
  companies, 80
Three-arrow picture,
  113–119
Tiffinwallahs, 100–101
Tipping points, 129–130
Tointon, Niels, 206, 209
Tools:
  grammar, 19–20, 125
  optimization and,
    158–159
  semantic stack, 20–33
Toyota Production System,
  81–82
Traceability, 28, 47, 48, 50, 76,
  164, 261
Transaction costs, 251
Transformation Program,
  195–196
Transformation Security
  Administration (TSA; Pat
  Schambach), 107–108, 112,
  120, 129, 130, 131, 220,
  225, 229, 239, 245, 260,
  261, 263
Transportation Worker
  Identification Credential
  (TWIC), 239
T-Shirts, Turtlenecks, and Suits,
  11–12, 131

U

UBS, 178, 187, 213
UISL, 206
Uncertainty, business, 109–110,
  113–119
Unemployment Insurance
  Division (UID) of
  NYSDOL, 144–153,
  156–157, 162, 165, 221
Unintended consequences, 69,
  181–184
Unisys Corporation, 95–96,
  231
Unisys Insurance Services Ltd.
  (UISL), 179, 206
Universal Modeling Language
  (UML), 5
UPS, 80
Use Cases, 66–70, 158, 159, 273
U.S. Postal Service, 228
U.S. Transportation Command
  (USTRANSCOM),
  219–220

V

Value:
  BPOs and, 209
  creation models, 212
  focus on, versus cost, 202,
    216

invisible, unlocking, 9–11
language of, 81, 201, 208, 211
Lean principle, 86, 142
Variability, process, 89, 102
Visibility:
    challenge underlying semantic
        disconnect, 41
    information advantage and, 261
    making the invisible visible,
        9–11, 69, 157, 244
    traceability and, 28, 47, 48,
        50, 76, 164, 261
Visible Commerce, 221, 228,
    233–245, 248, 254

W

Wal-Mart, 84–85, 219
Webb, Janice, 229
Web Services (emerging
    standard), 27
Wedge effect, 187–190,
    197
Wipro, 92

Woolever, Gerald, 234
Wright, Robert, 177
Wright, Steven, 47

X

X-Engineering, 84
XML (eXtended/eXtensible
    Markup Language), 26, 27

Y

Yoshida, Tatsuo, 82

Z

Zuboff, Shoshanna, 83

About the Authors

Ralph Welborn and Vince Kasten are "roll-up-your-sleeves" business transformation experts; they're getting used to being called the "tip of the spear for getting things done." They have both widely worked and presented throughout the world on topics such as disruptive business and technology trends, emerging innovation models, "stuff that works around global sourcing" and next-generation outsourcing, the "DNA of organizational transformation," and just plain "how to get stuff done." Their affiliations have included being managing partners of BearingPoint (KPMG Consulting), Unisys, and Bell Laboratories. This is their second book together, the first, *The Jericho Principle*, described emerging business collaborative models. They can be reached at Ralph.Welborn@gmail.com and Vincent.Kasten@gmail.com.

Ralph's 20-year career combines strategy with execution honed from years of making sure that "the heads in the clouds are well connected to the feet on the ground"—hence his focus on "pragmatic execution." During the past several years, Ralph has focused increasingly on how to exploit innovation "at the edges" of the market and throughout organizations as well as "what works around global sourcing."

His affiliations have included managing partner of business transformation responsible for new revenue sources at Unisys; BearingPoint (formerly KPMG Consulting), where he was senior vice president of solutions engineering responsible for global solutions, as well as managing partner of business strategy; Charles Schwab; the Advanced Technology Group at Coopers & Lybrand; and a startup in San Francisco. Ralph holds a doctorate degree in the Philosophy of Science & Technology from Boston University.

Vince's 25-year career combines leading (sometimes bleeding) edge business experience with deep technical experience, spanning business strategy, research and development, large-scale systems integration, program management, and commercial software product development. In the past several years, he has focused on how business meets technology in enterprise innovation and global sourcing. His affiliations have included Unisys, as managing partner of business transformation; BearingPoint (formerly KPMG Consulting), as managing director of application architecture and Web services; Lucent Technologies, where he specialized in large-scale system integration; Bell Communications Research (now Telcordia), where he was director of the High Performance Transaction Technology Group; Bell Laboratories; and two technology startups. Vince has published more than 40 papers on a variety of strategic, management, and technical topics. He holds three U.S. patents and received a master's degree in Computer Science from Columbia University.